ANIMATION
TECHNIQUES

STEVE ROBERTS

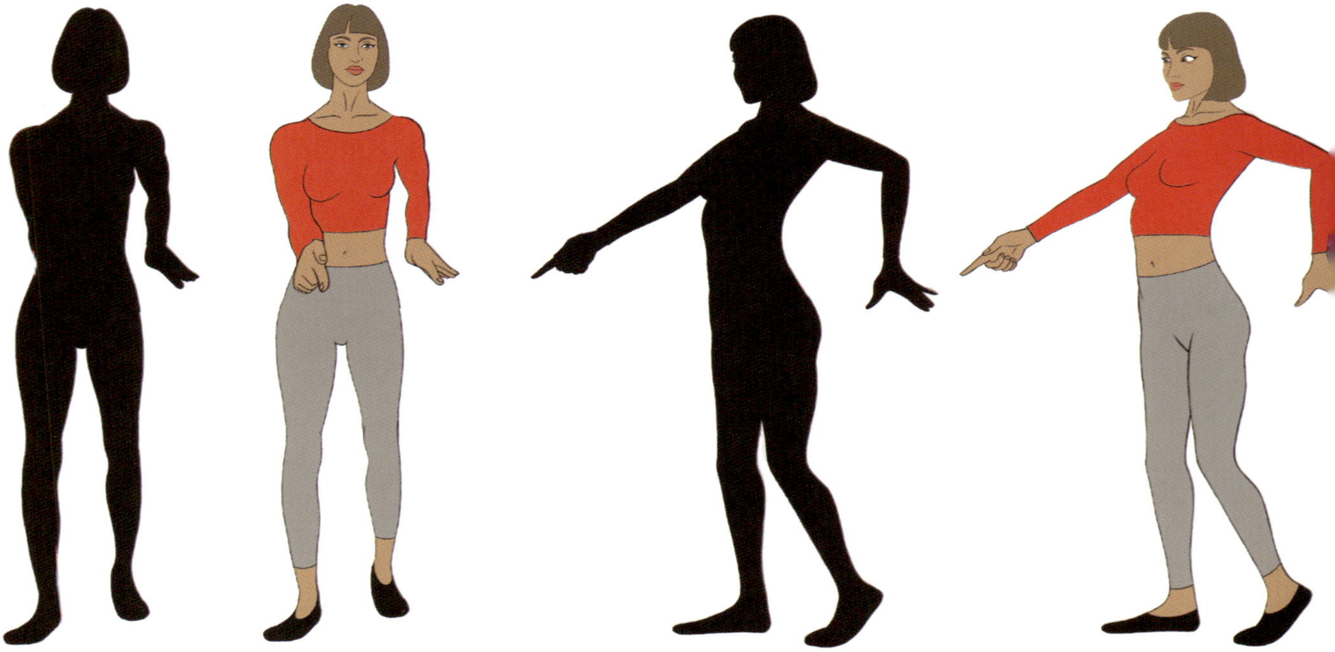

ANIMATION TECHNIQUES

STEVE ROBERTS

THE CROWOOD PRESS

First published in 2021 by
The Crowood Press Ltd
Ramsbury, Marlborough
Wiltshire SN8 2HR

enquiries@crowood.com

www.crowood.com

© Steve Roberts 2021

All rights reserved. No part of this publication may be reproduced or transmitted in any form or by any means, electronic or mechanical, including photocopy, recording, or any information storage and retrieval system, without permission in writing from the publishers.

British Library Cataloguing-in-Publication Data
A catalogue record for this book is available from the British Library.

ISBN 978 1 78500 935 8

Images from *The Koala Brothers* © Famous Flying Films and Koala Brothers Ltd.

Typeset by Simon and Sons

Cover design by Sergey Tsvetkov

Printed and bound in India by Parksons Graphics Pvt. Ltd., Mumbai.

CONTENTS

	DEDICATION AND ACKNOWLEDGEMENTS	6
	PREFACE	7
1	WHAT IS ANIMATION?	10
2	ANIMATION PRINCIPLES	20
3	PERFORMANCE IN ANIMATION	61
4	2D ANIMATION	82
5	PUPPET ANIMATION	103
6	3D COMPUTER ANIMATION	128
7	HOW TO MAKE AN ANIMATED FILM	147
8	PROMOTING YOUR ANIMATION AND WORKING IN ANIMATION	159
	GLOSSARY OF KEY TERMS	167
	FURTHER READING AND RESOURCES	171
	INDEX	172

DEDICATION AND ACKNOWLEDGEMENTS

This book is dedicated to the memory of Shaun McGlinchey (1962–2019), brilliant animator, inspiration and the best friend a person could have.

A huge thank you to Dee, Felix and Emily, the most important people in my life.

Thanks to Simon and Sara Bor for giving me my first job in animation.

An enormous thank you to David Johnson, Haemin Ko and Katie Chan for the case studies and the use of their images.

Thanks to Doreen Edemafaka for getting me into puppet animation and allowing me to show an image of her set.

Thanks to Adrian Gillan for being such a great life model and allowing images of him to be used in Haemin Ko's case study.

Huge thanks to Andy Blazdell (CelAction), Dean Cesaron (TVPaint) and Ton Roosendaal (Blender) for coming up with such amazing software and permission to use images of the brilliant tools we get to use as animators.

Big thanks to Roger Todd for help with casting latex puppet heads and Rich Metson for help with Blender.

Monumental thanks to my best animating mates, Paul Stone, Mal Hartley and Vanessa Luther-Smith. I would not be who I am without you!

Finally, a gigantic thank you to Central St Martins for employing me for so long, thanks to Shaun Clark for putting up with my foibles and thanks to all the students I have ever taught. I have learnt so much more from you than you have learnt from me!

PREFACE

MY BACKGROUND

I have worked in animation for almost forty years. In that time, I've seen a huge amount of change in the way that animation can be produced, but the basic principles of animation have remained the same. As a child, I was fascinated by animation, whether watching it on television or at the cinema. I found it amazing that drawings or puppets could move, as if by magic.

When I was ten years old, there was a series on BBC television in the UK called *The Do-it-Yourself Film Animation Show*, introduced by an animator called Bob Godfrey. In this series, Bob showed how to do cartoon animation using various techniques, how to write for animation and how to use sound for animation. It was a complete revelation to me. I was bought the book as a present and pestered my parents for a cine camera with 'single frame release'. Unfortunately, a cine camera that sophisticated would be incredibly expensive, so I stuck to making animated films as flipbooks in the back of my school exercise books. (In fact, I met an old English teacher of mine a few years ago and she asked me what I was doing now. 'I'm an animator,' I replied. 'Oh, that figures! You were terrible at English, but I always looked forwards to watching your latest movie in the back of your exercise books!')

In the early 1980s, I finally got to try some animation when I was doing a foundation course in art at the age of eighteen. I bought a second-hand Russian clockwork standard 8mm cine camera, built a rostrum to mount it on and had a go at doing cut-out animation. I can't really say the results were particularly impressive, but I was hooked. However, for some strange reason I decided to do

The Do-it-Yourself Film Animation book, linked to the BBC television series, *The Do-it-Yourself Film Animation Show*.

a BA course in fine art and sculpture. The problem with fine art is that you need to dig deep into your soul in order to produce decent work. Having looked deep into my soul, I discovered there was nothing there, so I dropped out of art college. I didn't have any plan of what I was going to do next, but then fate took a hand when my mother showed me an advert in a local newspaper, asking for a college leaver to work in an animation studio.

I went for the interview, showing the artwork I had done on my foundation course and got the

The advertisement in a local newspaper that changed my life.

job. I ended up painting cells on the kitchen table of a new start-up animation company and loved every minute of it. I found that my employers, Simon and Sara Bor of Honeycomb Animation, had studied at West Surrey College of Art and Design in Farnham. Simon had been taught there by Bob Godfrey. When I learnt this, I decided to study animation at Farnham. I also worked in animation studios at the weekends and during the holidays in order to supplement my income. Since that time, I have worked on television series, adverts, feature films and short educational films. I even worked for Bob Godfrey!

I started directing short animated films for the BBC in the early 1990s and in 1994 began teaching animation back at my old college in Farnham. From the late 1990s, I have specifically trained animators at Central St Martins College of Art and Design to work in the animation industry and over 600 people now have a career in animation as a result. I have devised my own class structure and worked out the best way to learn animation quickly and thoroughly.

From the late 1990s, I have used computers to produce animation, both 2D and 3D. It's always nice to experiment with new techniques and technology, but I still use the old-fashioned lessons learnt over my career. Recently I have moved into puppet animation and produced two films using puppets and clay.

So, all in all I have had a long career in animation and I'm sure it will keep me busy for a few years to come.

ABOUT THIS BOOK

Animation and the concept of continuous moving images have been around for thousands of years, predating live-action films (an animation device powered by an oil lamp was invented in China in 150BC). In fact, you could think of live-action films as a development of animation. But as well as having existed for such a long time and involving a lot of traditional techniques, animation is also at the cutting edge of modern technology.

Animation is brilliant at explaining difficult concepts and making them understandable to all. It can put over stories in an engaging way, ranging from being realistic to completely fantastic. Almost any artistic technique – for example, sculpture, drawing, painting, printing, textiles, flower arranging and make-up – can be incorporated into animation. If you have a visual style or artistic technique, you can animate with it.

There is always something new to learn about animation and you will never know it all. In order to make an animated film, you need to do lots of research and will end up finding out a lot about the world around you.

This book will go through the basics of animation in Chapters 1, 2 and 3. These incorporate the twelve rules of animation along with suitable exercises to illustrate these rules. Chapters 4, 5 and 6 will go through the different techniques of animation and you can try the exercises in your chosen animation style. The last two chapters will go through how to make a short animated film and how to get it seen by an audience.

Some people believe that animation is very expensive and takes a long time to do, but if you have a great script and keep the technique simple, you can produce an entire, amazing film on your own that will look magical compared to a live-action film. If you want a worthwhile hobby or a fulfilling career, animation has it all.

1
WHAT IS ANIMATION?

Many people have tried to sum up what animation is and it is consequently open to several different interpretations. According to the *Oxford English Dictionary*, animation means to 'Breathe life into; enliven, make lively'. This is a rather general interpretation of the word. For a more specific definition, the world's largest animation festival (Annecy International) defines it as 'Any audio-visual animation, created *frame* by frame whatever the technique, made for the cinema, television and any other screening platform may be entered.'

What's clear here is that animation is something that consists of a series of images played one after the other in order to create movement, each of those images being partly or completely created by some method.

The one thing that animation relies on is the persistence of vision. This is where the light receptive nerve endings in the eye continue to see an object, even after the light has ceased to be emitted from the object. It means that if we see a succession of images that change slightly from image to image, it will create the illusion of movement. This is helped by a 'shutter' which will create a millisecond of black between each image in order to help the eye register each picture.

A SHORT HISTORY OF ANIMATION

In order to understand animation, we need to look back in history to see its origins.

If we go right back to the first images created by *Homo sapiens*, often those images were there to help capture movement. Early cave paintings depict animals with multiple legs, giving the

A recreation of an early human being creating a cave painting with movement.

WHAT IS ANIMATION? 11

A recreation of a Greek vase showing sequential movement.

sequences of motion with drawings in his amazing and copious collection of sketches.

A Chinese inventor and craftsman called Ding Huan invented a device that created movement from a series of paintings on a cylinder, which was hung over an oil lamp and the heat of the lamp caused the cylinder to rotate. When the images were viewed through the slits of an umbrella type device, they would appear to move. This was invented in Han Dynasty China around 150BC.

Many centuries later, Joseph Plateau invented the Phenakistiscope, also known as the Spindle Viewer, in 1832. The Phenakistiscope was a disc split into equal segments, with an image drawn on each one. This was mounted on a stick. Slots were cut into the disc and the images would be viewed through the slots while holding the disc up to a mirror. When the disc was spun quickly, looking at one segment at a time would cause the images to create motion. The slots created a shutter between the eye and the images.

William Horner invented the Zoetrope in 1833. The Zoetrope consisted of a cylinder with slots in the side, balanced on a spindle. Inside was placed a paper strip of drawings, each showing a slight

impression of galloping. Centuries later, Greek vases depicted athletes going through sequential images of the sports in which they were engaging. During the Renaissance in fifteenth- and sixteenth-century Italy, Leonardo da Vinci created

The Ding Huan device used to produce animation – the first of its type.

The Phenakistiscope (or Spindle Viewer) was invented by Joseph Plateau in 1832 as a way of causing images to create motion.

The Zoetrope, invented by William Horner in 1833. When the cylinder was spun, the images on the inside of the cylinder came to life.

difference from one image to the next. Once the cylinder was spun, looking at the pictures through the slots created the illusion of movement. The slots acted as a shutter between each of the images.

The first flip-book animation appeared in September 1868 and was patented by John Barnes Linnett, under the name Kineograph. This consisted of a series of drawings displaying frame by frame movement, stapled together in a stiff book and the pages flipped one after the other by the thumb. (You can make something similar with a pad of sticky notes.)

A more elaborate version of this was called the Mutoscope (or a 'What the Butler Saw' machine). This was invented in 1894 by Herman Casler. A sequence of images on cards was mounted on a drum and viewed though a small peephole. A crank was turned to rotate the drum and show each image, one after the other. The images were taken from film and then printed on to the cards.

WHAT IS ANIMATION? 13

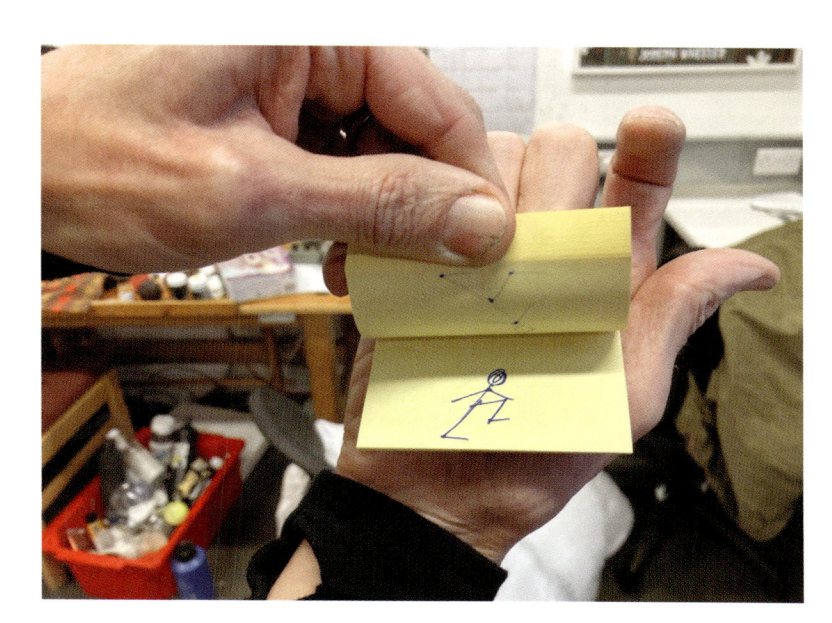

A flip book made from sticky notes (using the same principle as patented by John Barnes Linnett).

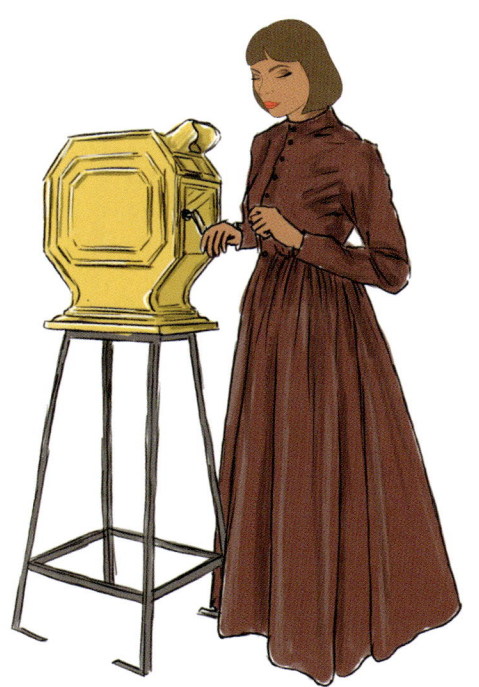

The Mutoscope (or a 'What the Butler Saw' machine). This was invented in 1894 by Herman Casler.

In 1877, Eadweard Muybridge developed a system of creating sequential photographs of animals and humans that displayed their movement in accurate detail. He was financed in this endeavour by Leland Stanford, a wealthy race-horse owner. He also created the Zoopraxiscope for projecting these sequential photographs in 1879. Not exactly animation, but providing lots of information for animators. His books *Animals in Motion* (1899) and *The Human Figure in Motion* (1901) are still in print today and are well worth buying by any budding animator.

At the same time in France, Charles-Émile Reynaud developed the Praxinoscope, which was an improvement on the Zoetrope, using light and glass mirrors in order to improve the animation of the images. He also invented the idea of projecting animation on to a screen. His Théâtre Optique device consisted of 300 to 700 gelatin plates (with images hand-painted on them) mounted in cardboard frames and taped together, and incorporating perforations to register against the gear wheels they ran around. A light would project through the images on to a screen and it created a soft, blurred impression of animated movement. In many ways it was also a development of magic lantern shows, which projected still or puppet-like movement images on to a screen. His invention could be thought of as the first ever cinematic experience.

All of these earliest examples of the moving image could be considered 'animation', so

A series of images similar to those captured by Eadweard Muybridge.

in many ways live-action film could be regarded as an offshoot of animation, not the other way round. Inspired by Eadweard Muybridge, in 1899, Thomas Edison created the Kinetoscope (though it was developed by his employee, William Dickson). It was a precursor to the 'What the Butler Saw Machine', where the movie was viewed through a peephole. It relied on a thin piece of film that ran past the eyehole, through a series of gears with a light to illuminate the film. Edison and Dickson developed the Kinetograph, a sophisticated (for the time) cine camera to shoot the movies.

One of the first uses of film to produce projected motion can be ascribed to the Lumière brothers. Auguste and Louis Lumière are considered the first ever movie makers. They both worked for their father, who was a pioneer photographer and photographic platemaker. Auguste and Louis developed machines that would mechanize the platemaking process. Later on, they set to work to make a film camera and projector. They acquired the rights to Léon Guillaume Bouly's Cinematograph (a combined film camera and projector) and incorporated it into their own device. These were demonstrated in 1895. Their films consisted of documenting real life and none was more than a minute long. The first film shows workers leaving the Lumière factory. The brothers never developed their system and refused to sell their cameras and projectors to any film-makers. They spent the rest of their careers developing colour photography.

THE HISTORY OF DIFFERENT ANIMATION TECHNIQUES

Drawn Animation

Probably the first ever drawn animated film was *Humorous Phases of Funny Faces* (using a chalkboard and cut-out technique) by James Stuart Blackton in 1906. Blackton was a comic artist, a 'chalk talk' music hall entertainer and a journalist with an interest in new technology. He interviewed Thomas Edison about his new invention, the Vitascope (a form of electric projector), and Edison invited Blackton to draw him as they were filmed with his new, hand-cranked, camera. When Blackton saw the film, he noticed that at certain points of the movie the drawn line would suddenly get longer. This happened when the camera had stopped filming, but Blackton had continued drawing. This intrigued Blackton. He was most impressed and bought a camera, projector and several prints of films from Edison. These films were incorporated into Blackton's stage shows.

One of the earliest films Blackton produced was *The Enchanted Drawing* (1900). This was more a demonstration of one of his stage shows than an animated film. He drew a wine bottle on a piece of paper, then the drawn champagne bottle turned into a real bottle of champagne. Obviously at this point they stopped cranking the camera and

A chalkboard music hall act, which led to some of the first film animation.

substituted the drawing for the real bottle, before cranking the camera again. This led to further experiments and Blackton worked out that a certain amount of rotation of the crank of the camera would result in one frame of film being exposed.

Humorous Phases of Funny Faces was drawn on a blackboard with chalk and the lines rubbed out and redrawn in order to move them, cranking the camera slightly between each of the drawings. The film consisted of a man smoking a cigar, then a man and woman looking at each other and the man then blowing cigar smoke in the lady's face. There is also a sequence involving a clown and a dog, with one arm and one leg drawn on black paper and moved (paper cut-out animation).

The first animated movie drawn entirely on paper and shot on film was Émile Cohl's *Fantasmagorie* of 1908. This film was made as a series of ink drawings on paper but was shot on negative film. It gave the impression of being white lines on a black surface, like chalk on a blackboard. It is likely that the camera would have been placed on some kind of rostrum. The camera would have been facing down, so that the drawings could be placed under the camera and shot one at a time more easily.

Another pioneer of animation was Winsor McCay. He did not invent animation and used basic techniques to produce his films, but he elevated animation to a form of high art. His first film, *Little Nemo*, made in 1911 is an amazing piece of animation and displays a wonderful sense of performance and movement, combined with the greatest artistry. His film was even coloured by hand and has a beautiful, ethereal quality.

Up to this point 2D animated films had emphasized the magic of drawings moving. They were not trying to be anything other than a collection of drawings and something that was created by hand. From here, there were further developments. Light boxes and a paper registration system were used so that the previous drawing could still be seen.

Around 1913, the Bray Studio in New York developed the use of cellulose acetate sheets. The characters were traced from the original drawings on to these sheets so that the background behind the character could be seen, rather than everything having to be shot on one sheet of paper. This made shooting a scene more complicated, so more sophisticated rostrums were developed and also things called *exposure sheets* (or *dope sheets*) on which to record the shooting information. (The Bray Studio made more money from the patent of this technique than it did from making cartoons.) The studio also divided the labour up into the different processes of creating a cartoon: animating (an *animator* would create *key* drawings and mark the timing on a dope sheet); in-betweening (an *assistant animator* would take the animator's key drawings and do the drawings between each of these keys to create smooth movement); tracing (the drawings would be traced on to the acetate sheets); and painting (a painter would colour in the characters on the reverse of the acetate sheets). A background artist would paint the backgrounds. A camera person would shoot the backgrounds and acetate sheets, combined, one frame at a time. An editor would cut the film together, ready to be printed and sent out to cinemas. All of this led to drawn animated films being made more efficiently.

Walt Disney used one of the early synchronized sound systems (Pat Powers' Cinephone system) in order to make one of the first sound cartoons, *Steamboat Willie* (1928), staring Mickey Mouse. This really revolutionized animation. Sound is almost 50 per cent of what is taken in when viewing an animated film. Walt Disney Studios was also the first animation company to secure the rights to use Technicolor, a three-colour film process, which really put the company ahead in the cinema. The first Technicolor film was *Flowers and Trees* (1932). Around this time, Walt Disney Studios began developing *storyboards*, which greatly added to the narrative structure of animated movies.

Walt Disney Studios also developed the use of the multiplane camera, which gave depth of field to a movie, creating a richer image. The first film to use this was *The Old Mill* (1937). It was also used to great effect in *Snow White and the Seven Dwarfs* (1937).

From this point on, drawn animation stuck to these basic principles for the best part of sixty years. The exception was the introduction of the Xerox process at Disney, which meant that a lot of money could be saved on the tracing process and a more accurate vision achieved of the drawings created by the animator. The first film to use this process was *One Hundred and One Dalmatians* made in 1961. It was only in the early 1990s that drawings were scanned into a computer and coloured on screen.

Each piece of technology added to the illusion that these were more than drawings moving and were the real living expressions of an artist's imagination.

Stop-Motion

James Stuart Blackton may also be responsible for the first ever *stop-motion animated* film, *The Humpty Dumpty Circus* (1898). In this film a collection of circus animal toys performs for a group of children. Unfortunately, only a few stills of this ground-breaking film exist.

Another contender for the first puppet animation is possibly *Matches: An Appeal* (1899 or 1914) by British film-maker Arthur Melbourne Cooper. This

Some of the earliest stop-frame animation involved the animation of matches.

is a rather hotly contested one! It was an advert for the Bryant & May Match company, thought to have been made in 1914 to encourage people to buy matches for soldiers on the front line during World War I. However, it has been suggested that it could have been made for soldiers serving in the Second Boer War in 1899. It consisted of figures made of matches, jointed by wire, playing football and cricket and writing the appeal on a wall.

Amongst the many films made by Cooper was *Dolly's Toys* (1902). This consisted of a group of toys that came alive while their owners were not looking (predating *Toy Story* by nearly 100 years)! A film with a similar theme was *Dreams of Toyland* (1908), where a boy and his mother went to a toy shop and bought lots of toys. When the boy went to sleep, he dreamed that his toys came alive. They engaged in several fights and ended up with a major car crash! Generally, most early puppet films involved inanimate objects coming to life in a magical way.

In Lithuania, Władysław Starewicz made several films as Director of the Museum of Natural History in the city of Kaunas. From this, he conceived the idea of making films with dead insects, jointed with wire. His first fictional animated film was *Lucanus Cervus* (1910).

Generally, stop-motion animators were very secretive about their techniques, none more so than Willis O'Brien, who made the animated sections in the feature film *The Lost World* (1925). O'Brien was very coy about what he was doing and how he did it. He was probably the first person to use jointed armatures and latex rubber to create realistic-looking animals and dinosaurs. Based on the Arthur Conan Doyle book, this was the first feature film to use puppet animation. O'Brien animated the dinosaurs and they were shown as if they were the real thing. When O'Brien disappeared into his studio, he shut everybody out in order to keep his techniques secret. He went on to animate the star of the feature film *King Kong* (1933).

It would seem that drawn animators were open about what they were doing and the fact that their

King Kong was animated by Willis O'Brien in 1933.

films consisted of drawings moving, like a kind of magic. They would also emphasize the huge amount of work involved and how many drawings had to be made to produce the movies. On the other hand, puppet animators tended to keep their techniques secret and tried to give the impression that what they were doing was the real thing and not animation at all. Dolls or matches had magically come to life, or 'real' dinosaurs were filmed in some exotic location. Early 3D computer animation also had a similar mystique!

Computer Animation

Some of the earliest computer animation was produced using military plotting applications. These produced abstract shapes that would morph from one thing to another. An early example can be seen in the title sequence of the Alfred Hitchcock film *Vertigo* (1958), animated by John Whitney.

In Canada, Peter Foldes made *Metadata* in 1971, using a computer that could calculate a metamorphosis from one plotted drawing to another. These images were then printed out, shot on a conventional rostrum camera and played back on film.

In 1972, Ed Catmull and Fred Parke produced *A Computer Animated Hand* at the University of Utah. This is one of the earliest examples of 3D

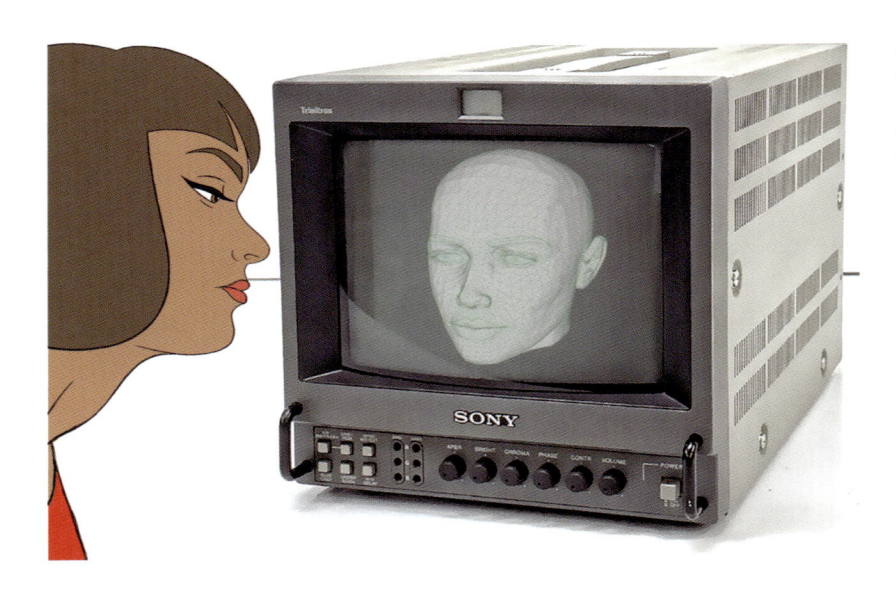

Early 3D animation was mainly done in wireframe and computers were not fast enough to play the animation back. Wireframe models constructed in the computer consist of wire-like edges for each shape, with no area coloured between the 'wires'.

computer animation. Some of this animation was used in the feature film *Future World* in 1976. Later, Catmull, Parke and John Lasseter went on to form Pixar with Steve Jobs.

So many advances have been made in 3D animation that it is almost impossible to document them all. The ability to articulate joints, the lighting, the *rendering* and shading of images and the use of *motion capture* (the interpretation of a real actor's movements to an animated character) are just some of the amazing advances that have been made.

We now have the prospect of animating and making films in virtual reality, using headsets. Animation has always relied on the latest technology, whether it was creating optical-illusion based toys, or using cellulose acetate sheets, engineered armatures or the computer.

WHERE TO USE ANIMATION

It is true to say that you can do anything with animation.

Sometimes the reason for an animated film existing is to show off the design style of the illustrations used. Animation tends to work better where it is used to do something that can't be done with live-action movies. If it can be done with live action, it's going to be much easier and look better if real people act out the plot. Animation can take you beyond everyday life.

Animation is great for recreating something that doesn't exist or can't be filmed. It has recently been used a lot in documentaries to fill in the gaps where live-action footage is unavailable. Sometimes it can be cheaper to commission animation, rather than buying archive footage.

Anything fantastical and imaginative will work well in animation. This is particularly true of Manga-style films, which cover fairly realistic people put into fantastical situations. If a film is well scripted and performed, it does not take long for an audience to suspend its disbelief and become engaged with the story.

The anthropomorphism of animals has always been a popular theme for animated films. In the early days it was the easiest way to get an animal or inanimate object to display life. What could be more amazing to an audience than to have an animal or an object behaving like a human being! The first real animated movie star was Felix the Cat. His creators (Otto Messmer and Pat Sullivan) were originally inspired by Charlie Chaplin and other early comedy film stars, but pushed this slapstick humour into a whole new surreal world, where the most amazing things could happen. Felix was dealt a fatal blow by the noisy Mickey Mouse, with Felix gaining sound far too late to compete. These early animated films were not just aimed at children, but at a much wider audience. They were also lauded by leading intellectuals and artists of the day. Walt Disney was considered an artistic genius.

Animation can also be used to illustrate, simplify and explain complicated subjects in a way that viewers will understand. This may range from basic 'explainers' for how to use a piece of the latest technology, to governments detailing their latest pieces of policy. You will see huge amounts of animation on Facebook, putting over different points of view, or delivering 'fake news'.

Animation is also great at selling things. Most adverts have some kind of animation in them, even if they are not fully animated. This could range from simple moving graphics or moving lettering, to special effects inserted into a live-action movie, or even to a full-on mini-animated feature.

Animation has been used in lots of multimedia events, such as projection on to buildings and large-scale video screens. It can make the ordinary seem fantastic.

So, keep your mind open and think about what you want to do with animation!

WHERE TO SEE ANIMATION

The best way to see animation is to go to animation festivals, or to film festivals that have an animation section. There may be an animation festival near you; various websites list animation festivals all over the world. At these festivals, you will get to see some of the latest animated films, long before anyone else. It is good to understand the breadth and scope of what animation can do and all the different styles that are used nowadays. It is worth noting that the latest animation produced by individuals tends not to be available on the web. A lot of animators will keep their movies to show at festivals first and when they have done their 'festival run' will release them for open viewing to the world by the internet. This is usually about two years after the first release date.

Browse websites like YouTube and Vimeo. Often, you can come across some little gem that may be a few years old, but that you find really inspirational. A fantastic place to see some revolutionary animation is the National Film Board of Canada website. The National Film Board of Canada has been producing ground-breaking animation for over eighty years and most of its output is now free to watch.

Television is a good place to see animation, though mainstream TV tends to be rather conservative as its scheduling of animation is aimed mainly at children. One of the most popular and long-lived TV series in the world is animated: *The Simpsons*! Some of the web streaming services such as Netflix, Amazon Prime and Apple TV are commissioning animation aimed at a far wider audience than purely children's entertainment. Audiences these days have grown up with computer games and animation via the web, so are far more receptive to entertainment delivered to them in this form. Indeed, computer games consist almost entirely of animation, ranging from the hyperrealistic to the incredibly imaginative.

So, what is animation? I believe anything that constructs a movie, frame by frame, can be considered animation. Watch as much animation as possible to make up your own mind. Whatever you decide, animation has never been so popular!

2
ANIMATION PRINCIPLES

This chapter will go through the basic principles of animation and suggest exercises you can try in order to understand them. This chapter will also cover basic animal and human locomotion. The next chapter will be about performance in animation and the subsequent chapters will show how you could complete these exercises in your chosen animation medium.

STRAIGHT-AHEAD AND POSE TO POSE ANIMATION

There are two ways to do animation: straight ahead and pose to pose (otherwise referred to as key to key animation). Each has its own benefits and the two approaches are often combined.

Straight-ahead animation involves animating one frame after another from start to finish. This type of animation will provide a more fluid, spontaneous type of movement, but with drawn animation it can lead to a lot of distortion of the character and the characters can also tend to float and show less weight. It can also be more difficult to work out really sharp timing of movements. You also have to keep the idea of the movement in your head while you are doing it, which can become rather confusing. Puppet animation is all straight ahead, but does not have the problem of the character changing shape and size. Drawn animation and 3D animation can be either straight ahead or key to key.

With the pose to pose (or key to key) technique, you create a pose at the beginning frame and then create major key frames through the movement until the end frame is reached. Then you go back and do the *in-between* frames, or let the computer do this job for you. This technique gives more

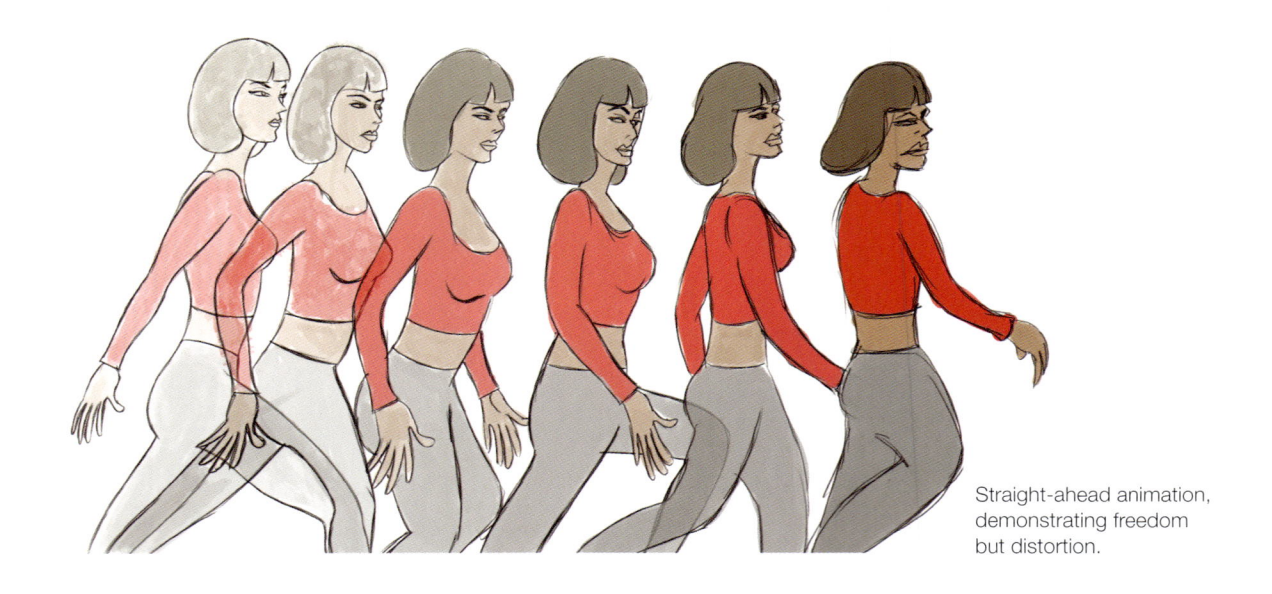

Straight-ahead animation, demonstrating freedom but distortion.

control within the scene. You can also use *timing charts* and *x sheets* to write down the information of the movement; this way you don't have to keep all this information in your head and can just get on with the creative bit.

While this technique is more suited to drawn, digital 2D and 3D animation, it can also be used by puppet animators. You put your puppet in a sequence of key positions and with the software you are using give each key (or pose) an appropriate amount of frames and play it back. When you are happy with the timing of this *pop through*, or pose test, note down which frame each key is at. When you go on to animate the piece fully, you will then know roughly at what position your character needs to be at each frame of the animation.

Unfortunately, pose to pose animation gives less scope for spontaneity, as it is not possible to change things when you are doing the in-between frames, unless you redo a whole section of the key positions. It is also necessary to have a good understanding of the movement in the scene in order to work out what the major poses are. This comes with practice and experience.

One thing that can really help your animation is to act it out first. Look at yourself performing a particular motion in a mirror, or video yourself doing the action and view it back. From this, you can establish the major key positions, then work out the timing between these key positions, especially if you are doing drawn animation, digital 2D or 3D animation. With puppet animation, while you are shooting the frames, you can keep referring back to your video footage to see what position you need to put your character in at any given point.

Exercise

Animate an action one frame at a time, then repeat, but this time doing a key position at the start and at the end of the shot, then in-betweening the actions. For example, you could animate a ball rolling along the ground (*see* Chapter 4 for details of how to shoot this animation).

First, animate the ball, one drawing after the other as it moves along the ground, from one side of the screen to the other.

Pose to pose animation can be more controlled, but can also lack spontaneity.

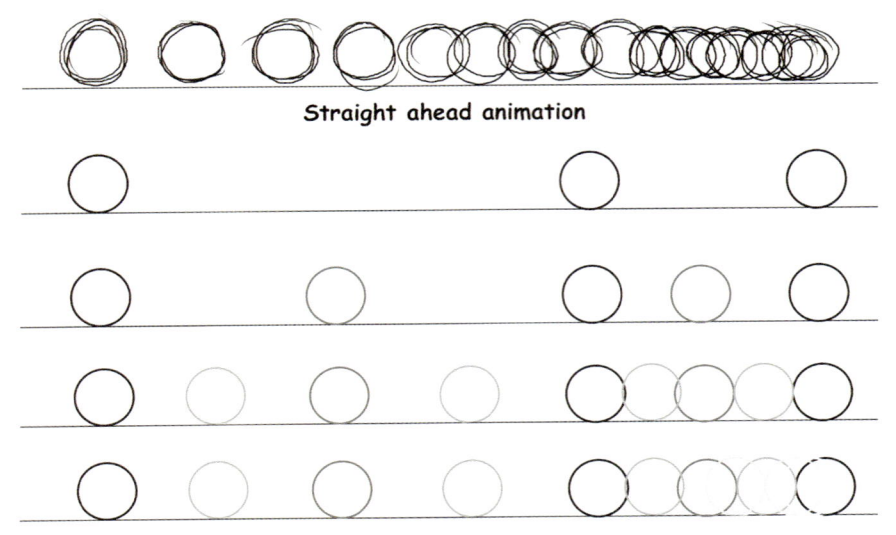

Straight-ahead and pose to pose exercise, animating a ball rolling along the ground.

Straight ahead animation

Pose to pose (key to key) animation

Next, animate the ball by starting with the first drawing of the sequence (ball at the left of the screen). Then, on another piece of paper, draw the last ball of the sequence (ball at the right of the screen). On another piece of paper, draw the ball in the middle of the two other balls. Then, on another piece of paper, draw a ball between the first drawing and the middle drawing. On another piece of paper, draw a ball between the middle drawing and the last drawing. Finally, on separate pieces of paper draw a ball between each of the balls you have drawn.

You will probably find that the straight-ahead animated ball will change size and shape and might move erratically. The pose to pose animated ball's size and shape will stay more consistent and the movement will be more regular.

SQUASH AND STRETCH

Any object or character that is not completely solid (by solid, I mean something like a statue that is very hard and inflexible) will display some kind of squash and stretch – that is, the volume of the object or character will stay the same, but its shape could change depending on its circumstance. It might get thinner and longer, or shorter and fatter, as a result of the effect of gravity and the environment in which the object or character exists. For example, a rubber ball when dropped will display squash when it hits the ground and stretch when it accelerates into a bounce. A solid ball (like a snooker or pool ball) will not squash or stretch.

The use of squash and stretch will give an audience an idea of how the object is constructed and make it more believable. Animation needs to make something believable to an audience. Everyone who watches your animation has a certain amount of life experience and knows how things move, even unconsciously. If your animation moves in a way that is not correct, the audience will realize and not believe in it.

So when it comes to animating something, you will first need to do some research. This could be as simple as dropping a rubber ball on the floor, or as sophisticated as acting out a scene and videoing the result to use as a guide for your animation. You will also need to work out a few things about the construction and weight of the object.

ANIMATION PRINCIPLES 23

Squash and stretch demonstrating a consistent volume when distorting an object.

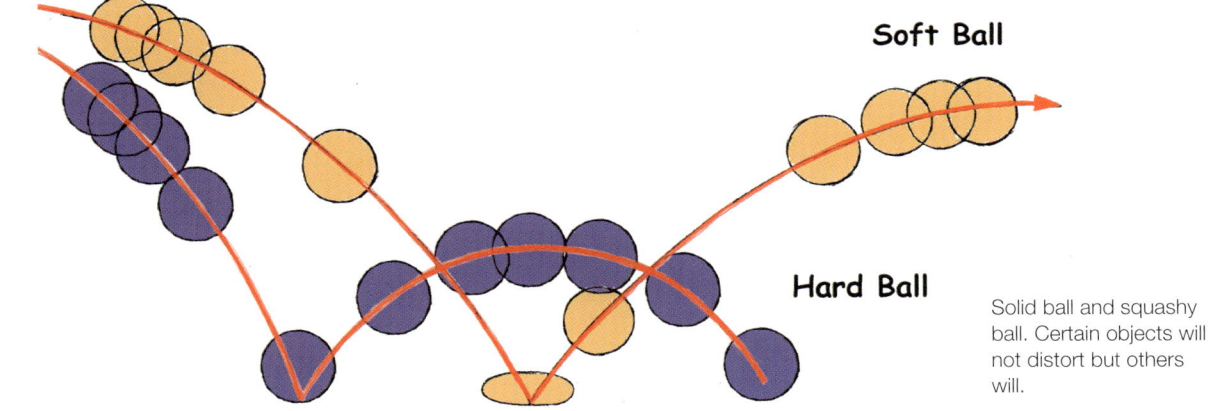

Soft Ball

Hard Ball

Solid ball and squashy ball. Certain objects will not distort but others will.

How heavy is the object? A heavy object such as a bowling ball will move in a very different way to a balloon.

What environment is it being animated in? An object on the moon or floating in water will move in a different way to an object on planet earth or on dry land. For example, a wooden railway sleeper is big and heavy, but will float on water.

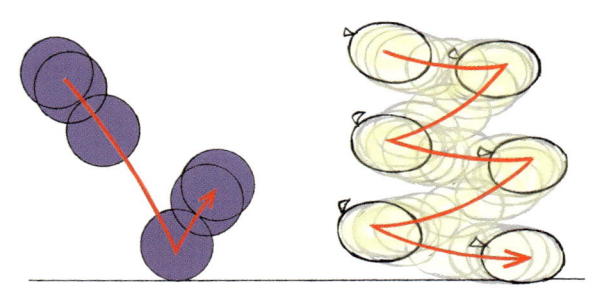

Weight of object: a balloon will move in a different way to a bowling ball.

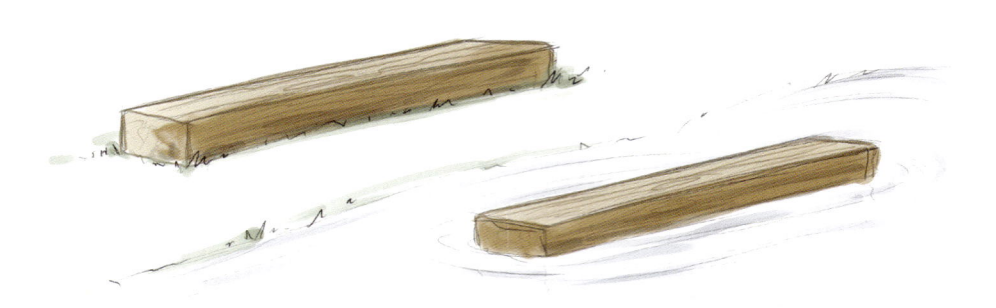

Environment: something heavy on land will be light in water.

How much force is being applied to the object? An object pushed gently will move in a different way to an object that is given a good shove.

How is the object constructed? A solid object will not distort at all, but a balloon full of water will distort a lot.

How is a character constructed? These considerations also apply to a statue of a human being and a real human being. A real human being will have bones – a character will have a head with a skull within it. The cranium of the skull will always stay the same shape, but the jaw could distort a great amount.

Force: how much effort is being applied to the object?

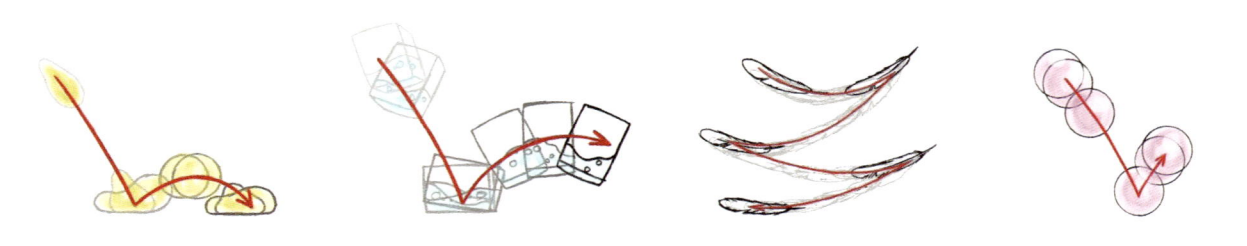

Construction: make sure you know how your object is constructed.

ANIMATION PRINCIPLES 25

twenty-five frames per second (or maybe even higher, depending on the system of recording). At certain points, the object will be moving so fast that the captured image will be blurred and out of focus. With animation, this can be replicated by distorting the shape of the object, even if it's solid. This should only be done at the point where the object is moving at its fastest. If it distorts when moving slowly, it will cease to be believable.

If a character jumps into a scene, bounces on a trampoline then flies out of the scene, it will look better if blurring or distortion are used at the point where the character moves fastest. The fastest points of movement will be where the character comes into the screen, up to the point of hitting the trampoline, then when the character leaves, having slowed down in mid-scene as the trampoline absorbs the energy. The character should be blurred or distorted at the two fastest points – this will make the movement more believable.

Character construction: you need to understand how a character is constructed in order to animate it correctly.

Blurring (Smearing)

When an object moves through the air at great speed it will distort because of blurring. When we shoot video, we capture that video at a certain *frame rate*. This could be twenty-four or

Exercise
Bouncing a ball
Imagine a ball being tossed into a scene, it hits the ground and bounces out of the scene (*see* Chapters 4, 5 and 6 for how to animate these balls as 2D, puppet and 3D animation). Animate different sorts of balls being tossed into the scene and showing, by the way they bounce, what sort of ball they are. Each ball should be a basic circular shape and the same size.

Soccer ball A soccer ball will animate into the scene in a graceful arc, hit the ground with a squash, then bounce out of the scene in another arc, but slightly lower than the first. Through each of the arcs the ball will distort slightly along the line of the arc.

Solid ball A heavy, solid ball, like a bowling ball, will follow a steeper arc. It will remain a circular shape and when it hits

Blurring and smearing. When something moves fast it will blur as it moves. Animate this blur.

Smear body at fastest points of the movement

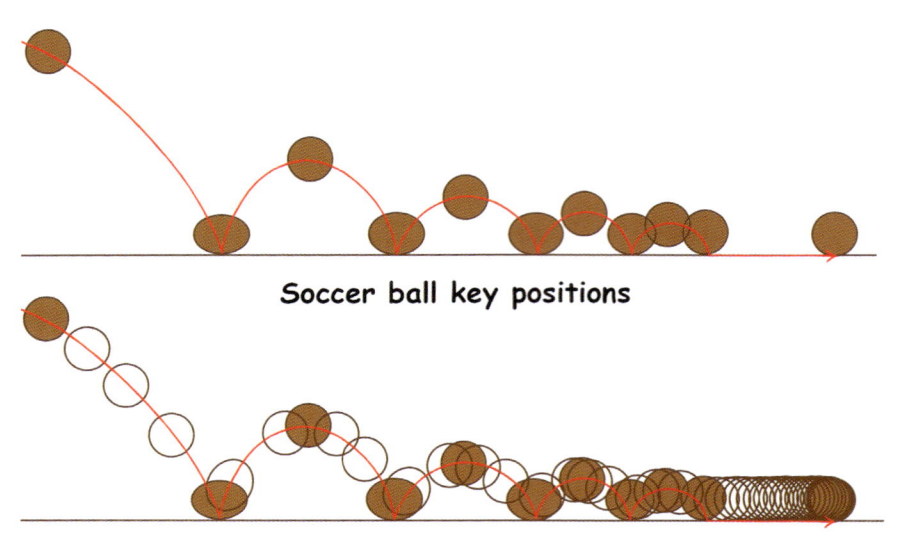

The trajectory of a soccer ball bouncing on the ground.

Soccer ball key positions

Soccer ball inbetween positions

the ground will not bounce as high. It also will not display any squash or stretch. It will bounce several times, but nowhere near as high as the soccer ball. It could then roll along until it reaches a stop. It will also move much faster than the soccer ball (the gaps between the ball in each frame will therefore be larger than with the soccer ball). As a solid ball is heavy, it takes a larger amount of energy to lift it up in order to drop it. This energy is transferred to the ball when it is dropped. Consequently, the ball contains a lot of energy and will take further to roll to a stop than a soccer ball.

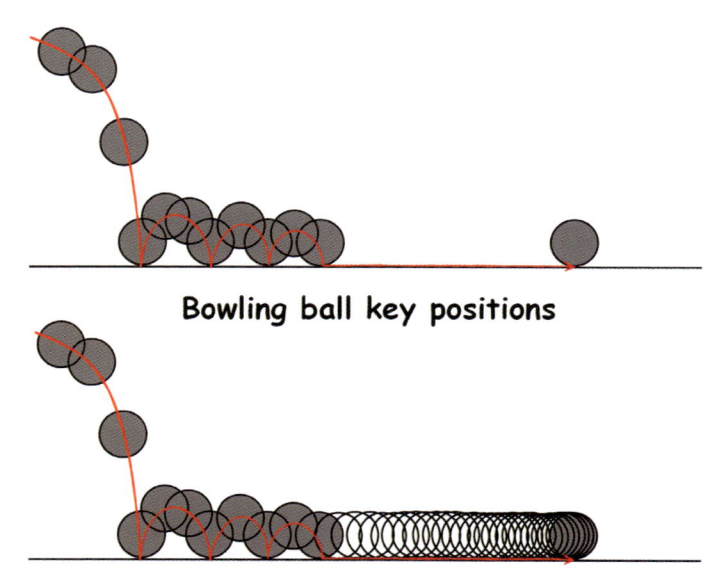

Bowling ball key positions

Bowling ball inbetween positions

The trajectory of a heavy ball bouncing on the ground.

ANIMATION PRINCIPLES 27

Beach ball A beach ball will almost float into the scene through an arc. It will move slower, so the gaps between each of the balls will be smaller than with the soccer ball or pool ball. Because it is so light, it won't squash as much as the soccer ball when it hits the ground. The lower part of the beach ball seems to 'crush', while the top part remains ovoid. It will also touch the ground more delicately, as if a cushion of air above the ground is slowing its descent. Adding an extra drawing, just before it hits the ground, will make it impact with the floor in a softer way.

Water-filled balloon A water-filled balloon, being quite heavy, will move though the first arc quite quickly (big gaps between the balls on each frame), but will squash a huge amount when it hits the ground and then only give a little bounce out of the squash. It could bounce several times, then roll to a stop. The balloon will distort through the arcs of the bounces and while it is rolling along. The reason for this is that the energy is absorbed by the liquid in the balloon. The energy pushes the sides of the balloon outward to its elasticated limit and then returns, upward towards the top of the balloon. The energy will then go downward, through the middle of the balloon and push outward again, producing a slightly smaller squash the second time. This will continue as it rolls along the ground, wobbling up and down as it rolls to a stop.

You could elaborate on this exercise by having a character jump from a cliff and bouncing on a diving board, then bouncing up and diving into water, showing squash and stretch, blurring and smearing, and acceleration and deceleration.

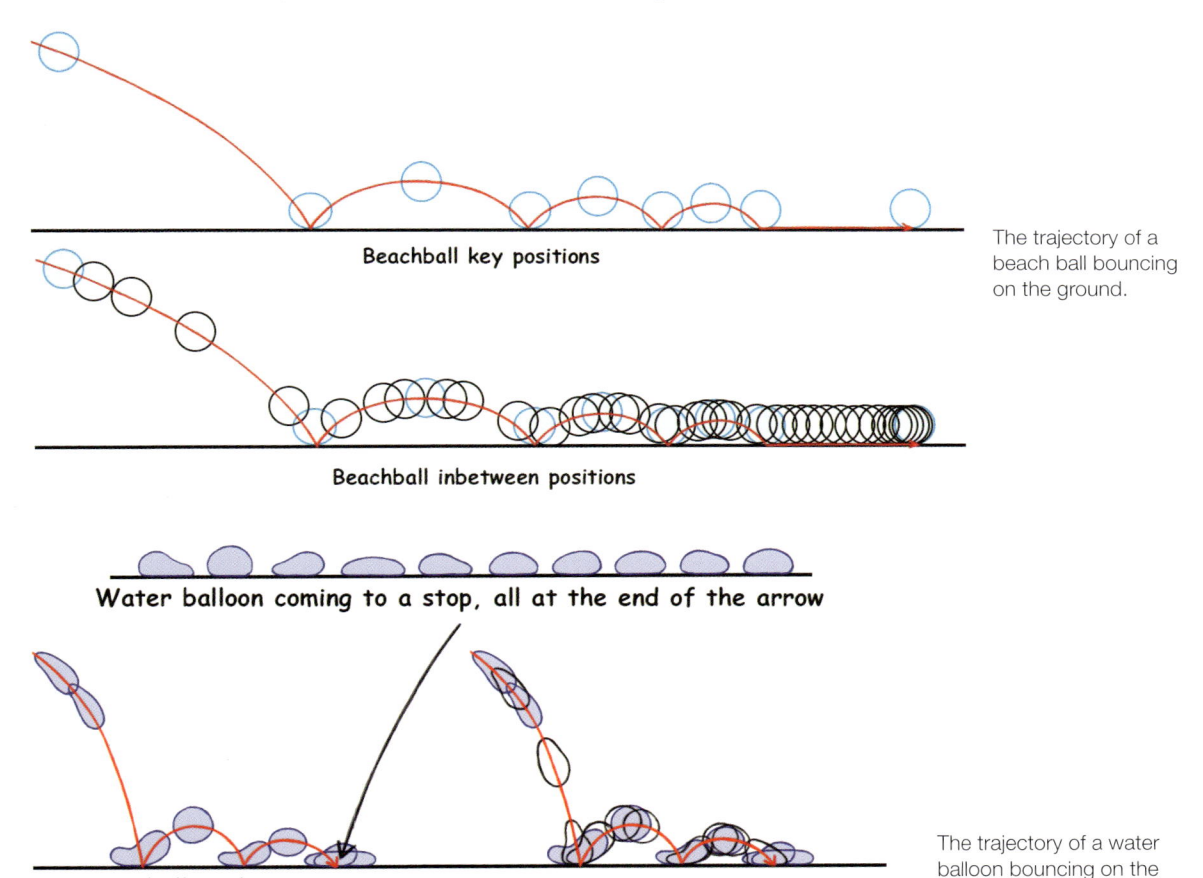

Beachball key positions

Beachball inbetween positions

The trajectory of a beach ball bouncing on the ground.

Water balloon coming to a stop, all at the end of the arrow

Water balloon key positions   Water balloon inbetween positions

The trajectory of a water balloon bouncing on the ground.

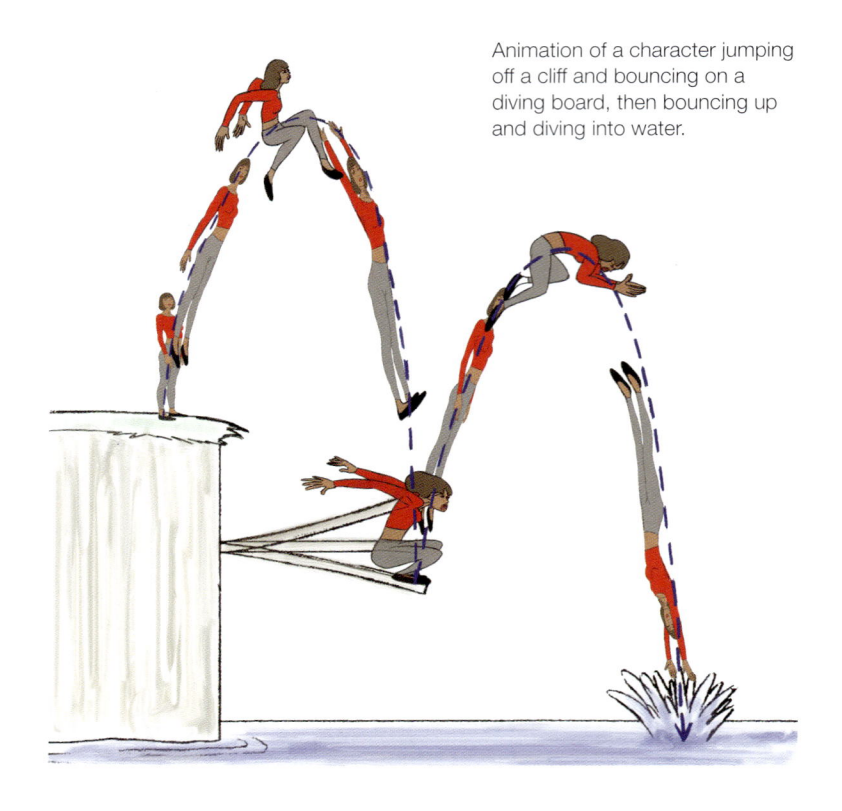

Animation of a character jumping off a cliff and bouncing on a diving board, then bouncing up and diving into water.

EASE IN AND EASE OUT

Whenever something moves, it will usually accelerate to its optimum speed, then decelerate to a stop. A motorbike or a car will accelerate when it moves off, travel along the road at a safe speed (if the driver is not breaking the law) and decelerate to a stop when the brakes are applied.

This can be done smoothly and evenly, or it can be done with a certain amount of variation in the acceleration and deceleration to give an idea of character, weight, influence from external sources and so on. This will give an idea of character and intention. Keys give the plot and in-betweens give the character. Move an object from one position to another and try different in-between positions to see what they do.

In drawn animation, timing charts can be drawn on to the bottom of your drawings to show how the movement will ease in and ease out of each key position. In the following illustration, drawing 5 is halfway between the two key positions at drawing 1 and drawing 6. So in the timing chart, an arc is drawn between numbers 1 and 5 and numbers 5 and 6 to indicate that drawing 5 is halfway between the two key positions. Drawing 5 would be regarded as a *breakdown*. A breakdown is the most important in-between drawing. Drawing 4 is halfway between drawing 1 and drawing 5. Drawing 3 is halfway between drawing 1 and 4. Drawing 2 is halfway between drawing 1 and 3.

Exercise
Animating the object without any ease in and ease out

Take an object like a toy car, toy motorbike or a coin. Place it at one side of the screen and then shoot one frame. Move the object along by a short distance. Take a shot. Move it by the same distance. Take another shot. Keep doing this until you reach the other side of the screen. Play the animation back. You will find that it seems to move very suddenly when it starts moving and stops very

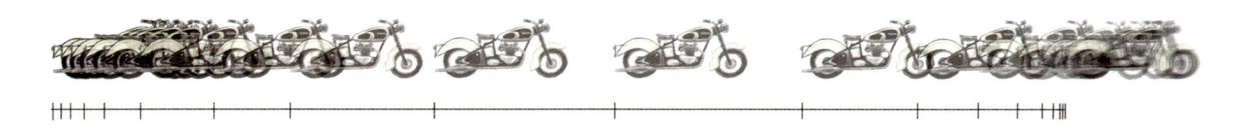

Toy motorcycle accelerating and decelerating along a path.

ANIMATION PRINCIPLES **29**

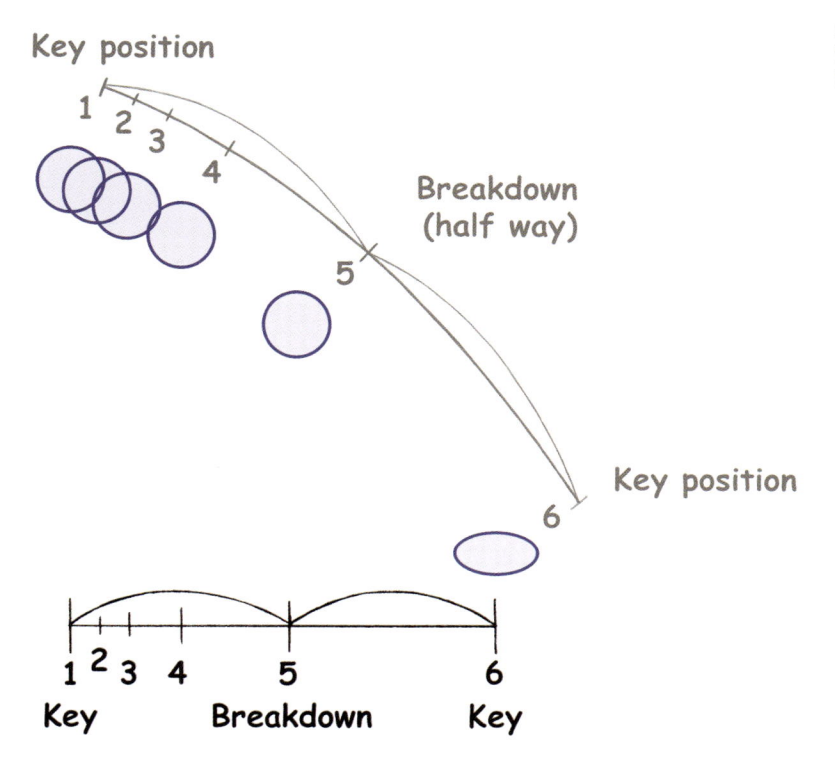

A timing chart is there to hold information, so that you don't have to remember it.

Ease in and ease out exercise that shows how real things move.

suddenly at the end (*see* Chapter 5 for how to animate this as puppet animation).

Animating the object with ease in and ease out
Take the same object. Place it at one side of the screen and then shoot one frame. Move the object a very small amount forwards and take a shot. Move it a slightly larger distance and take a shot. Move it an even larger distance, then take another shot. Increase the distances between each shot until you reach the middle of the screen. From this point onward, decrease the distances between each shot until you come to a stop at the other side of the screen. Take a look at it. You will find that the object moves in a more believable way.

ARCS

Most objects, when moving, will follow an arc. If you throw a ball ahead of you, it won't follow a straight line – gravity will make it fall towards the ground in a smooth arc. When the ball hits the ground, it will bounce up in an arc.

Most movements within a character's body will follow arcs. The part of our brain (the occipital lobe

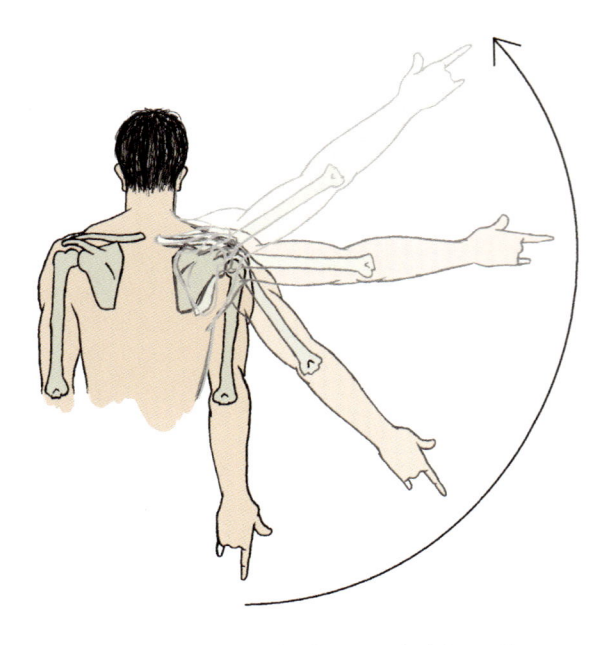

Whenever a human or an animal moves, the joints will move in arcs.

things further away. The animal in the distance could be dinner, or it could want us for dinner. We needed to work out how it moved and react accordingly.

Human Anatomy

In order to understand how a character moves, we need to learn a bit about human anatomy. A human consists of the following parts.

The spine At the centre of the human skeleton is the 'S'-shaped spine. This can flex backwards and forwards, from side to side, and can also twist. It consists of twenty-four individual bones, called vertebrae. The lower part of the spine is called the lumbar. This is the most flexible part of the spine and a large amount of emotion can be expressed through it. If the lumbar is bent forwards, it pulls the chest down and has the effect of pulling the arms in and covering the front of the body. This gives a closed, defensive and negative feeling to the mood of a character. If the lumbar is bent

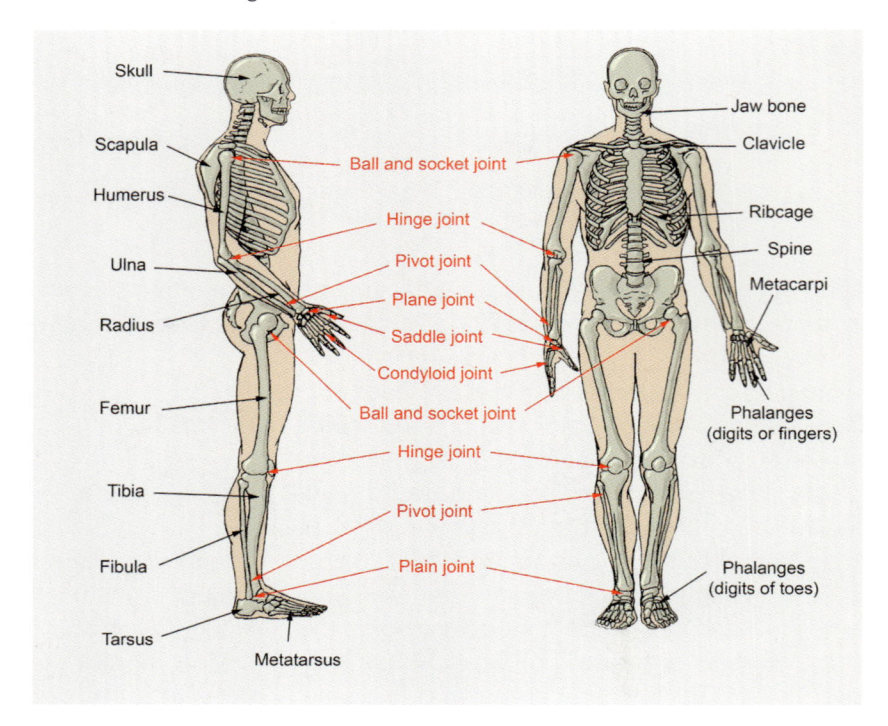

of the cerebrum) that interprets movement is conditioned to look for arcs. The reason for this is that when our primate ancestors evolved from being tree dwellers to living on savannahs (large open plains) due to climate and environmental change, they needed to be able to interpret movement from a long distance. When our ancestors had lived in a jungle in small groups, they had a lot of intimate contact; anything further away would have been obscured by vegetation. When our ancestors became upright walking apes living on the savannah, they had to interpret

The skeleton is the basis of all characters.

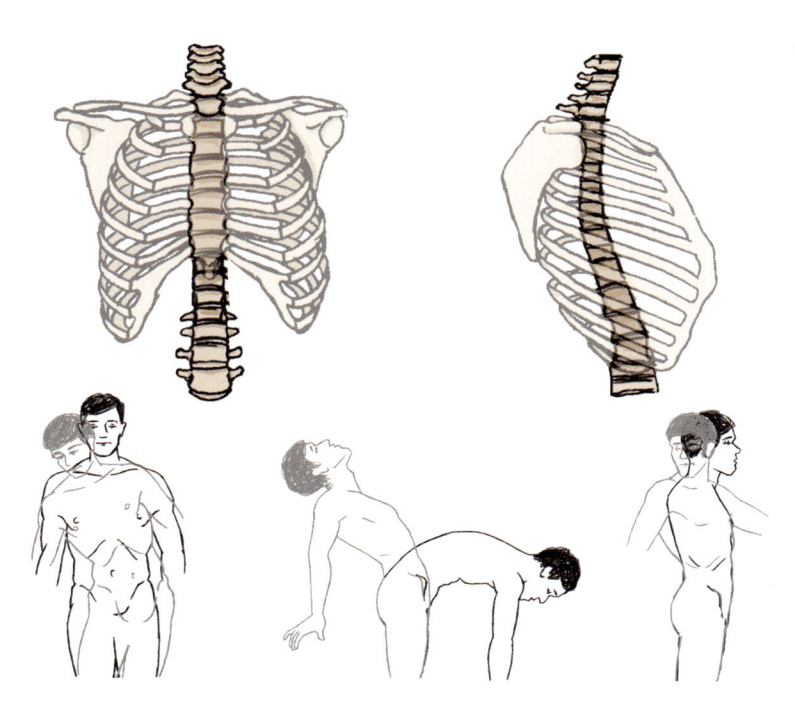

The spine is the basic shape of the skeleton.

backwards, it pulls the chest back, pulling back the arms and opening up the body. This gives an open, positive and confident posture.

The ribcage The upper part of the spine has a ribcage that provides solid protection for the heart and lungs. This part of the spine will have slightly less movement than the lower end (the lumbar).

The pelvic girdle At the base of the spine is the pelvic girdle. This solid set of bones plays a role in keeping us upright. The spine attaches to the top of the pelvic girdle and the legs are attached to it with ball and socket joints. It is also attached to the largest muscle in the body, the gluteus maximus (basically the muscle that makes up the bottom). This muscle holds us upright and provides us with

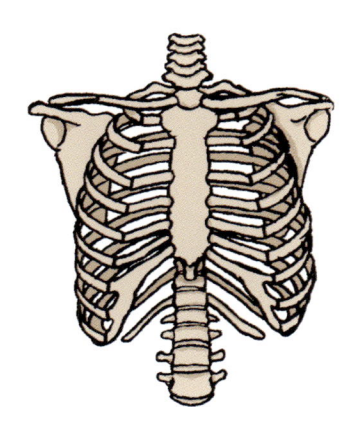

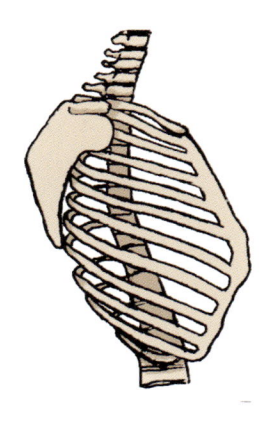

The ribcage is the upper, solid part of the body, protecting the heart and lungs.

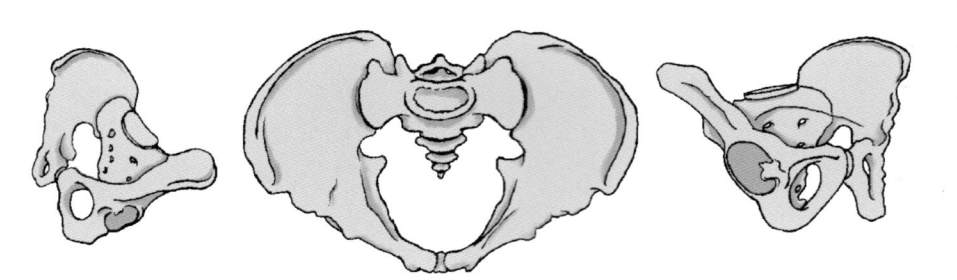

The pelvic girdle is the solid part of the lower body; the muscles attached to it hold the body upright.

balance, as well as the main thrust from the legs in walking, running and jumping.

The skull At the top of the spine is the skull. The skull consists of several plates that sit together loosely when we are born, then fuse together as we grow up. Attached to the skull is the jawbone, which hinges from the point at which it meets the skull. It has up and down and side to side movements, which aid chewing, facial expressions and talking.

The shoulders At the top of the ribcage are the shoulders. They consist of two collarbones (clavicles) at the front and two shoulder blades (scapulars) at the back. The scapulars are free-floating and can be moved from side to side and up and down. The upper arms are attached to the shoulders by ball and socket joints. A lot of expression can be conveyed by the shoulders. Raising the shoulders up gives a shrug or can show excitement, while lowering them indicates exhaustion or depression.

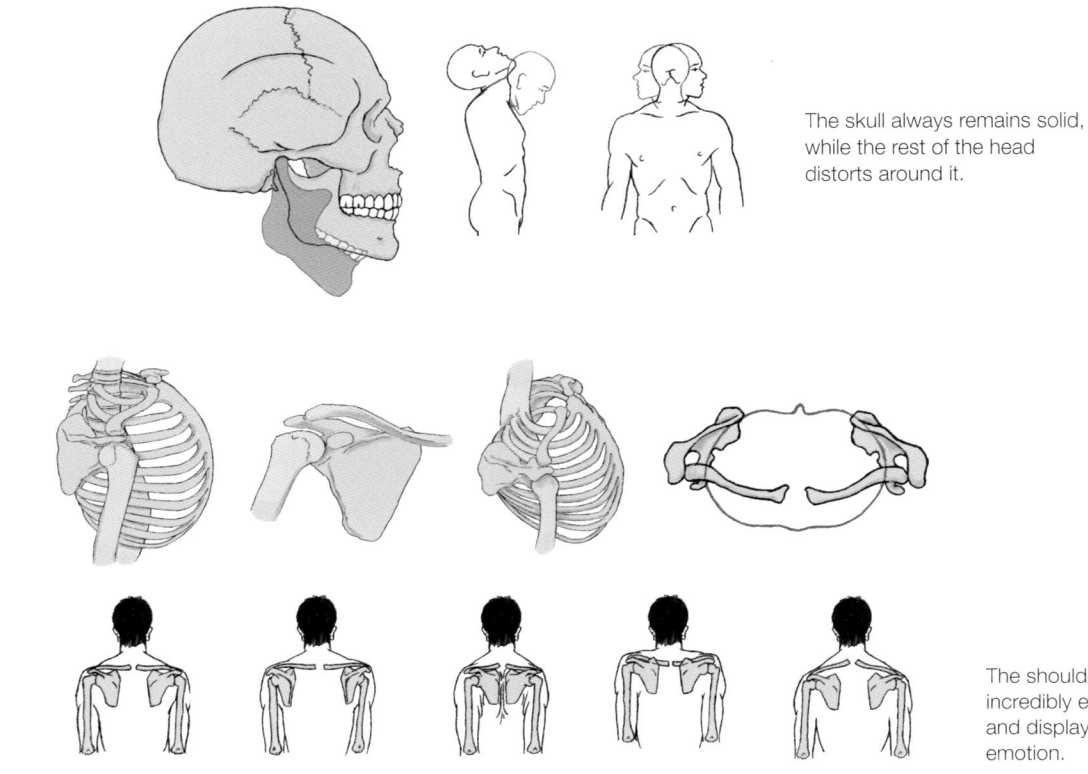

The skull always remains solid, while the rest of the head distorts around it.

The shoulders are incredibly expressive and display a lot of emotion.

Different Types of Joints

The arms, legs, hands and feet are attached with different types of joints.

Ball and socket joint The arms are attached to the scapulae and legs are attached to the pelvic girdle by ball and socket joints. The ball and socket joint allows a huge amount of circular movement in most directions. It consists of a ball at the end of the arm or leg and a socket in the scapula or pelvic girdle.

Hinge joint The knees and elbows are connected by hinge joints, which work just like a door hinge. These give about 180 degrees of movement forwards and back, but very little lateral movement from side to side.

Pivot joint The lower arm and (to a lesser extent) the lower leg are joined by a pivot joint, giving a rotation movement to the hands and feet. This allows the radius and ulna (in the lower arm) and the tibia and fibula (in the lower leg) to rotate around each other. With the forearm, this is really

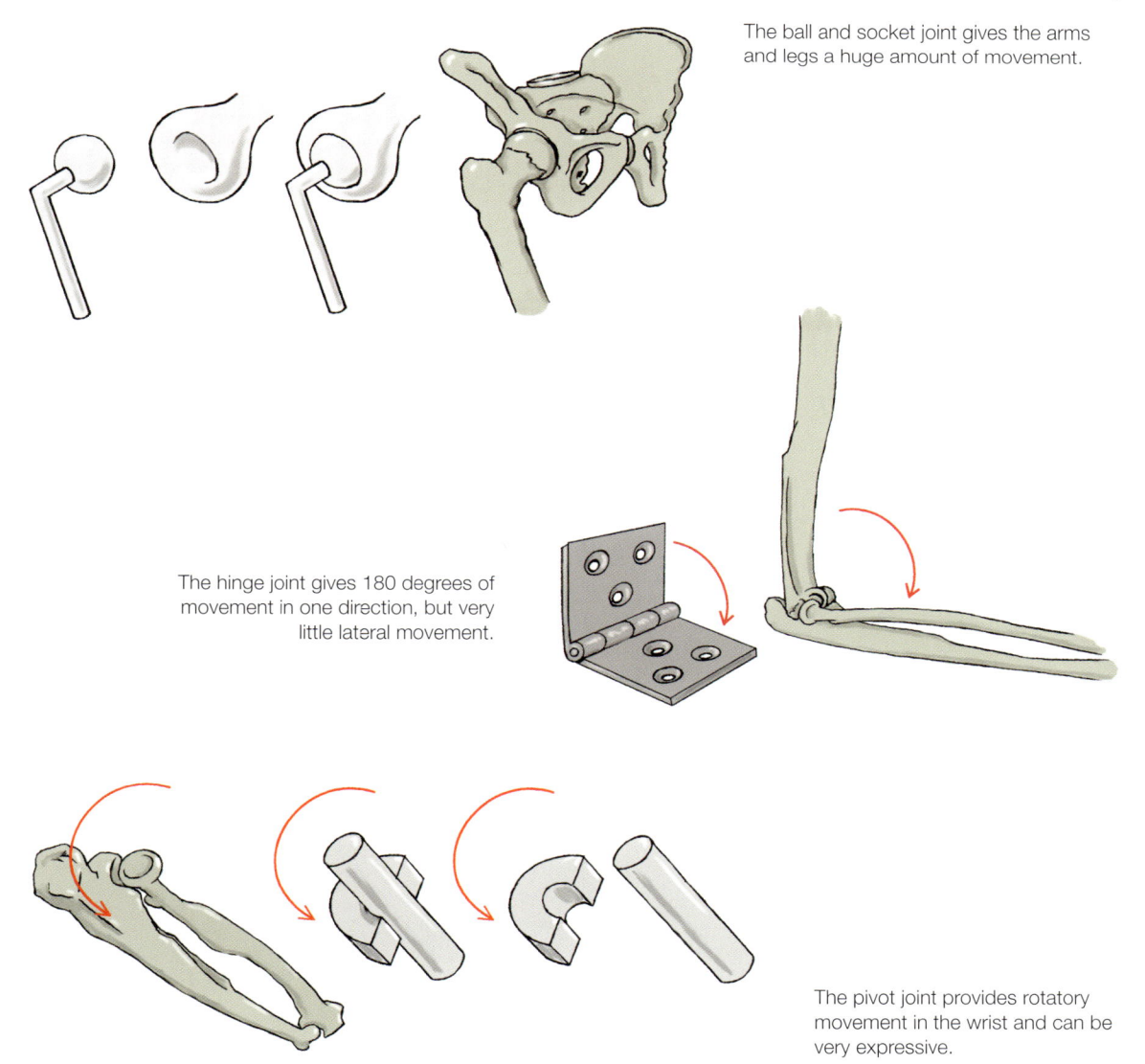

The ball and socket joint gives the arms and legs a huge amount of movement.

The hinge joint gives 180 degrees of movement in one direction, but very little lateral movement.

The pivot joint provides rotatory movement in the wrist and can be very expressive.

useful for delicate wrist movements that can help to demonstrate the character of a person.

Plane joint The part where the lower arm meets the wrist and where the lower leg meets the ankle is a plane joint. This is like a cross between a hinge joint and a ball and socket joint and allows for further rotation of the wrist and ankle. As with the pivot joint, this can be used to give delicate, expressive poses with the wrist.

Saddle joint The thumbs are attached to the hands with a saddle joint. This gives a limited rotational movement. It also means that we, as human beings, can pick up things with our inverted thumbs, such as pencils, sculpting tools, computer mice and tablet styli. The saddle joint is why we can be creative and do animation!

Condyloid joint The fingers and toes are attached to the hand and foot with condyloid joints. These are a bit like hinge joints, but with more sideways movement. It means that we can flex our fingers outward in order to pick up larger objects with a suitable amount of purchase. The rest of the fingers and toes are jointed with hinge joints.

Each of these joints provides movement that results in an arc. So whenever you move any part of a creature, it should move in some sort of an

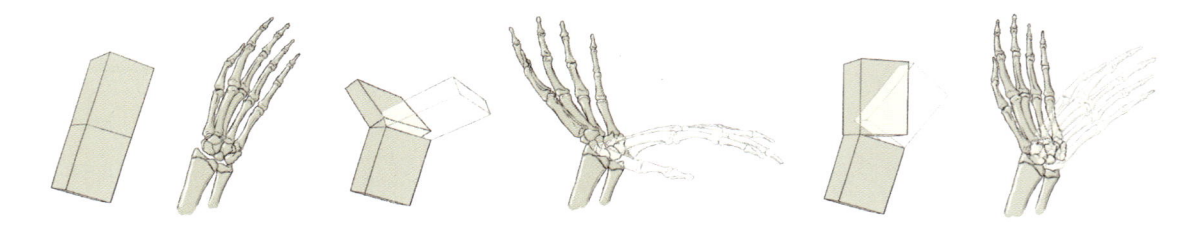

The plane joint gives about 160 degrees of movement backwards and forwards and about 45 degrees of movement side to side.

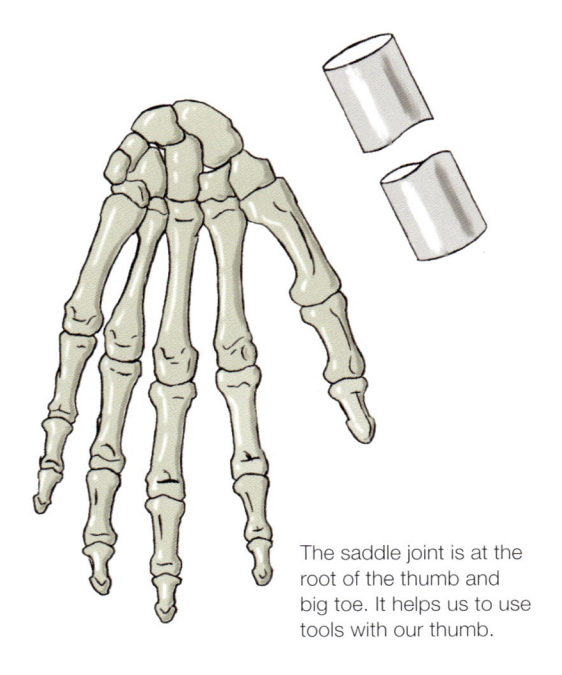

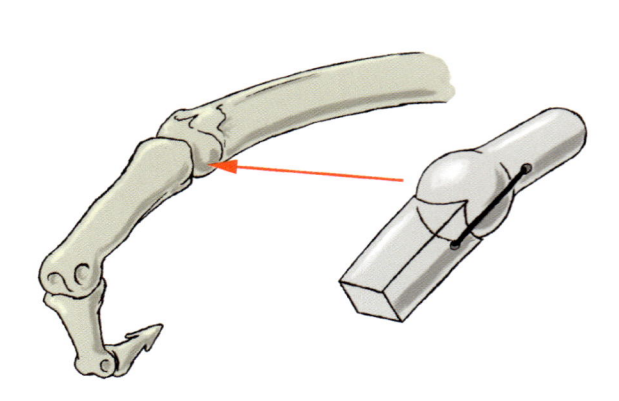

The saddle joint is at the root of the thumb and big toe. It helps us to use tools with our thumb.

The condyloid joint helps the fingers and toes to move from side to side. It enables the fingers to pick up different sized objects.

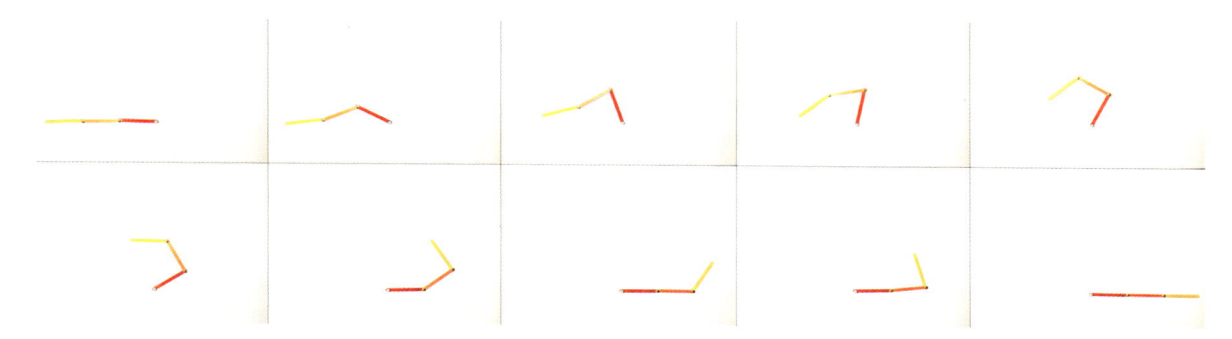

This exercise helps you to understand how joints work.

arc. As I said above, part of our brain is attuned to look for these arc-like movements. It is very important!

Exercise

In this exercise we will move three sticks joined together with hinge joints (*see* Chapters 4, 5 and 6 for how to animate these sticks as 2D, puppet and 3D animation).

Take three lollipop sticks and join them together with pins or clips (or create three sticks joined together in 3D, or draw three sticks on paper). Arrange the first stick in the middle of the shot, with the other two sticks hanging down.

Move the first stick to the left side slightly, pivoting from the bottom (taking a shot with the camera). Have the other sticks following it in an arc. Continue moving the sticks to the left, taking a shot each time. When the first stick has moved to about 45 degrees, move it in the other direction. The attached sticks will continue moving to the left, following the first stick.

WEIGHT AND BALANCE

In order for an audience to believe that a character is in front of us, on planet earth it must demonstrate weight and balance.

Weight

Any character will demonstrate its weight. When standing up, the legs will be slightly bent to show the weight of the character. The bigger and heavier the character, the more the legs will be bent.

When a character is holding a heavy object, the legs will be more bent and the centre of gravity will be lower. A heavier person will be slower in their movements in order to move their weight around. A person carrying a heavy object will also move

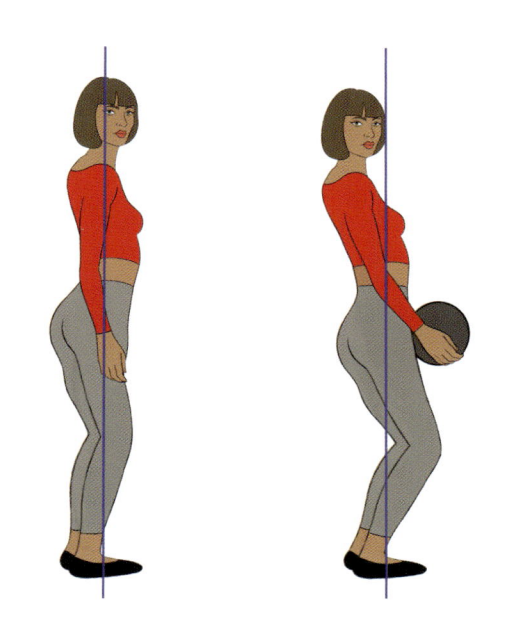

The weight of a character must always be equally balanced.

slower. There must always be an equal amount of weight either side of the line of balance.

Balance

The stability of an object is affected by its shape. The wider the base, the more stable it will be. For example, a cube is a very stable object that is difficult to push over or roll down a slope. A ball, on the other hand, is much less stable and is easy to push along or roll down a slope. Because of this instability, a ball is much more susceptible to the force of gravity.

Our character maintains stability by spreading its legs. The wider the legs are spread, the lower the centre of gravity and the more difficult it is to knock over the character. To ensure that your character looks balanced, imagine a plumb line running top to bottom through the centre. There should always be an equal amount of weight either side of this line.

As the character leans in one direction, the plumb line will move with the centre of gravity. If it swings far enough to reach a leg, then other parts of the body will need to be moved to maintain balance and to stop the character from falling over. For example, if a person leans forwards, to maintain their balance they will need to stretch their arms out behind them. If they lean further, they will then need to stretch one leg out behind them. If a person holds a heavy bucket of water, they will lean their body at the opposite angle to the arm holding the bucket. Someone who is overweight will need to lean back to balance his or her large stomach.

One good way of seeing if your character is correctly balanced is to look at a mirror image of it. If you are doing a drawing on a piece of paper, turn it over and look at the back of it on a light box. Does it still look balanced? If it does not, redraw it so that it looks correct. If you are doing puppet or 3D animation, look at your computer screen via a mirror. If it looks unbalanced, move the character until it appears correct.

Certain objects will be easier to push than others.

A character with the legs spread will be more stable than a character with the legs together.

ANIMATION PRINCIPLES **37**

When carrying a heavy object, a character will have to lean in the opposite direction to the heavy object.

Exercise

To understand weight and balance we will animate a human character lifting a heavy object. The three exercises have been set out step by step below.

Working out the key positions I have included timing charts with each of the key positions to show where the in-betweens should be placed.

In-betweening the key positions If you are doing this exercise as puppet animation, you can do a test first with just the puppet in the key positions (a *pop-through*), work out the timing and then redo the animation straight ahead, following the timing you have worked out (more of this in Chapter 5). If you are doing the exercise in 3D, do the key positions first, then adjust them using the Curve Editor, or by adding extra key positions (more about this in Chapter 6).

You can follow the exercises as shown below, or use them as a rough guide and animate something that you have acted out yourself. In this exercise we will get our character to pick up a heavy ball. For the majority of the time, the character should be balanced, that is, there should be an equal amount of weight on either side of the imaginary plumb line.

Before you do the animation, act out the movement. Find an object (I would suggest a bowling ball, though not everyone has one of these lying around) and have a go at picking it up. Remember to lift the ball correctly. Keep your back as straight as possible and bend your legs to bring yourself down to the ball. Use your legs to provide most of the momentum (the largest muscle in the body is at the top of the leg, the gluteus maximus) and keep your back straight. Please do not pick up something too heavy. Just to be on the safe side, pretend that the object you are picking up is heavier than it is.

It is a good idea to video yourself doing this action. That way, you can play back the video and see how you picked up the ball. Videoing yourself for an animation you want to execute is called a Live Action Video Shoot (LAVS). When working professionally, most animators will do LAVS in order to help with their animation and it can also be a good thing to show a director, just to make sure that you are on the right track.

It is always a good idea to act out a movement that you want to animate. Here is an example of me acting out lifting a ball (you don't have to wear such a strange outfit to do this).

Thumbnail sketches are a good way to sum up the movement quickly and to simplify what you do.

By acting out this sequence, you should have an understanding of the movement, getting the different stages clear in your head. I have provided some *thumbnail* sketches, but use these as a guide. Use your own research to guide your animation for this sequence so as to personalize it.

When you act out the sequence, exaggerate the weight of the object you are picking up. This will help the animation to work better. Exaggerating the weight of the object makes the action clearer to the audience. It can also help to study mime artists. These performers are trained to give the illusion of acting with props that do not exist. In animation the props exist, but they have no substance.

A good idea is to have a go at drawing very rough thumbnail sketches that sum up the movement as key positions.

Working out the key positions
The first stage is to draw the key positions and then shoot them on a *line tester* (a line tester is a camera attached to a computer, where you can shoot your drawings and then, with an animation program such as Dragonframe, give each of the drawings a certain amount of frames to see the movement played back at roughly the right speed. More about line testers in Chapter 4). There are ten key positions for this sequence. The sequence is about 100 frames long. When you work out these key positions, you may have to give more time to the action than when you acted it out. A piece of animation often needs more time for an audience to watch it than a piece of live-action footage. So slow down the action slightly when you animate.

I have numbered the drawings according to the frame numbers to which they relate. When I first did the key positions for this sequence, I shot them on a line tester, then guessed how many frames it would take to get me from one key position to the next. On the line tester, I gave each of these key drawings a certain amount of frames and played it back. When it looked right, I then guessed how I would space the in-between drawings. The timing charts below the drawings of the lift show how I would space out the in-between drawings.

- The first key position is at frame 1. Begin with your character standing over the ball. Make sure that the ball is not too far away; otherwise as the character bends, they will end up having to reach too far forwards.
- The second key position is at frame 9. Move your character up slightly. This is the anticipatory move.
- The third key position is at frame 19. This is where our character is grabbing hold of the ball. The hands should be placed at the lower part of the ball.
- The fourth key position is at frame 29. As the character starts to pick up the ball, their body will lean backwards and their bottom will go down. The weight of the ball causes the arms to become straight and even stretch a bit.

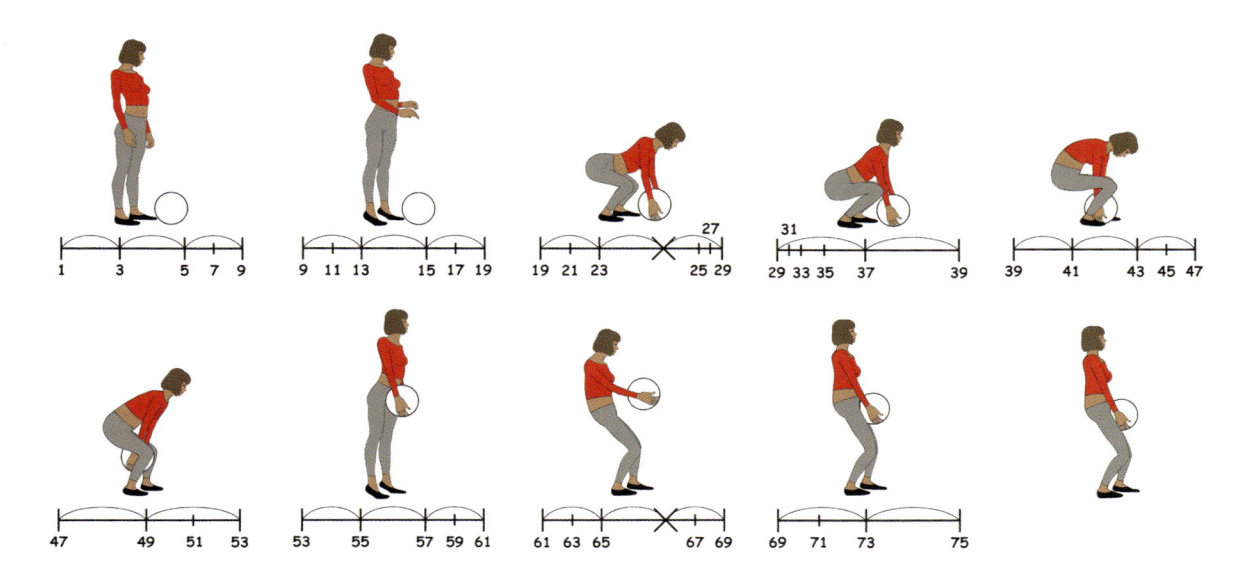

The key positions of the action of lifting a ball.

- The fifth key position is at frame 39. As the weight of the body is moved backwards, the arms straighten and the ball leaves the ground. The ball swings between the character's legs. Think of the arms being straightened by the weight of the ball and swinging like a pendulum. As the ball travels between the legs, it crosses the plumb line and causes the character to lean forwards.
- The sixth key position is at frame 47. As the body is raised further, the ball will swing further between the legs of the character, causing the body to lean backwards.
- The seventh key position is at frame 53. The character slows down as they go on tiptoe. This is the overshoot position (more about overshoot below).
- The eighth key position is at frame 61. As the character starts descending towards the resting position the ball keeps moving upward. This is because the ball contains momentum from being picked up and wants to keep going.
- The ninth key position is at frame 69. Our character has moved up slightly from the last key position and the ball has fallen down against her legs.
- The tenth key position is at frame 75. Here the character has dropped down slightly and is leaning back and bending the legs to take account of the weight of the ball.

These key positions are established by working out how long you think it will take to put over the action to an audience. Shoot the key positions with a number of frames and see how it works. If it is too quick, add more frames to each key position. If it is too slow, take frames away from each key position. When it looks correct, you can then work out how many images are needed between each key position.

In-betweening the key positions
When we were animating the bouncing balls, we could stick quite closely to the timing charts. With a human being it's not that simple. The timing charts should be regarded as a rough guide as to where the in-betweens should go. You may find that you will have to make some parts of the character's body move faster than others, or leave other bits behind in order to make the movement more believable.

Drag the hand

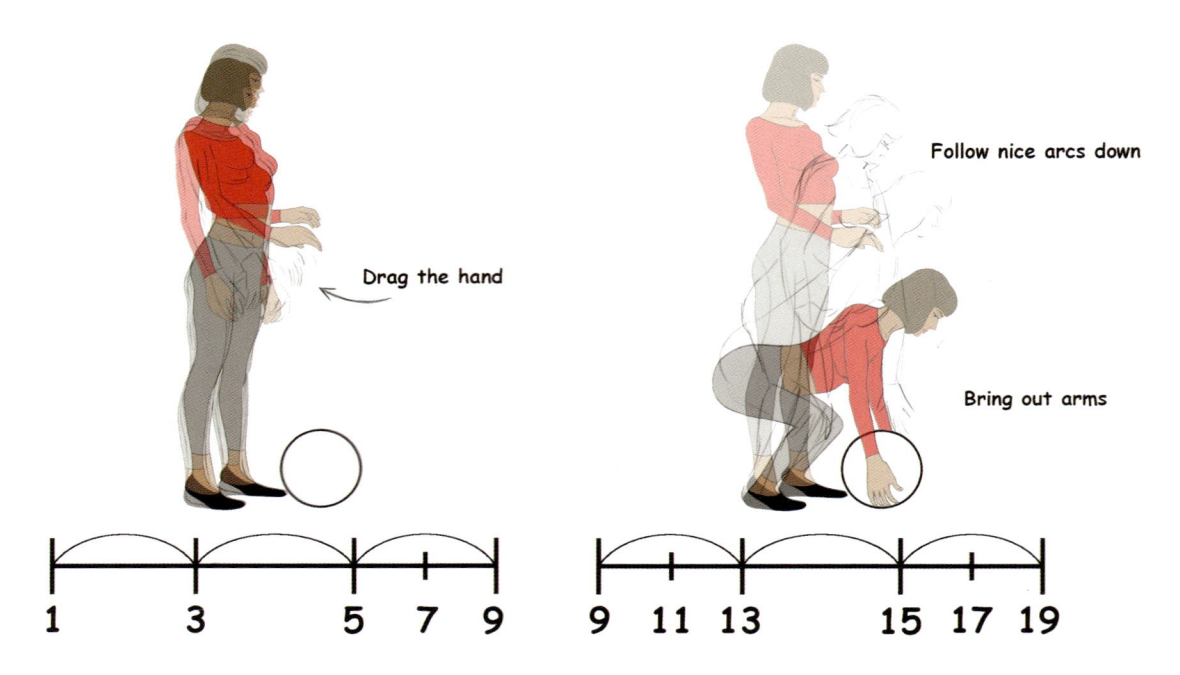

Follow nice arcs down

Bring out arms

1 3 5 7 9   9 11 13 15 17 19

The in-between positions of lifting a ball.

Between key position one and key position two (frames 1 and 9), make the hands drag a bit to make the wrist movement seem more fluid.

Between the second and third key positions (frames 9 and 19), make the hands flail upward as they move out of the second key position. As the hand goes downward towards the ball make it move outward towards us to give the idea that it is going to grasp the ball.

Between key positions three and four (frames 19 and 29), the first bit of the movement is quite slow (frames 19, 21 and 23 are close together) then there is a sudden movement as the arms become taught (a big gap between frames 23 and 25). At the very end of the movement there are three drawings very close to key position four to decelerate quickly (frames 25, 27 and 29 are very close together).

Between key positions four and five (frames 29 and 39), there is a slow movement until the halfway point (frames 29 to 37) and then a sudden movement as the heavy ball 'gives' (between frames 37 to 39). At frame 37 the body is positioned halfway between 29 and 39, but the ball is positioned about a third of the way between 29 and 39. This will give the impression of the ball being heavy.

Between key positions five and six (frames 39 and 47), the ball swings between the character's legs, then slows as it reaches the end of its swing to the left (43, 45 and 47). The arms stay straight and they swing like a pendulum.

Between keys six and seven (frames 47 and 53), the character reaches their highest position and the ball swings slightly to the right as it is picked up. The arms stay straight and the character goes up on tiptoe. They slow down as they reach this position (frames 49, 51 and 53).

Between keys seven and eight (frames 53 and 61), the character comes back down to earth, but the ball continues moving upward, slowing at its apex (frames 57 and 59).

Between keys eight and nine (frames 61 and 69), the ball falls to a resting point against the character's tummy with the arms at full stretch. The ball comes out of its apex slowly (frames 63 and 65), falls quickly (gap between frames 65 and 67), then

ANIMATION PRINCIPLES **41**

slows into the next key (frame 69). This slowing down is caused by the body moving upward and the arms stretching slightly, the body slowing to its highest point at key nine (frame 69).

Between keys nine and ten (frames 69 and 75), the figure comes down to the final resting position, slower out of key nine (the drawings between frames 69 to 73 are closer together).

TIMING AND SPACING (PERFORMING WITH IN-BETWEENS)

Unlike the ease in and ease out principle (which works better for inanimate objects like cars), most characters will move in an uneven way between each major pose, for example:

- If a person is hesitant about touching something, the initial part of the movement of the hand will be slower and then the movement will be faster towards the end.
- If a person is desperate to touch something, the movement will be faster at the beginning and relatively slower at the end.
- If the person is indifferent about touching the object, the movement will be more even, with ease in at the start and ease out at the end.

One way to help with this is to use timing charts. These are a graphic interpretation of the movement, mainly used in drawn animation. At the bottom of each piece of paper with a key position drawing on it, a timing chart is drawn as a guide to how the character will move from this key position to the next. All timing charts incorporate a certain

The timing and spacing of an action can affect how an audience interprets what is happening.

amount of guesswork. You try to imagine how the movement will be and then guess where each of the in-between images will be placed to get the kind of movement you want.

Exercise

Animate someone having a drink of water. All of the key positions for this exercise are the same, but the way that the movement between them is done will be different. This is done by changing the positions of the in-between images. One way to work this out is by using timing charts, as noted above.

So if a character is going to move their hand down to pick up a glass of water, they may move the hand quickly at first and then slower at the point where the hand touches the glass.

The arcs between the lines on the timing chart indicate where the major in-between drawings, otherwise known as breakdowns, are positioned. If there are two arcs between the key drawings and one breakdown drawing in the middle, it shows that the breakdown drawing is in the middle of the two key positions.

If the breakdown drawing is one-third closer to the first key position and two-thirds further away from the second key position, it means that the breakdown drawing is nearer key one. This will mean that the movement is slower at the start and faster at the end.

So, if a character is really thirsty, they will move quickly at the start of each movement because our character really needs a drink.

STAGING

Staging in animation is a lot like composition in a painting. Everything in a scene should guide the viewer's eye and draw attention to what's important within the scene. The motion of everything else should be kept to a minimum. Use background objects to direct the eye to the part of the screen that you want the audience to look at and make sure that the area behind the character is not cluttered up with lots of stuff that will distract an audience. You can also use light and shade to illuminate the main object or person. Make a strong silhouette to highlight

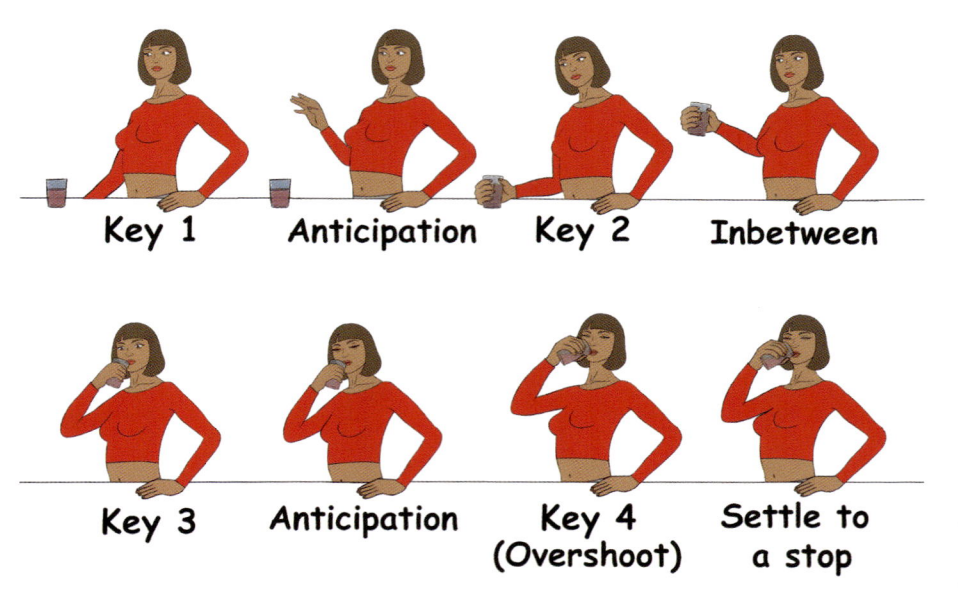

These are the key positions of a timing and spacing exercise.

the character, or use vivid colours – the audience will be drawn to anything bright on a dull background.

Make sure that your characters demonstrate strong silhouettes – for example, if the character is completely black, could you tell what the character is doing? If not, come up with a pose that has a stronger silhouette.

When designing a scene, it is often better to make the design asymmetrical. Having a character right in the middle of the scene is easy for an audience to see, but is also boring to look at.

Staging is important for ensuring that your audience is looking at the right part of the screen.

Strong silhouettes are very important and help an audience to understand what is happening in a shot as quickly as possible.

Exercise

Draw a background that leads the audience's eye to the part of the screen that you want them to look at.

ANTICIPATION

Anticipation does two things. It gets an audience to look at the right part of a screen just before a major event happens and prepares an audience for that action. It also 'winds up' a character like a spring before they do something. For example, if someone is going to jump up into the air, they need to move their body down first before they jump. When they jump up into the air, they will slow down into the apex of their bounce before falling towards the ground. When they hit the ground, they will squash down and come back up to a stop (this is called follow-through; *see* next section). It is almost impossible to get a character to jump without bending the knees first.

If a person throws a ball, they will move the arm and body backwards in order to gain momentum for the throw.

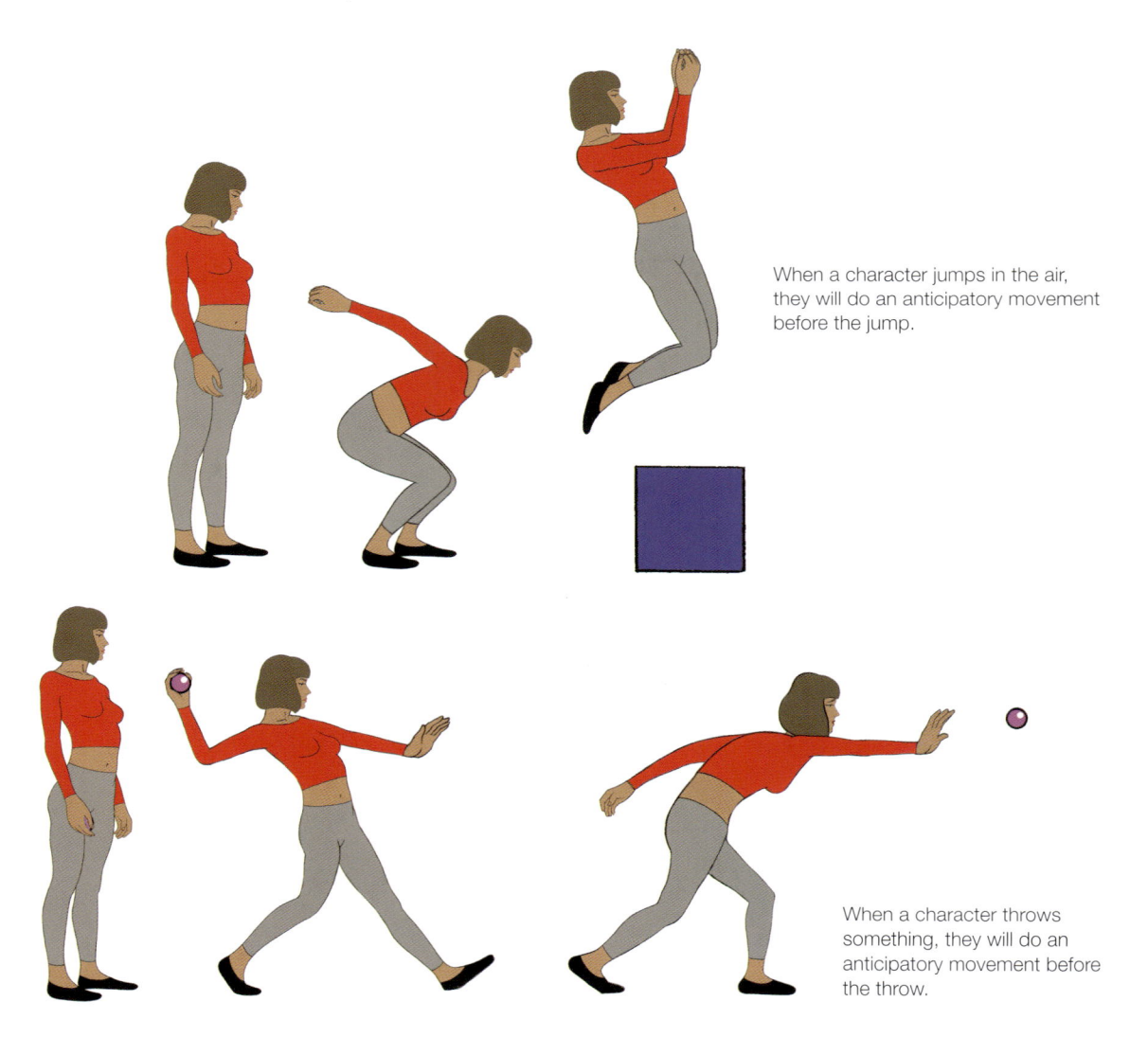

When a character jumps in the air, they will do an anticipatory movement before the jump.

When a character throws something, they will do an anticipatory movement before the throw.

ANIMATION PRINCIPLES   45

Exercise

Animate a character, standing mid-screen. They then walk, run or jump out of screen, demonstrating anticipation before they exit.

When a character walks out of screen, when they start to walk somewhere, or for that matter almost any movement will have a preceding anticipatory movement to get it going.

OVERLAPPING ACTION AND FOLLOW-THROUGH

When a character walks out of screen, they will do an anticipatory movement before they start to walk.

When objects come to a standstill after being in motion, different parts of the object will stop at different rates. Similarly, not everything on an object will move at the same rate. (A good example is the squash-down at the end of a jump, as shown below.)

If your character is running across the scene, their arms and legs may be moving at a different rate from their head. This is overlapping action. Likewise, when they stop running, their hair will likely continue to move for a few frames before coming to rest. This is follow-through. These are important principles to understand if you want your animation to flow believably.

It is often a good idea to animate the main movement of the character first and then animate the part of the character that demonstrates overlapping action. You could do the main action as pose to pose animation and the secondary action as straight-ahead animation. This gives it a bit more spontaneity. For example, when animating a dog walking, animate the dog first and the tail second.

When a character lands at the end of a jump, they will overshoot beyond their resting point.

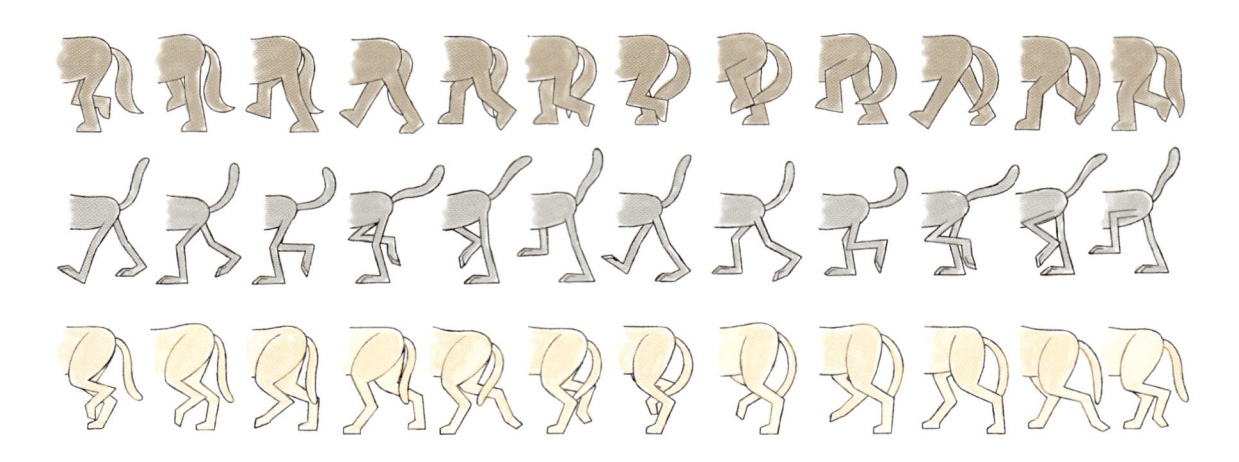

A tail of an animal will display follow-through and overlapping action.

Exercise

Overlapping action
Animate a character making a jump over an object. They anticipate the jump, jump over the object and then land, displaying overshoot and coming to a stop.

Follow-through
Have a go at making a round creature with a tail bounce up and down. We can start with a ball shape bouncing up and down on the spot. This will demonstrate the basic principle of the bounce up and down.

Overshoot exercise consists of a character jumping over an object.

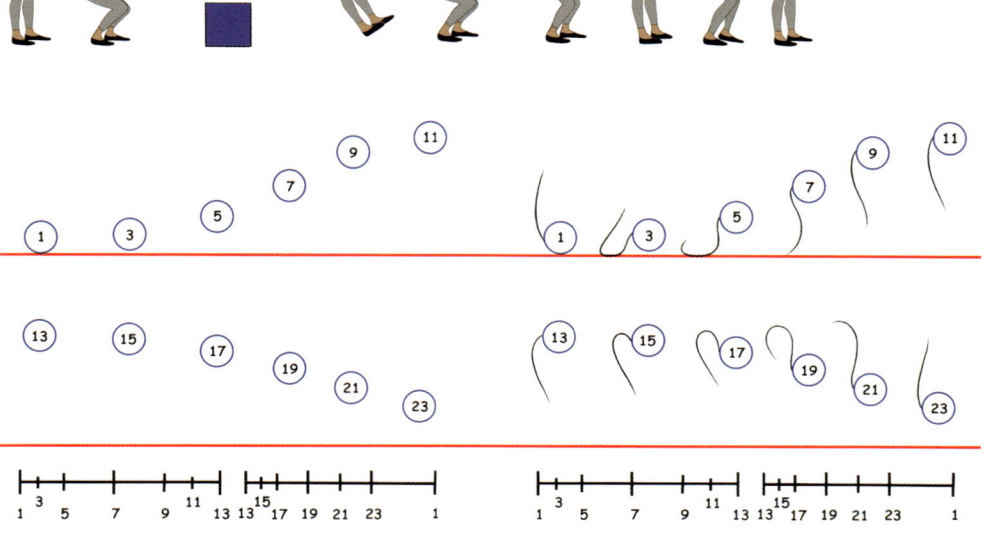

By animating a bouncing ball with a piece of string attached to it you can learn about follow-through.

Adapt the bouncing ball animation to make a cute creature showing follow-through with its tail.

Then turn the ball shape into a creature of your choice. Add a tail, which will follow through the action of the body of the creature.

SECONDARY ACTION

Secondary actions are used to support or emphasize the main action going on within a scene. They add more dimension to your characters and objects. For instance, the subtle movement of your character's hair as they walk, or perhaps a facial expression or a secondary object reacting to the first adds more dimension. However, this secondary action should not distract from the primary one. You should not notice it, but you would miss it if it were not there.

Exercise

Take any animation of a character you have done and add some secondary action. You could add long hair to the character or loose clothing. These additions would show secondary action as the character moves.

EXAGGERATION

In animation, realism is boring. Instead, add some exaggeration to your characters and objects to make them more dynamic. Animated movement and acting have much more in common with theatrical acting than film acting. In the theatre, an audience is a long way from the actor, so the actor's actions have to be big and demonstrative. In a live-action film, we can cut to close-ups of the character in order to put over emotions with subtle facial expressions and tiny movements. Generally, animation works better if the acting and movement is big and over the top. Why animate a realistic movement in animation, when you could as easily video a real person with a camera?

Exercise

Animate a double-take. This involves a character seeing something and because the thing that they

Head moves through an arc... and comes to a stop.

The hair will follow the path of the head and continue moving when the head stops.

A person's hair demonstrates secondary action, in the way that it comes to a stop after the head has ceased movement.

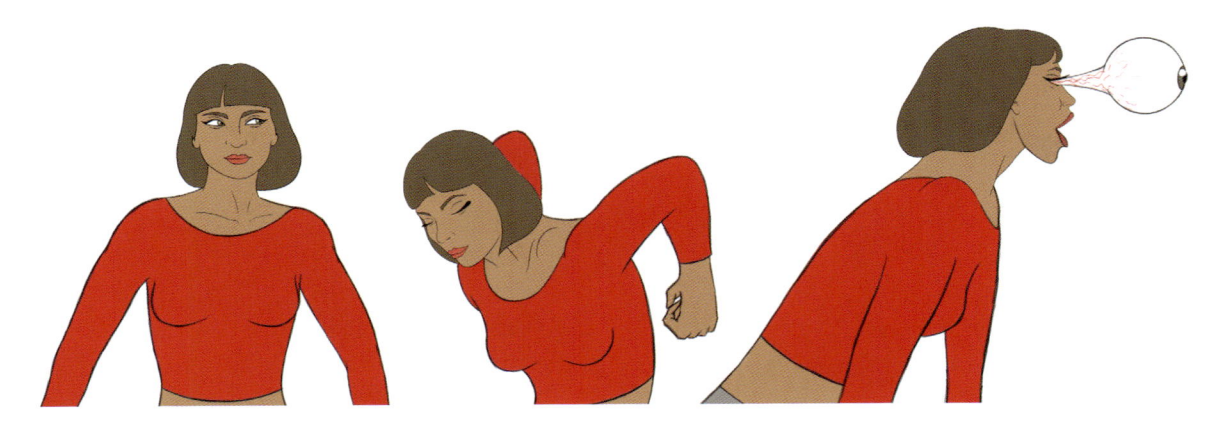

By exaggerating an action, it can be more interesting for an audience to watch.

have seen is so amazing/scary/interesting, they then take a really big, exaggerated second look.

SOLID DRAWING

As an animator, it's a good idea to have some basic drawing skills. The best way to learn to draw is to draw, lots and lots. Go to life drawing classes and draw a nude model. This will give you a good idea about how the human body is constructed and how it moves. Do quick sketches and do lots of them, no more than ten minutes long. Do not just draw out the basic shape of the model, then spend ages shading bits in. The more drawings you do, the more you will learn. Think of where the spine is first, then how the legs, arms and head attach to it. Do this with a simple line that shows the curve of the spine. Then work out the bulk of the body with a simple ovoid shape. Then use similar, but smaller ovoid shapes to bulk out the arms and legs. Finally, use a darker line to work out the outline of the model.

Do observational drawings of people. Keep a sketchbook with you all the time and draw people discreetly. Sit in a park or a café and draw the people around you. Try to understand from the positions they are in what their character is like or how they are feeling. What emotions are they demonstrating? Are they happy, sad, bored or tired? Draw quickly and roughly. You learn so much more by doing lots of quick drawings, rather than a single drawing that takes a long time.

Go to a zoo or a public farm and draw the animals. Try to work out how they are constructed and how they move. Because animals move around a lot, you have to draw very quickly. Study animal anatomy books, or look at animal anatomy on the internet. Draw animal skeletons, so that you know what is going on under the skin of the animal. Work out how the muscles relate to the bones. You do not need to have a really detailed knowledge of human or animal anatomy, but an idea of basic construction will really help with your animation.

You could always draw from a picture in a book or from the internet, but this doesn't help much with your understanding of how a living thing is put together. Drawing from real life is so much better. It makes you look at the subject a lot more intensively.

Exercise

Go out and draw something!

CHARACTER DESIGN

Your characters and objects and the world in which they live need to appeal to the viewer. This includes having an easy to read design, solid drawing and a personality. There is no formula for getting this right, but it starts with strong character development and being able to tell your story through the art of animation.

Work out what the character needs to do in the movie you are making. What story will they go through? What are your character's personality traits? Are they happy or sad? How old are they? What is their motivation in a scene?

The basis of a character design is the model sheet. This is a drawing that consists of a front, side and three-quarter view of your character. It would also have some character studies that show how the character would look if they were happy, sad, surprised, disgusted, angry and any other emotions that they may demonstrate. You also need to show information about how the hands hold things, mouth shapes for *lip-sync* and whether the character has teeth or not.

As well as a full-coloured model sheet, you should also do a model sheet that shows the construction of the character, so that other animators would be able to work out how the character is constructed.

Always think about the following when you are designing a character. How would somebody else be able to draw this character? (If you were drawing a character, what would you need to know?) How would the character move? What are they feeling? What is their overall outlook on life (glass half empty or glass half full)?

Exercise

Design a character and create a model sheet.

A good model sheet helps to make sure that the character remains consistent during a movie.

A construction model sheet is useful for an animator to understand how a character is constructed.

ANIMAL AND HUMAN LOCOMOTION

Birds

Birds are designed to fly. They do this by having wings with huge muscles in them, a stiff, fused skeleton and feathers that are light but can produce a huge amount of thrust when the wings are flapped.

To achieve flight, a bird will flap its wings up and down. On the downstroke, the wings will be spread out as far as possible in order to push air downward and backwards to provide lift and forwards motion. On the upstroke, the wings will be

The skeleton of a bird is constructed for flight. The backbone is fused together, there is a huge bone at the front of the chest to attach the wing muscles and the bones are lighter than those of a non-flying animal.

ANIMATION PRINCIPLES 51

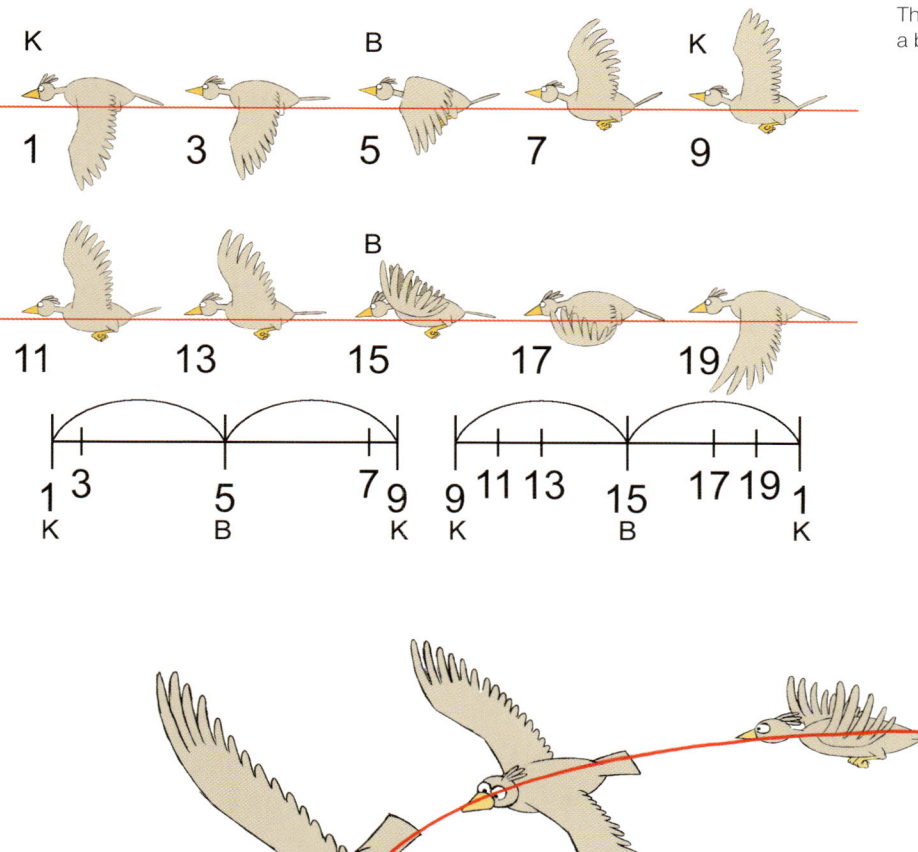

These are the basics of how a bird flies.

When a bird turns a corner, its body will bank over in the direction of the turn.

tucked in so as to create as little resistance as possible to the air. The body tends to go up on the upstroke and down on the downstroke. The illustration is a *cycle*. That is, if you animate the bird on the spot, the last image will animate into the first image, so that it can be repeated over and over.

In order to change direction whilst flying, a bird will bank into a turn. The inner wing of the turn will be dipped lower and the outer wing raised higher.

Exercise

Animate a flying cycle of a bird. Follow the drawings in the illustration of a bird's flying cycle, but design your own bird.

Fish

A fish consists of a strong, flexible backbone running along the body. It also has fins and a tail, which provide thrust and aid direction. Fish swim by sending a wave along their body that pushes water backwards, while propelling them forwards.

In order to turn, the fish will use its tail like the rudder of a boat. The tail will point into the turn to slow the fish down on one side.

Exercise

Animate a swimming cycle of a fish.

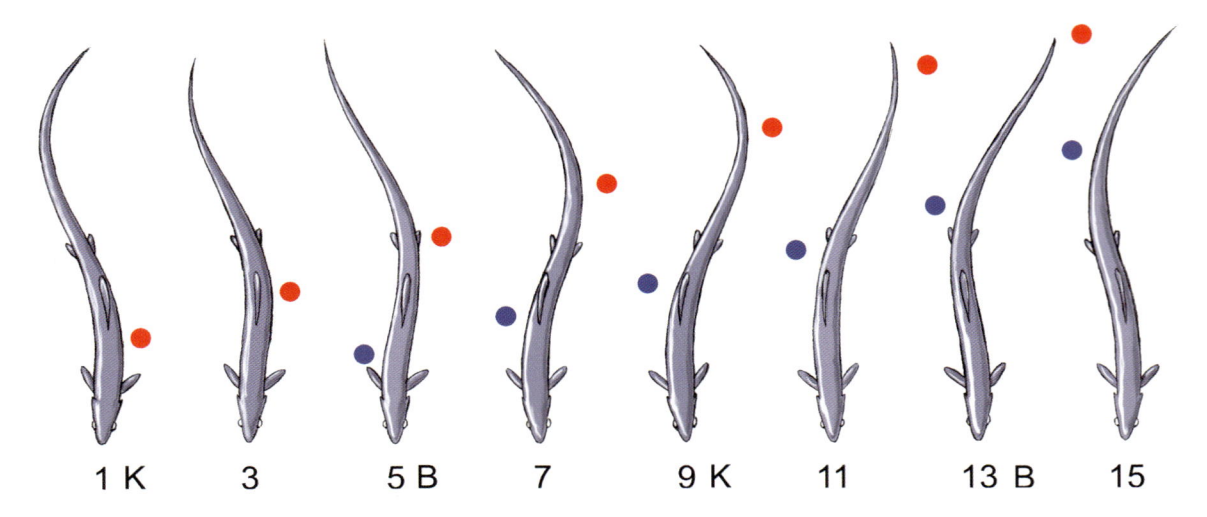

1 K   3   5 B   7   9 K   11   13 B   15

Fish movement consists of a wave that runs down the body of the fish, propelling itself through the water.

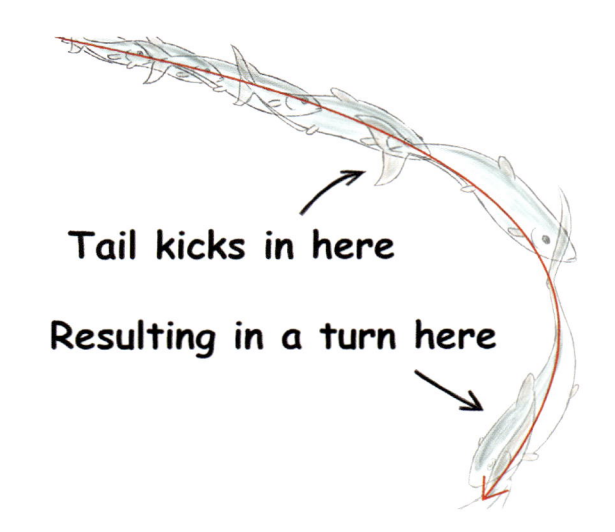

Tail kicks in here

Resulting in a turn here

When a fish turns, it waves its tail into the direction of the turn, to move the front part of the body inwards like the rudder of a boat.

Snakes

Snakes consist of an elongated body with a backbone running its length and ribs attached to almost all of the vertebrae of the backbone. Snakes move by flexing the ribs backwards and forwards. Snakes have several forms of locomotion, the most basic being the serpentine movement. Certain snakes can also move with a sidewinder movement to help them to propel themselves over hot sand.

When doing a serpentine movement, the snake will follow a wave-like path along the ground. It is best to plot out this path and then move your snake along it. Always have at least two waves in your snake so that it will convincingly look as though it is moving along the path. If the snake is too short, it will end up looking like a slug.

For the sidewinder movement, a snake pushes a loop of its body from its head and then the loop moves through the body until it reaches the end. The head is then lifted up and placed forwards and another loop will flow through the snake's length.

Exercise

Animate a snake along a path. Make sure that the snake is long enough to have at least two waves in its body length. If it is too short, it will look like a slug following a path.

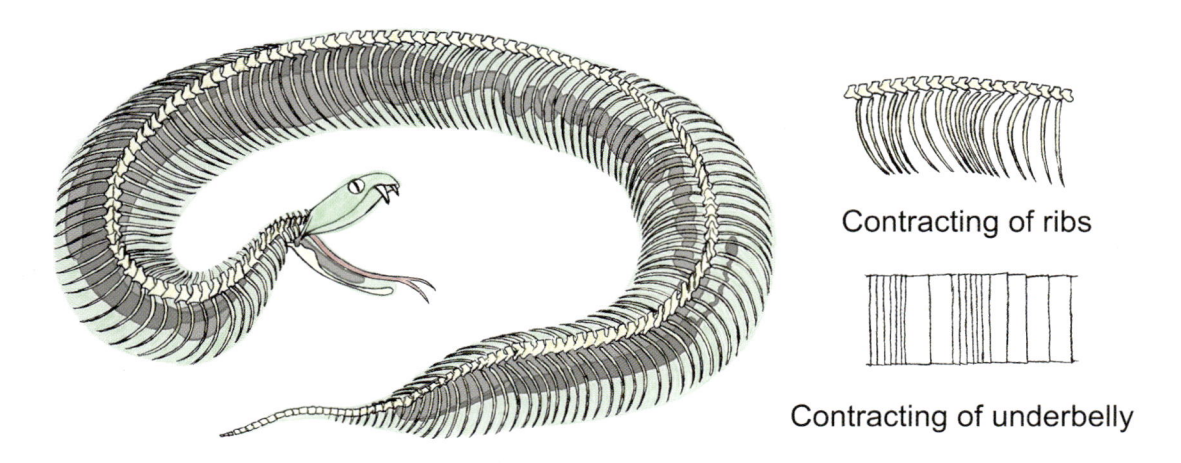

Contracting of ribs

Contracting of underbelly

A snake skeleton runs along the whole body of the snake and is used to produce movement.

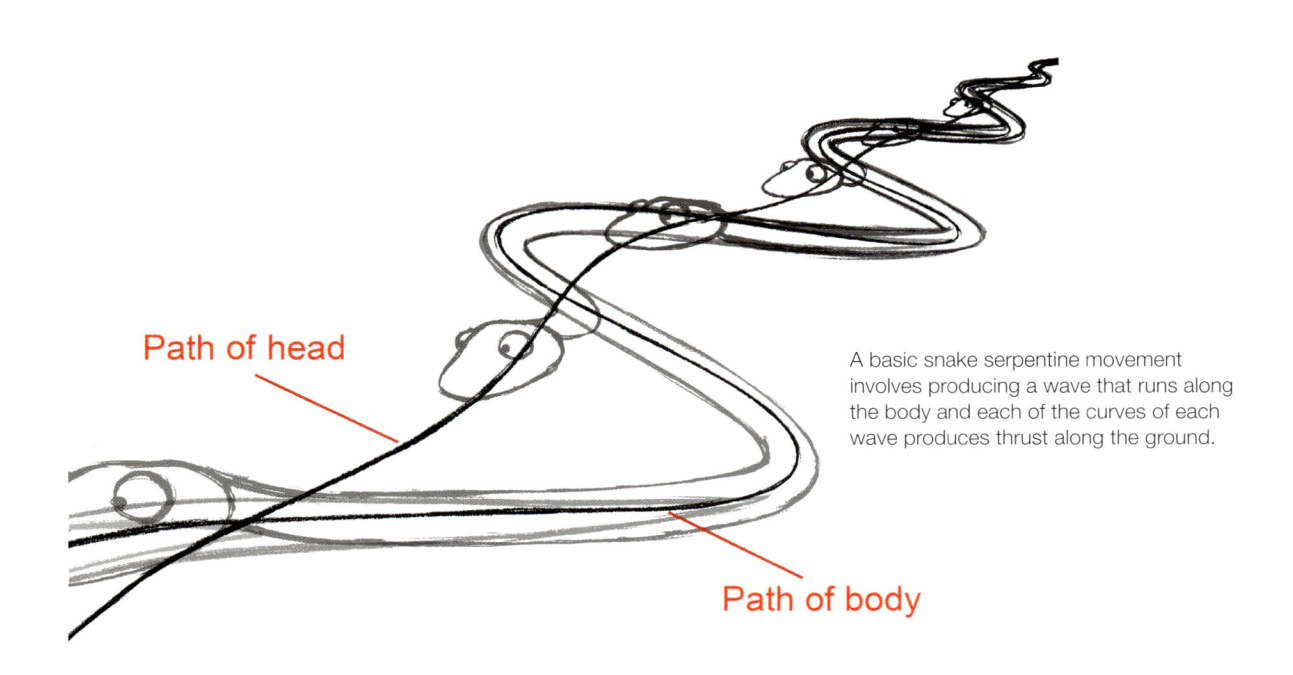

Path of head

Path of body

A basic snake serpentine movement involves producing a wave that runs along the body and each of the curves of each wave produces thrust along the ground.

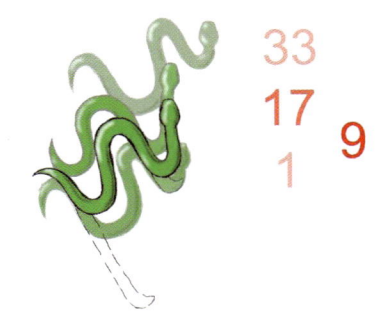

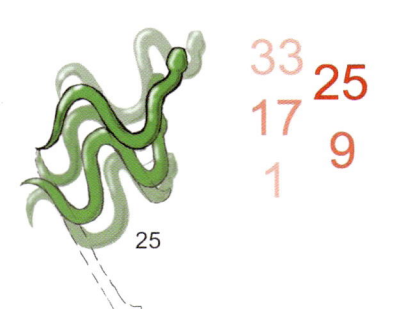

With the sidewinder movement, the snake pushes a loop of its body beyond its head and then the loop moves though the body to the tail.

Then, if you are feeling brave, have a go at animating a sidewinder movement.

Four-Legged Animals (Quadrupeds)

Four-legged animals have a long spine running along their back, which is very flexible to help with running. They have a narrower, deeper ribcage than a human being, with the shoulder blades to the side and the shoulder joints towards the front of the body. The upper legs attach to these shoulder blades with ball and socket joints. Four-legged mammals have no collar bones. They also have a solid pelvis with the legs attached to ball and socket joints. All of the remaining joints of the legs act as hinge joints. A four-legged animal is a bit like a human being on all fours.

The front legs are like human arms, but the palms of the hands are much longer and the feet are basically finger bones extended to the end of the limb. The rear legs are like human legs, but the foot is extended and the feet are like extended toes.

The main difference between most animals is how the feet are constructed. These can be divided into paws (for example, dogs and cats), cloven feet (pigs, sheep, deer) and hooves (horse, zebra).

With paws, the four toes are elongated and the second two digits of the toes rest on the ground.

With cloven feet, two toes are elongated and the final digit rests on the ground.

With hooves, a single toe is elongated, the final digit forming the hoof.

Quadrupeds have four basic forms of movement.

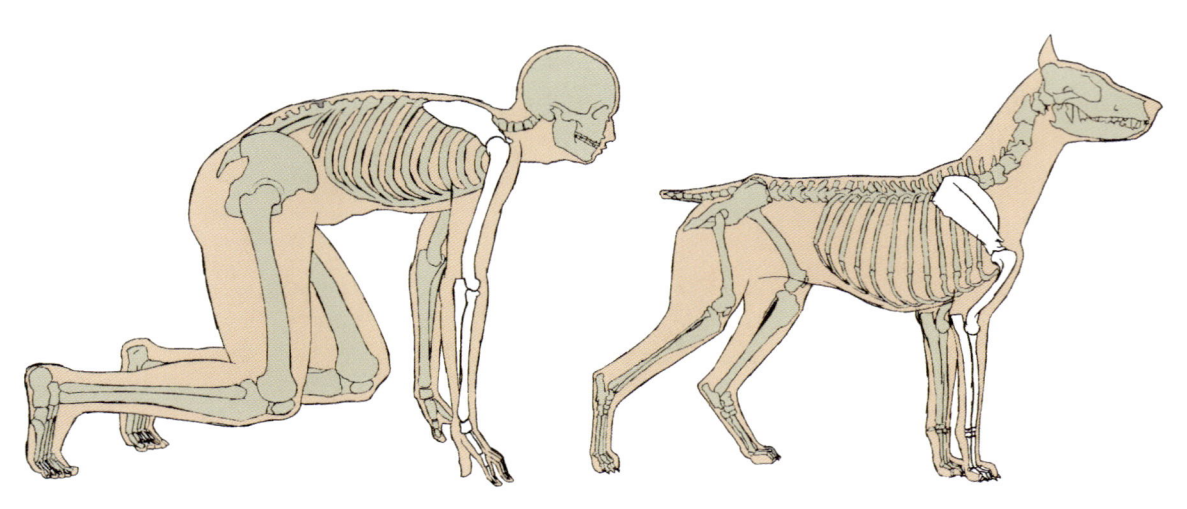

With the construction of a four-legged character, think of them as being a human on all fours (with a few differences).

ANIMATION PRINCIPLES 55

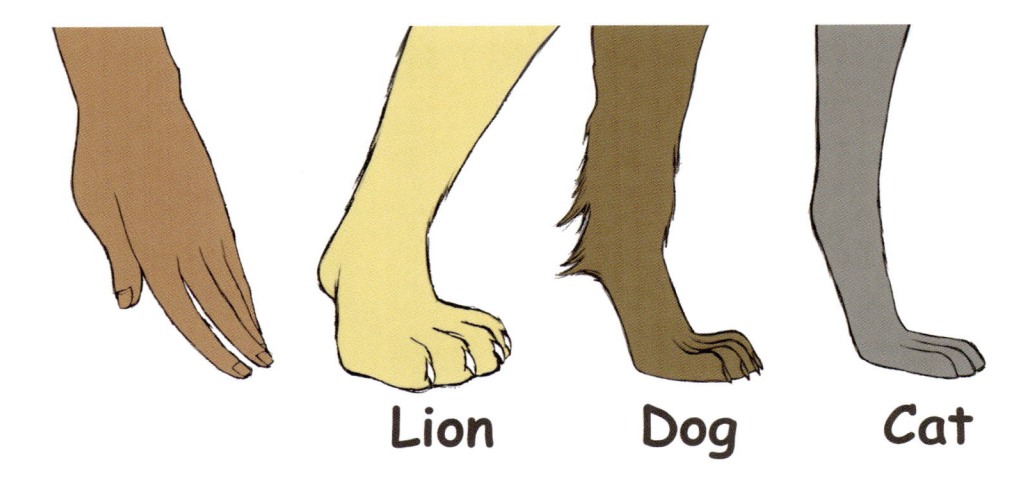

Lion Dog Cat

The construction of the feet for animals with paws.

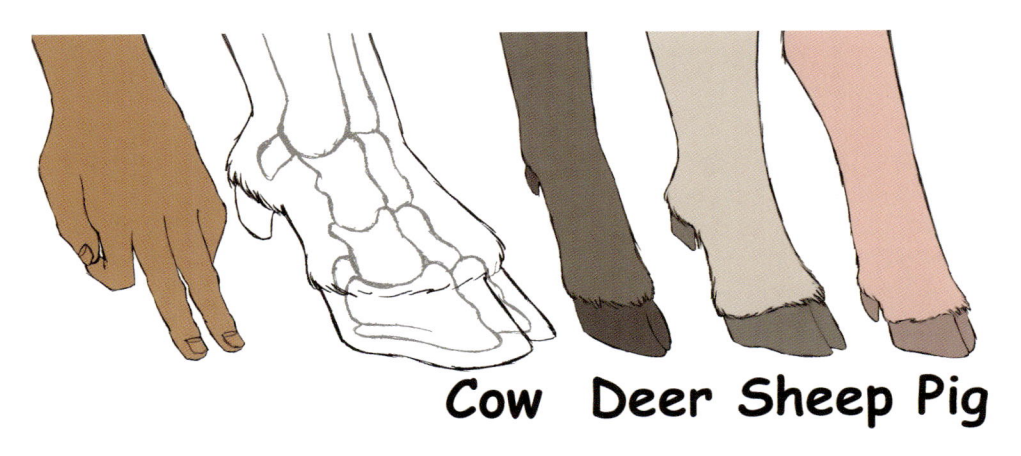

Cow Deer Sheep Pig

The construction of the feet for animals' cloven feet.

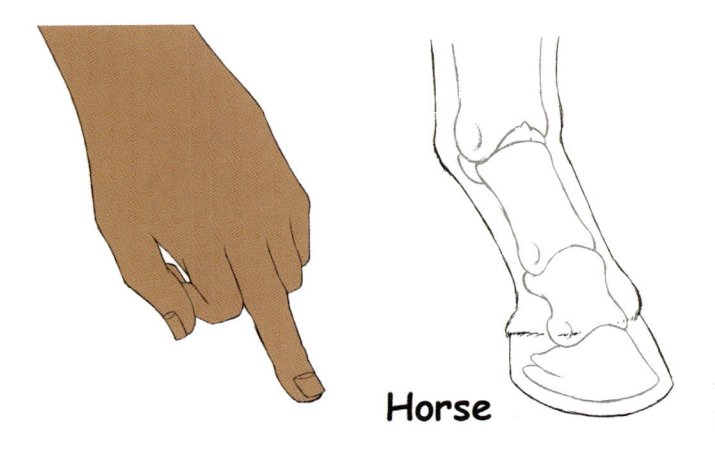

Horse

The construction of the feet for animals' hooves.

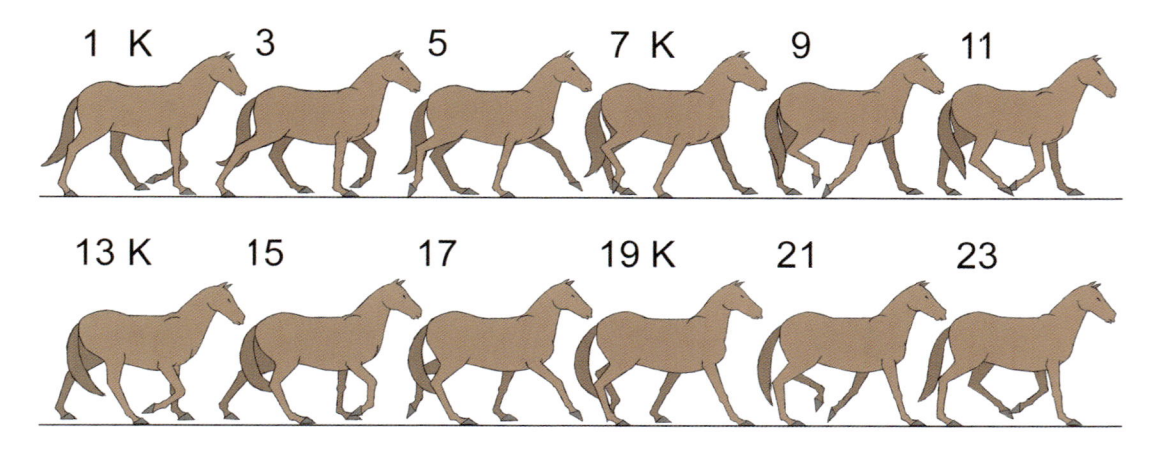

A horse walk will consist of four key positions that have strides at the back or the front.

Walking The walk is the slowest and most stable form of movement. The legs move from a stride position to a crossover position, where one of the legs crosses over the other leg that is on the ground.

At its most simplistic, a horse walk will consist of four basic key positions. First key position is a stride position at the front and a crossover at the back. The second key position is a stride at the front and a crossover at the back. The third key position is a stride position at the front and a crossover at the back, but opposite to the first key position. The fourth key position is a stride at the front and a crossover at the back, but the opposite of the second key position.

There will always be two feet in contact with the ground and most of the time three feet. Usually, the rear foot steps into the same position occupied by the front foot. The stride at the back should be the same as the stride at the front.

Trotting The trot is a slightly faster gait. The legs work as diagonal pairs and do the stride and crossover at the same time. At the stride position, the animal will do a little jump into the air in order go that little bit further.

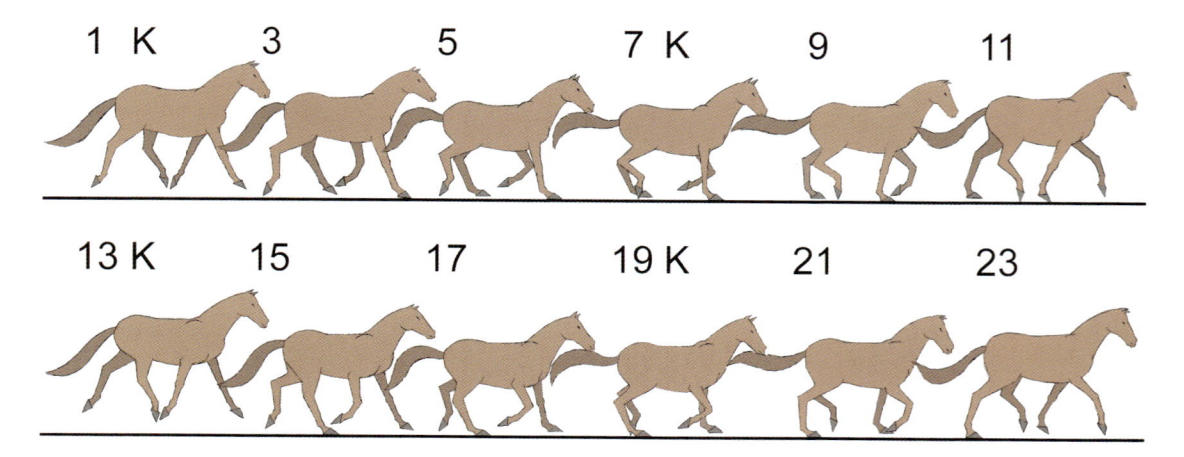

Trot: the horse will use the legs in unison to lengthen the stride with a jump.

ANIMATION PRINCIPLES 57

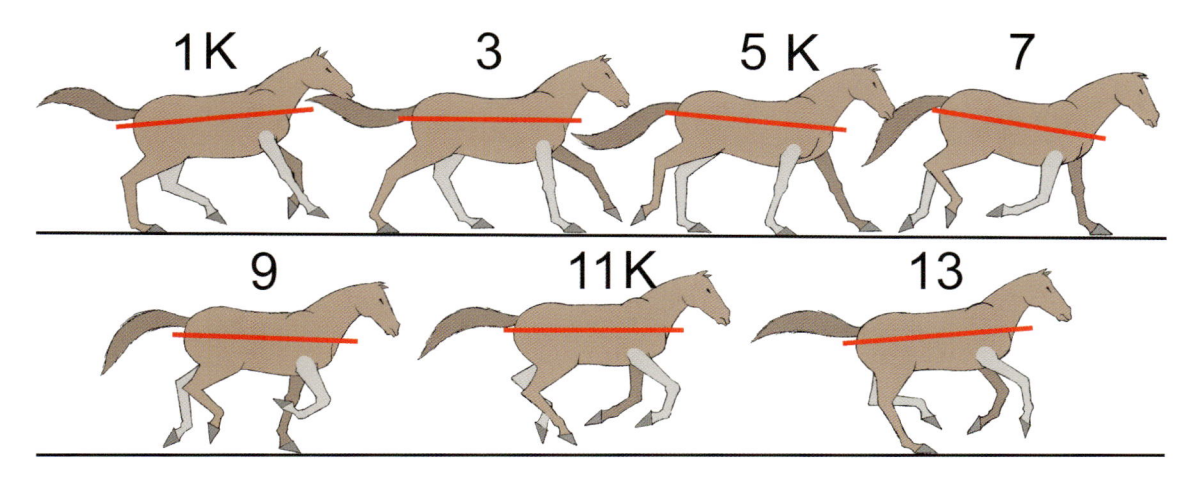

Canter: one diagonal pair of legs works in unison and the other two legs work independently.

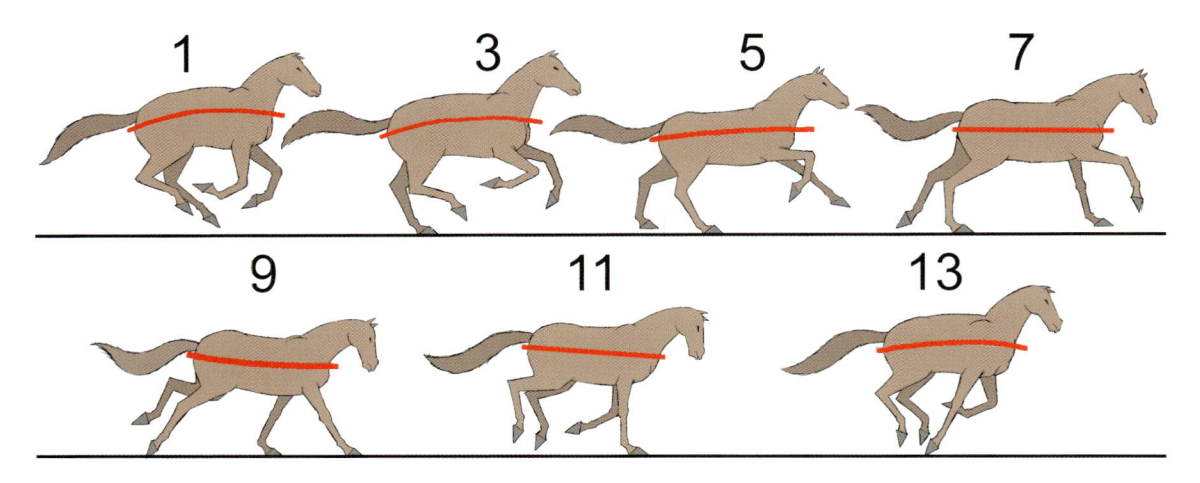

Gallop: all legs move independently and the spine is flexed as much as possible to extend the length of the stride.

Cantering The canter is slightly faster than the trot. One diagonal pair of legs works in unison and the other two legs work independently. There is also a slightly longer jump into the air to achieve more speed.

Galloping The gallop is the fastest gait and is achieved by the front legs working together and the rear legs working together. All legs touch the ground at different times and there is much more flexing of the spine to help with a much longer jump at the point where all legs are off the ground.

Exercise

Animate a four-legged walk, trot, canter and gallop. The illustrations are shown as cycles, that is, if the body of the animal stays in the same place, relative to forwards and backwards movement, the animation can be repeated over and over, on the spot.

Human Locomotion

Humans have two basic forms of locomotion, walking and running. A human walk is one of the most difficult things to get right in animation. We have all been walking since we were about a year old. We see people walking all the time. Basically, we are walking experts, so doing a human walk convincingly is open to a huge amount of scrutiny on the part of your audience.

Walking A walk consists of two basic key positions, stride and crossover. The stride position is where both legs are on the ground and there is a large distance between them. There will be a twist through the spine and the arms will be elongated in the opposite direction to the legs in order to balance the body. In the crossover position, one foot is on the ground and the other leg crosses over, to be placed in front of the leg on the ground. One arm will be swinging backwards and the other will be swinging forwards.

To do the in-betweens, the body will bob up and down. From the stride position, the body will move downward as the weight is shifted on to the front foot and then come back up again as it moves into the crossover position. From the crossover position, the body will go up in order to give enough room for the leg to be brought forwards of the leg that is in contact with the ground. The body will then lower into the next stride position. The stride positions each take approximately half a second (about twelve frames).

Walk cycles A walk cycle is where a character continues a walk on the spot, a bit like walking on

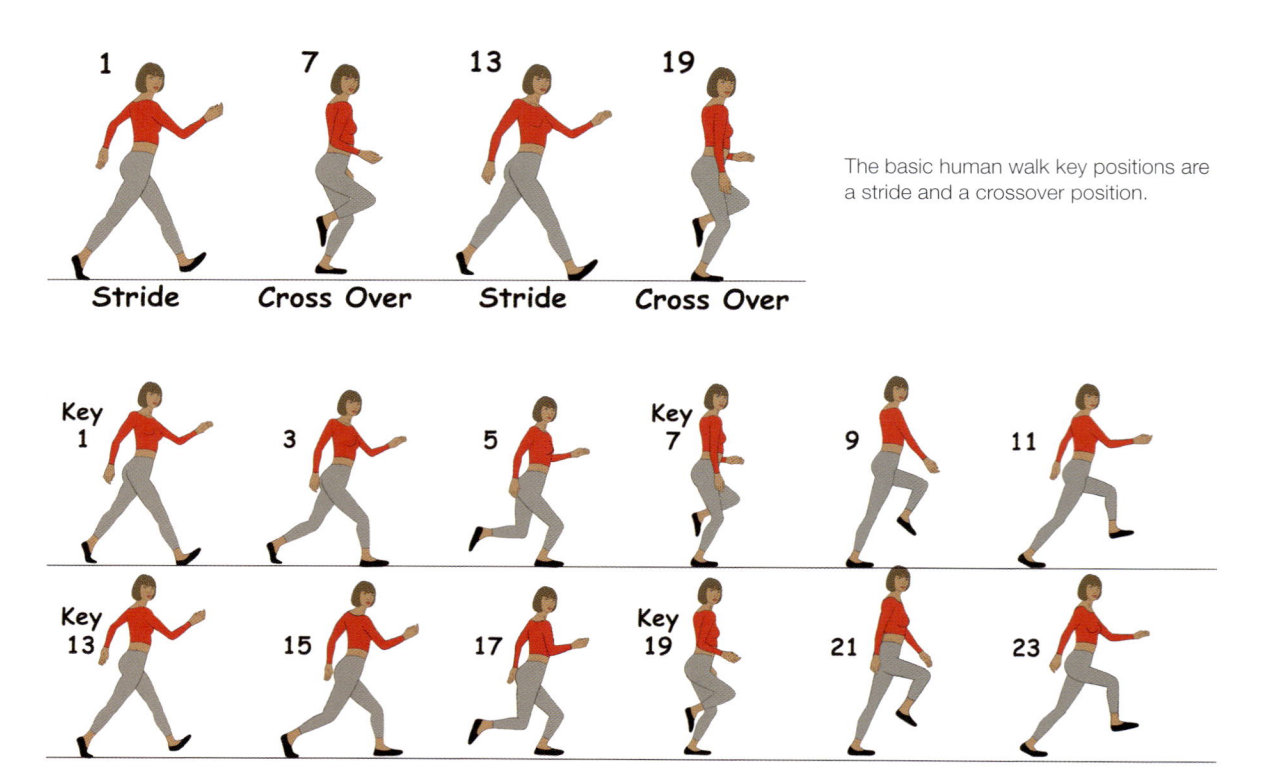

The basic human walk key positions are a stride and a crossover position.

The human walk in-betweens involve the body going down, out of the stride and up, from the crossover position and into the next stride.

ANIMATION PRINCIPLES 59

With the human walk, it is possible to put over certain types of emotions.

Happy walk A happy walk consists of the character leaning back slightly (the lumbar bent backwards) with the chest open and an exaggerated up and down movement.

Sad walk With a sad walk the character bends forwards (the lumbar bent forwards), with the weight of the world on their shoulders. The legs drag, because walking is such an effort, and the rest of the body follows through with as little effort as possible.

Angry walk An angry walk is where the hands are held in fists and the legs stamp down into the stride position.

Cartoony walk A cartoony walk consists of a double bounce at the stride position. As the stride is completed, the body bounces down, following through the touching of the front foot on the ground. Just before the foot is then lifted off the ground, there is a second bounce of the body up into the crossover position.

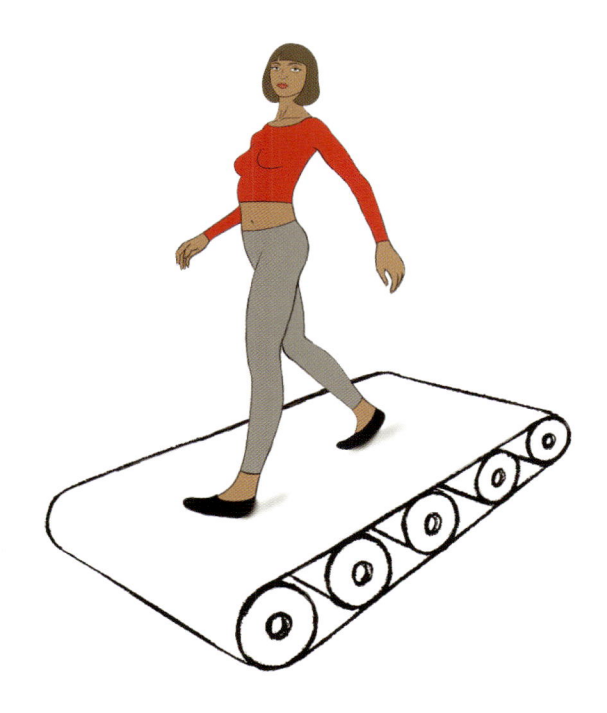

A walk cycle is like a person walking on a treadmill.

a treadmill. This is a rather artificial way of doing a walk, as it only shows what a character is thinking, feeling or doing for one second (two strides, half a second each), then it is repeated over and over again. In reality, as we are walking we change pace and speed, we look this way and that, we hold things, look at our phones, eat things, look in shop windows and hundreds of other influences. However, animating walk cycles is a good way to understand how a human walks.

Exercise

Animate all of these walk cycles in your chosen animation technique.

A happy walk involves the character leaning back and holding the body open.

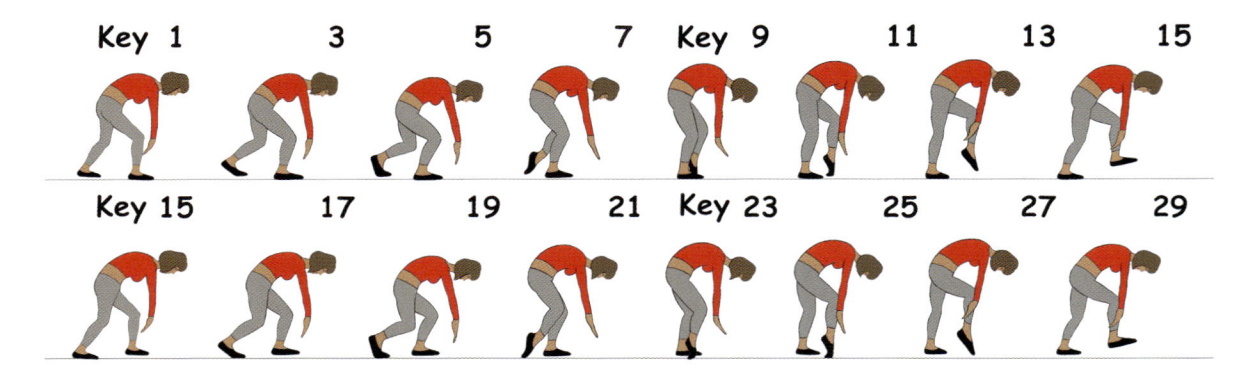

A sad walk involves the character bending the body forwards and the legs being dragged from stride to stride.

An angry walk involves the legs stamping down on to the ground, with the arms held stiffly and the hands clenched into fists.

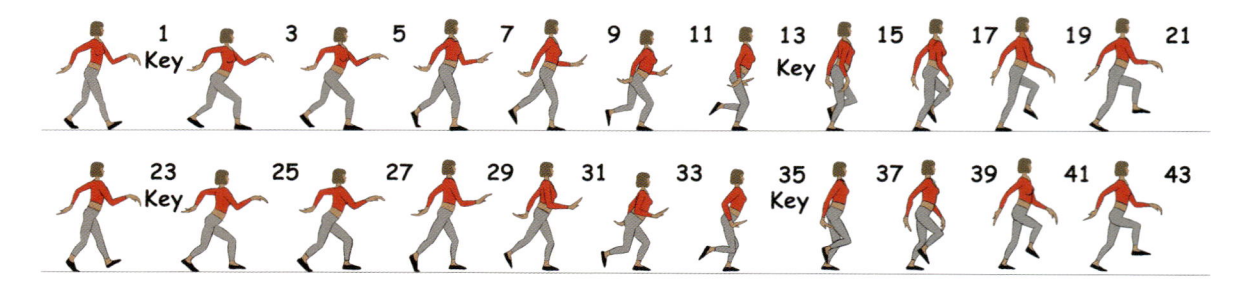

A cartoony walk involves a bob up and down at the stride position.

3
PERFORMANCE IN ANIMATION

STUDY ACTING

The key to doing a great piece of animation is paying attention to the performance. You need to know how to act out any given shot that you want to animate, so the study of acting can be very useful. If you have a chance to perform in an amateur theatrical group or club, give it a go. Nothing is better for getting an idea of timing and putting over an idea to an audience.

Animation performance has much more in common with theatrical acting than film acting. Go to see plays, operas, dance and any other live performances. How does the dancer or actor portray themselves to an audience? Generally, their actions and diction are very big and over the top, compared to acting for the screen. Because of the distance between an audience and the actor, everything has to be far more demonstrative in order to be understood. On the stage, there is not the luxury of the close-up, like on screen, where a subtle performance can be achieved with the merest raising of the eyebrow or small facial expression to demonstrate the emotion the actor wants you to see. You can do close-ups in animation, but they tend not to work so well. The closer you get to a character, the more obvious it is that the character is not real and just a drawing, a lump of clay or rubber or a collection of rendered pixels. When the audience sees this and realizes that the character is not real, it stops believing in the character.

LIVE ACTION VIDEO SHOOTS AND ACTING OUT A SCENE

One way in which to achieve a good animated performance is to act out the shot first. This performance can then be videoed to use as a reference when animating. Act out the shot in several different ways. This can work as a rehearsal of your scene and mean that when you do start animating you will have a good idea what to do. BUT, don't just copy the video reference. Use it to work out the basic key positions of the piece by simplifying what is in the video reference. Some animators argue that LAVS limit spontaneity, but as long as you use this video reference footage as a starting point and then develop it within your animation, you should avoid this problem. Also, by acting out a scene you will have a better 'feel' of how to move a character.

The concept of sports visualization is a useful tool. When an athlete is about to complete a sporting task like the high jump, they will visualize their body during their performance. They imagine the twist of the body as it jumps up and works its way over the bar in slow motion. This mind exercise links up synapses in the brain so that when the athlete does the high jump, they don't have to think about it, the body just does it automatically. Sports visualization is used in many sports. Car racing, downhill skiing, long jump, pole vault, gymnastics – the list goes on. It has helped to achieve

LAVS are very useful to work out how to animate a scene.

many world records. An ice skater can't jump any higher now than thirty years ago, but they can fit more elaborate movements in that metre or so of height, due to sports visualization. Acting out the animation will link up synapses in the brain that will help when you are animating.

ACTING STYLES

There are many styles of acting, but the ones I have found most useful are as follows.

Method Acting

Method acting was developed by Constantin Stanislavski. He was a Russian actor, director and producer of stage plays and a founder of the Moscow Art Theatre in 1898. His book, *An Actor Prepares*, is well worth a read.

Method acting is where an actor will imagine themselves internally as the character. The actor will research the character, work out a backstory and, in extreme cases, try to live like the character and react to situations in the same way. They will also use their own memories to evoke emotions from within. A method actor works from the inside out. So, for example, if they want to portray a character looking sad, the actor will remember a time in the past when they felt sad (for example, when their pet cat died) and the actor's body language, facial expressions and voice will reflect this. It will come over to an audience as being a genuine portrayal of sadness.

Method acting involves an actor trying to experience the emotion that they wish to portray, so that their acting comes across as more authentic.

Obviously this acting style is not that useful for your actual animation, but it can help when you are working out the way that your character could behave in a given situation and when performing LAVS.

Theatrical Acting

With theatrical acting, the actor will study what a given emotion looks like and then replicate it with their own body, face and voice. So if an actor wants to look sad, they will put on a sad face and weigh the body down with drooped shoulders and hanging arms. They may lean the spine forwards to close the body and bend the legs to look heavy. They may study examples of sadness in books, films or on the internet and practise in a mirror or video themselves in order to achieve this. A theatrical actor works from the outside in. This style of acting is much closer to what we are doing in animation – each emotion that an actor has to do as a reaction to something could be seen as a key position.

With theatrical acting, an actor represents the emotions that suggest what needs to be conveyed to an audience.

LABAN MOVEMENT THEORY

As well as different acting techniques, it is also good to understand basic movement. There are also several different concepts of movement study, but the most useful I have found is Laban Movement Theory.

This approach to acting and dancing was developed by Rudolf Laban (1879–1958). Laban was not only a choreographer, dancer and actor, but was also interested in all forms of movement. He was involved in time and motion studies for industry and applied his theories using mathematics, geometry and drawing.

I am not going to even try to cover all aspects of Laban's Movement Theory, other than the absolute basics. The best thing would be to try to find a Laban movement class locally and do some exercises. Failing that, you could look up the Laban theory on the internet, or buy the book *Laban for Actors and Dancers* by Jean Newlove. Remember, nothing beats doing the movement yourself to really understand it.

The great thing about Laban Movement Theory is that it makes you very body and movement aware. Through a series of exercises, you will become familiar with the way the body moves and how external and internal influences can affect it. It also ascribes movements to things like character and emotion.

Kinesphere

Laban's kinesphere is as an area of personal space around the body, a bit like a large bubble. Within this, the body can move forwards–backwards, up–down and left–right. The body can also move diagonally across this space. It is a similar, but more sophisticated, way of thinking about movement than the idea of just

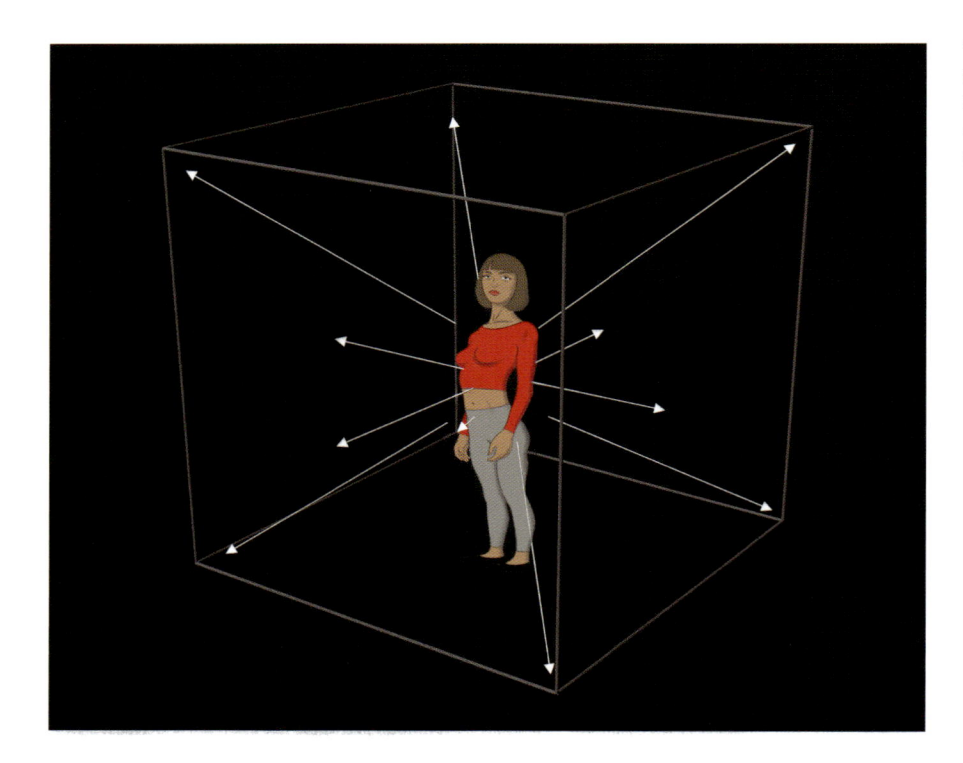

The kinesphere is the area around a person's body that can be used to demonstrate movement and emotions.

forwards–backwards and open–closed body positions.

Diagonal movements are more furtive because they will unbalance the body and either have to be completed quickly, or some sort of counterbalance will have to come into play. There will always be a specific reason for a diagonal movement or stance, such as to balance yourself while holding an object or pointing at something. Standing on one leg and adopting the necessary diagonal posture to remain balanced makes a person look vulnerable, but it can also give a feeling of confidence in that person. It would be easy to push that person over, but the character is confident enough to know this is not going to happen. Asymmetrical postures are always more interesting to look at than symmetrical ones, so use them as much as possible.

Space, Time, Weight and Flow Continua

Anything we do involves the movement of our body through space. Often during a life-drawing class a tutor will refer to the model as occupying space and it is that bit of space you are drawing. When we leap about, pull a facial expression, or just breathe we are moving in space.

Time is not only the amount of time it takes for an audience to understand a certain point that you want to put across. It can also be the changing of the seasons, the phases of a human's life, the fast-moving modern world, or the idealized notion of a slower-moving bygone age.

The depiction of weight is one of the fundamentals of producing a convincing piece of animation. A balanced person will look right, planted in the middle of the screen. An unbalanced person will look as if they are going to fall over, and if they don't either fall over or correct their balance, they will start to unnerve an audience. There is also the other 'weight' a person may be carrying, such as the weight of responsibility, guilt or misery. They could also be affected by the lightness of relief or a lack of responsibility, or being in love.

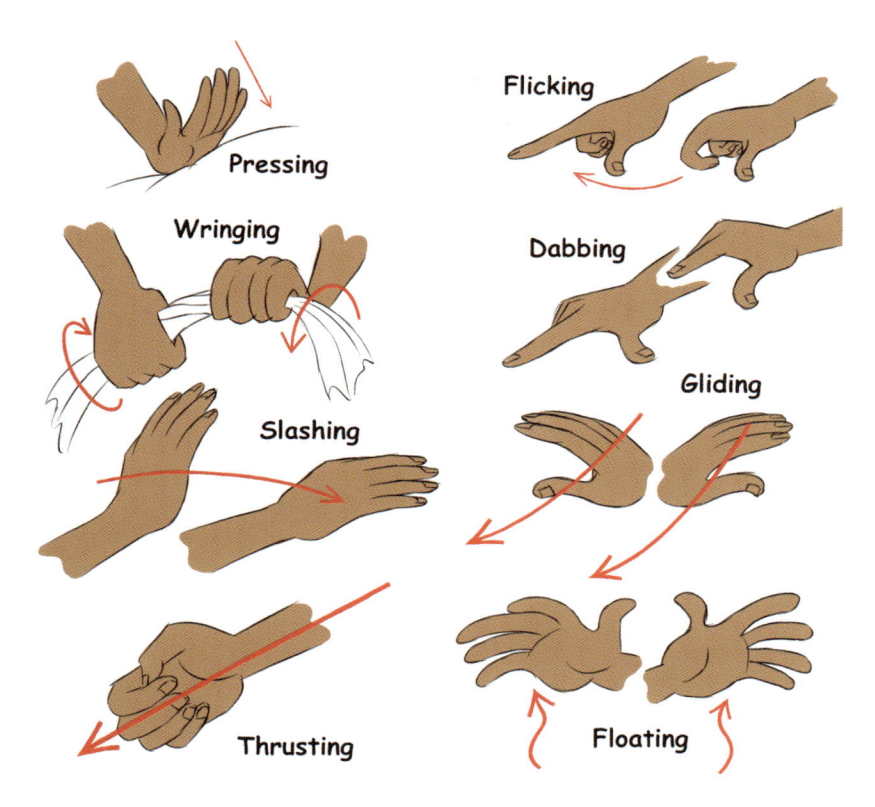

Space, time, weight and flow continua can be used to represent the main types of movement made by an actor or an animated character to portray the emotions they are feeling.

Flowing movement is the continuous movement of one action into another. If your animation has too much flow, it will be difficult for an audience to define each of the individual movements and what they mean. A series of movements that stop and start could be described as jerky and again can be off-putting to an audience. It is always best to use a mix of approaches.

The Eight Efforts

Laban Movement Theory divides movement into eight basic Efforts. One way to give a scene you are animating more depth is to decide which of these Efforts applies to the personality of your character and the situation they are in. Have a go at physically doing these Efforts yourself. Subconsciously, you will take on board the movements required and this will be reflected in your animation.

Pressing This movement is direct, sustained and strong. It could be pushing or pulling something, lifting or leading something. It suggests a character that is determined and indefatigable and could be applied to someone who has a definite goal.

Flicking This movement is flexible, sudden and light, such as flicking dust off clothes, or moving the head round in response to a sudden noise. This, to me, sums up a more nervous person, twitching and reacting to things that happen to them.

Wringing This movement is flexible, sustained and strong. It can be a movement like wringing out wet clothes, but could also be interpreted as gut-churning internal emotions within somebody who is frightened or embarrassed, somebody in inner turmoil, or somebody who is worried about something.

Dabbing This movement is direct, sudden and light. It is somewhat like flicking but with a directness to it, such as poking somebody on the shoulder to get their attention. This could be a busybody type of person, bossing other people around.

Slashing This movement is sudden, strong and flexible. Think of it like slashing a sword in all directions, or slashing the arms about to escape from something. An angry person who is annoyed by everything and anything would slash.

Gliding This movement is sustained, light and direct. I think of it as being how a butler would glide silently into a room, very confident and aloof. It has a definite direction to it. A quiet, confident person who is in control of themselves and everything else (or who gives a good impression of it) would glide.

Thrusting This movement is direct, sudden and strong. It is like slashing, but with a definite direction to the movement, such as one person punching another or somebody punching the air. It describes a person who exists on short bursts of energy, either aggressive or delighted.

Floating This movement is flexible, sustained and light. It is a dreamier feeling of movement, like thistledown drifting in the air, or a cork bobbing on the ocean. I picture somebody dreamily skipping through the woods, at one with nature.

You may find that a character you are animating is using one of these basic Efforts all the time when they move, or they may adopt different ones as their emotions change. For example, if someone is feeling really embarrassed, they may take on the Effort of wringing, twisting themselves up. If they are in love, they may adopt the Effort of floating, dreamily moving around and thinking of the person they are in love with. A confident person will glide into a room, while an angry person will display slashing or thrusting.

THE BASIC EMOTIONS

We spend all our time on this planet expressing emotions, whether briefly or for long periods of time. They may be subtle, normal or exaggerated. We can read another person's emotions by their body language, their facial expressions and the intonation of their voice. We've been learning this since the day we were born and a lot of this information is taken in subconsciously.

An emotion demonstrated by a human being is usually a consequence of some kind of external influence. The things we see, hear, smell, touch and taste will cause a reaction, and the posture of the body, distortion of the face and the sounds we make will be as a consequence of these things we have sensed. We sign to the world the way we are feeling (or covering up the way we are feeling) by the body language, facial expressions and intonation of voice we are demonstrating. There are eight basic emotional states – happy, sad, anger, surprise, disgust, fear, interest and pain – plus lying. These can then be mixed and matched to produce many different emotional states.

Body language is a key tool for the animator to use to describe an emotional state and can be divided into four basic positions – forwards, backwards, open and closed. In the forwards positions, the body leans towards the thing to which the person is reacting. In the backwards positions, the body leans away from the thing that is engaging the person. In open body postures, the arms could be apart, the palms open, the legs apart and the spine arched back to reveal the chest, with the head held high. In closed body postures, the arms could be crossed over the body, the legs crossed and the spine bent forwards to close up the chest and the head held low. Most emotions will show a mixture of these body postures.

As well as the body postures, we have the face pulling different facial expressions. When combined, these body postures can be thought of in four ways: responsive (open and forwards, for example happy, interested); reflective (open and

PERFORMANCE IN ANIMATION 67

Open   Closed   Forward   Back

The basic body postures that a person adopts are forwards, backwards, open and closed.

Responsive   Reflective   Combative   Fugitive

The main body postures adopted by a character can be interpreted as responsive, reflective, combative or fugitive.

backwards, for example thinking about something); combative (closed and forwards, for example angry, determined); and fugitive (closed and backwards, for example frightened or disgusted).

Happy When someone is happy, the body generally will be open – arms wide apart, shoulders back, chest out and head held high. If your character is particularly interested in something, they could lean forwards, towards the object of their interest. Even if the hands are rubbed together in excitement, the elbows will be held up to maintain an openness to the body. If a character is happily contemplating something, the body could be pulled backwards, but the openness of the body will suggest a positive air. The face will have a smile.

Sad When someone is sad, the body will be closed. The spine will be bent forwards, the shoulders dropped down, the arms could be crossed over the chest, the legs bent to suggest a heaviness and the basic body posture will be backwards. If the arms are not crossed, the hands could hang down limply and the elbows will be held in towards the body. The face will have a frown.

Anger When someone is angry, the body is held forwards, usually in a closed position. The hands could be clenched into fists, elbows tight into the body and the head down but facing forwards in a confrontational way. The shoulders are forced up and tensed, while the legs are apart but bent to suggest weight and tightness. The face will have an angry look, with teeth clenched.

Examples of happy, sad and angry body postures.

Surprise With surprise, the body will be held upright and backwards. Depending on the type of surprise the person has received, the body could be open for a nice surprise, or closed for a nasty one. For a nice surprise, the body would initially move backwards, but then forwards when the character has realized what they have sensed is something they like. For a nasty surprise, the spine could be bent backwards slightly at the lumbar and remain like that. The legs will be straighter. The face will have a surprised look, mouth and eyes wide open.

Disgust If your character is disgusted by something, the body will be in a backwards position, with the body closed. The hands could be held up to reject the object of their disgust, or the arms could be crossed over the body in protection. The head could also be angled away from the thing that disgusts them. The face would be screwed up

Examples of surprised, disgusted and fearful body postures.

with the eyes closed to slits and the lips puckered into a disgusted look.

Fear If your character is scared by something, the body will be in a backwards position, with the body closed. The hands could be held up to protect the character from what they are scared of. Generally, the body will go up.

Interest Interest is usually done with a combination of the six emotional states above. If your character is happily interested in something, the body will be forwards and open. If they are disgusted but morbidly interested, the body will generally be backwards and closed, but the head might be pulled forwards.

Pain Pain is probably the rawest of emotions. It could be a reaction to pain being inflicted on the body, or an emotional pain being felt inside. Generally, the body posture will be closed and backwards, away from the thing that caused the pain, or weighted down, backwards and closed, for something more internal.

Lying One thing we are all good at is lying. We often have to cover up our real emotions or our internal thoughts in order to get along with each other and get through the day. Anyone engaged in a service industry must remain professional, even if the customer they are dealing with is abhorrent. They have to try to deal with the situation in a way that covers up their real emotions.

Having said that, the further we move down the body, the worse we are at lying. The face is excellent at covering up emotions, the body and arms slightly less so, and the legs even less. A person could look happy, but inside they are sad. So there may be a smile on the face, but if the body is closed and backwards, the body language will tell a different story.

Emotional Expression Using Hands, Arms and Legs

People often use their hands, arms and to a lesser extent their legs to express the emotions they are feeling.

Hands Hands with the palms open and upward tend to signal honesty and openness. Hands with palms open but facing downward suggest dominance or dishonesty. Hands that are clenched into fists or aggressively pointing suggest anger. Rubbing the palms together suggests eagerness, excitement and expectation.

Arms Crossing the arms across the body is a way of closing off the body from other people. Clenching the fists while crossing arms suggests anger. Gripping arms tightly with the hands whilst crossed suggests tension or nervousness. Partially crossing the arms suggests lack of confidence. Crossing the arms at the wrist suggests humility.

Legs Generally, the legs tend to be bent to show weight and heaviness. They may be straight to give confidence, spread apart to show dominance, or crossed to cover up or close the body to show nervousness or fear.

The way that a character crosses their legs can give a clue about what kind of person they are. Legs crossed at the knee suggest defensiveness,

Examples of interest, pain and lying body postures.

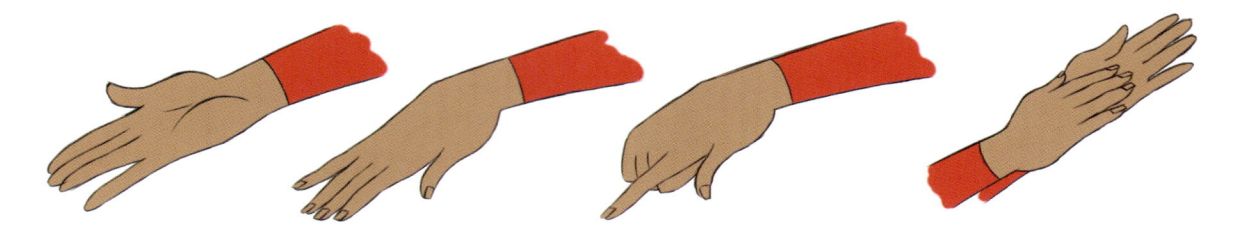

Examples of how hands can express emotions.

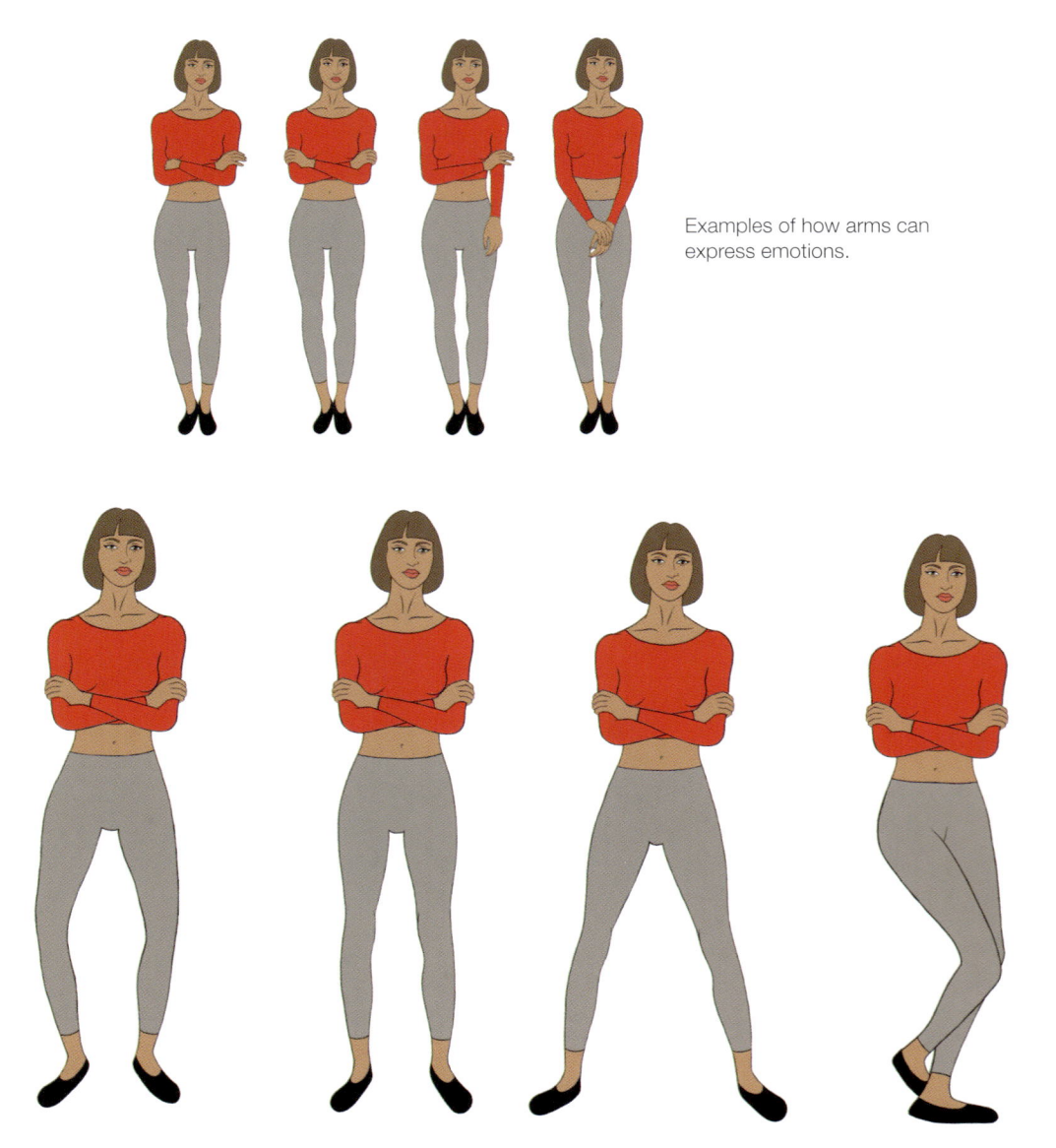

Examples of how arms can express emotions.

Examples of how legs can express emotions.

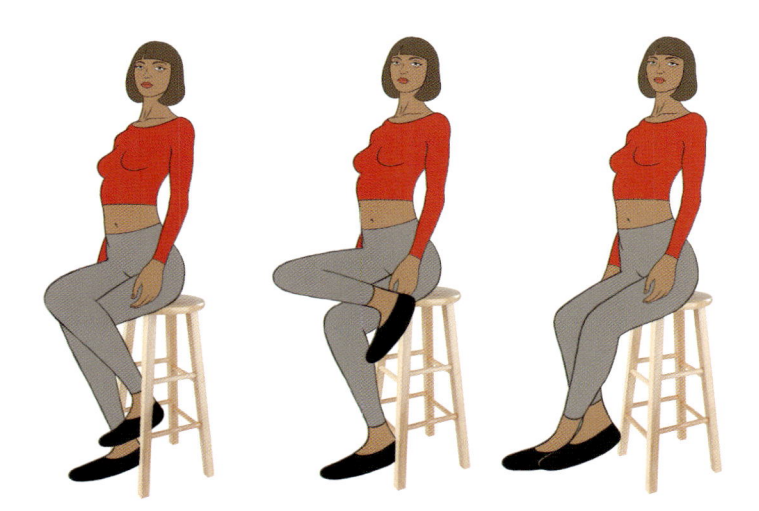

Examples of how crossing legs can express emotions.

legs crossed with the heel at the knee suggest aggressiveness or confidence, while legs crossed at the ankles give a prim and proper look.

KNOW YOUR CHARACTER

A useful thing to do before you start animating is to research your character. You could write a full biography with a huge backstory, but the quickest way to get to the soul of your protagonist is to ask the seven questions of character. These were formulated by Constantin Stanislavski to enable an actor (or screen writer) to understand the basis of the character and how they would act in a given situation. They are interpreted below to apply to an animated character. The first three questions are more general about what the character is like, where they are and when they are situated. The last four questions tend to be more specific to a given scene or shot that you are about to animate (but could apply to a movie as a whole).

Who is Your Character?

This can include the character's backstory, gender, race, height, weight, temperament, what they believe, whom they are inspired by and so on.

Where is Your Character?

This can include general things like the country in which the character lives, or be more specific to a shot, such as whether they are in public (the street, a café), or in private (in their house, bedroom). Characters tend to act differently in public than they do in private and they will react differently to an environment that they are familiar with compared to a strange environment (different planet, different country, dark old house).

What Era Does Your Character Exist in?

What era is your movie set in and how does this affect the way the character would behave? A character existing in the Victorian era would behave very differently to someone living today.

What Does Your Character Want?

This question is more specific to the shot you are about to animate, but could relate to an entire movie. Does your character want a drink? Do they need to tell somebody something? What is the motivation for the character in this shot?

Why Does Your Character Want It?

There has to be a reason why the character wants this and why they want to do something about it. Do they want a drink because they are thirsty, or are they an alcoholic? Do they need to tell somebody something to avert a disaster, or say some spiteful gossip? How important is it that they are able to do this thing?

How Will Your Character Get What They Want?

Your character will need to work out a way to get what they want. It may be as simple as going to a tap and pouring water into a glass, or they may be in the desert and have get water from an oasis. They may have to run to the other person to tell them something, or they may just have to cross a room or butt into a conversation.

What is Stopping Your Character Getting What They Want?

Almost every story involves a character being confronted by a problem. To get that glass of water, they need to find a tap and a glass, or they need to look for an oasis in the desert. They may have to travel far to tell someone something, or they could be bound and gagged and can't speak. If you have a character without a problem, you don't have a story.

Exercise

This exercise can be done with any animation medium, but you will need a character. For 2D animation, you will need to create a model sheet to refer to. For digital cut-out animation, the character will need to be built up from their constituent parts. For stop-motion animation, you will need to make a puppet and for 3D animation, you will need to build a character, or download one from the internet.

When doing this exercise, it is always easier to have a character respond to something that is visual, rather than a sound or a thought. So have something on screen for the character to react to.

Your character is stood centre screen with some kind of small object. This could be an object on the floor or on a small table. The character sees the small object in the shot and it interests them. They pick it up to have a closer look. They

In the body acting exercise, the character reacts to something that they engage with on a table.

react to what they see. The small object then needs to do something. It could magically change shape. If it's a small animal it could bite the character, or if it's a box they could try to open it. The character reacts to what the object does. They could be amazed by the magical transformation. They react in pain to being bitten, or they struggle to open the box and get frustrated. Finally, they get rid of the object. The magically transformed object could be put in a pocket and the character looks happy. The animal that has bitten our hero could jump out of the character's hand. The character throws the box away in disgust, unable to open it.

This exercise is open to interpretation and could be done in many ways. Act it out first and video yourself (LAVS). You will then have something to refer to. Don't just copy what you have videoed. Take it as the starting point and exaggerate it. Work out the basic key positions and do little thumbnail sketches to reduce down to the minimum information needed for an audience. You might find that your character will need to move more slowly than the video you have taken.

FACIAL EXPRESSIONS

As with body language, the basic emotions expressed on the face boil down to happy, sad, anger, surprise, disgust, fear, interest and pain, plus lying. The face can express far more than the body, so these basic facial expressions combine to produce many different emotions. The face can also cover up the underlying emotion felt by the character, but the contrasting body language can give it away.

When designing a character, you will need eyes, eyebrows and a mouth to get these emotions across. The ability to use the forehead to produce furrows is useful, as is the capability to produce wrinkles around the eyes. A jaw that can open and close and also lengthen and squash the face helps as well, but you can get away with just eyes, eyebrows and a mouth.

You will need to keep the acting much simpler with facial expressions than you would with whole-body language, because the camera is closer. If you move the character around too much, the animation will be far too busy to take in. Below are the basic facial expressions.

Happy The mouth will have a smile; it could be closed or open. The eyebrows are raised (or with an evil smile the inner ends of the eyebrows are lowered, the outer ends raised). The cheeks push up against the eyes, narrowing them slightly and producing crow's feet at the outer corners of the eyes. The pupils of the eyes may be dilated and look large.

Sad The mouth will be pulled downward and be either open or closed. The inner ends of the eyebrows are raised and the outer ends lowered against the brow. The top eyelid will be lowered over part of the eye.

Anger The mouth adopts a square shape to bare the teeth. The inner ends of the eyebrows are pulled inwards and downward. The eyelids are narrowed. The pupils will constrict and look tiny.

Surprised The mouth is open in a rounded shape. The eyebrows are raised; the eyes bulge open. The pupils will constrict and look small for a nasty surprise, but dilate and look big for a nice surprise.

Disgust The mouth is pulled into a small, puckered shape. The eyebrows are pulled down

Examples of happy, sad and angry facial expressions.

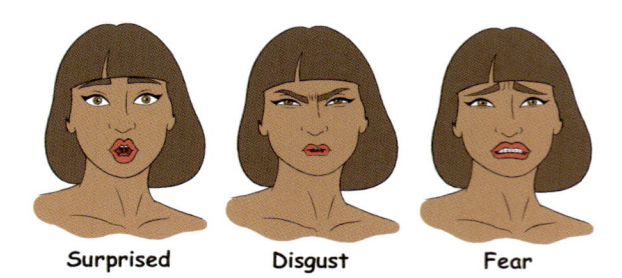

Examples of surprised, disgusted and fearful facial expressions.

horizontally and the eyelids narrowed. The pupils could be dilated and look small.

Fear The eyes bulge wide open. The mouth will be open, with the bottom corners pulled out to make the bottom lip look straight. The pupils will constrict and look tiny.

Interest Usually a person showing interest will have another expression, with interest exaggerating the expression being felt, for example happy and interested, or disgusted and interested.

Pain Pain produces a very pure, raw form of expression, with the eyes shut or half open, the mouth contorted and the eyebrows screwed up.

Lying face A lying face is one where the expression is forced and does not seem quite right. The eyebrows may be uneven and the eyes bulge. The mouth may be fixed and artificial looking. With a fake smile, you don't get crow's feet at the corners of the eyes.

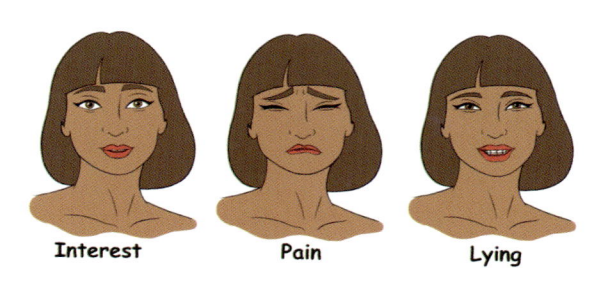

Examples of interested, painful and lying facial expressions.

Eyes

Human beings are always looking at something. The eyes should therefore always be looking somewhere (unless the character is dazed or sleepy, or the eyes are bulging outward or crossed). If your character does not appear to be looking at something, they will seem doll-like. When a character does a head turn to look at something, the eyes will lead the turn. So have the eyes move first and then move the head in a nice arc.

- Eyes with large pupils will make a character look loving and cute (like a puppy or a baby).
- Eyes with tiny pupils will look evil or scared.
- Eyes tend to move quickly; they almost 'click' from one position to another. In real life, moving the pupils slowly is very hard to do.

Blinks

- When a character does a normal blink, the eye will shut slower than when it opens.

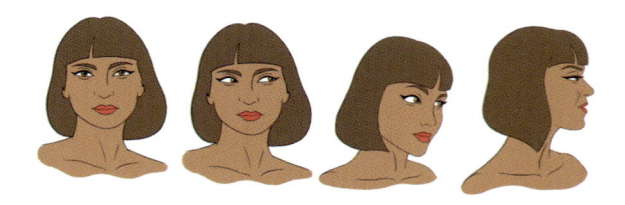

The eyes will always lead a head turn.

Dilated pupils seem attractive and loving, while contracted pupils seem evil, mean, angry or scared.

PERFORMANCE IN ANIMATION 75

- When a character is tired or a bit dim, the eyes will shut slowly and open even more hesitantly.
- A baby's blink will be deliberate, even when the eyes open and shut, and will be repeated a few times.
- A sexy flutter of the eyelashes will be quick and repeated several times. The eyelid will only open halfway.

HAND TO FACE GESTURES

We touch our faces all the time. Often this can be related to what we are seeing or hearing, or things that we are saying. It's a bit like three wise monkeys – see no evil, hear no evil and speak no evil.

- Touching around the front of the face near the mouth can give the impression that someone is saying something that is untrue, or is hearing something that is untrue.
- Touching around the ears can give the impression that the person is hearing something that they think is untrue, or can't believe.
- Touching around or rubbing the eyes gives the impression of the character having seen something that they don't believe, or that they are feeling tired.
- Touching or rubbing the back of the neck is usually a result of stress (hairs stand up on the back of the neck and irritate).

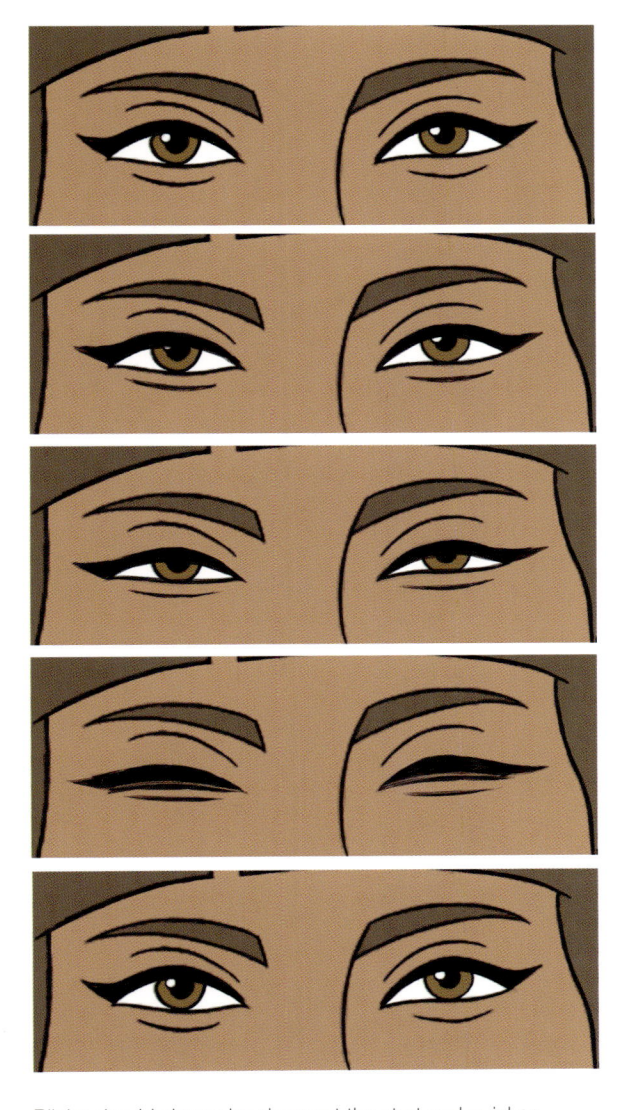

Blinks should always be slower at the start and quicker at the end. Make the eyes pop open to give a fresh, wide-awake look.

Hand to face gestures give clues about how a character is feeling and if they are being honest or not.

In the facial expression exercise, a character reacts to what they find in a box.

Exercise

Position your character centre screen, sat at a desk. There is a box on the table, slightly to the side, in front of them. The character reaches into the box and pulls something out. The character then reacts to the object they have pulled out. They could look quizzical and interested at the start, then be happy or disgusted about what they see in their hand.

To make the exercise more elaborate, the object could do something – explode, bite, change into something else, open up and so on. The character would then react to this thing happening.

TWO CHARACTERS ON THE SCREEN AT THE SAME TIME

When animating a shot with two characters on the screen at the same time, you need to make sure that the audience is looking at the correct character at the correct time. This is done by making sure that the character we are meant to be looking at is moving around and attracting attention, while the other character is more muted. When the attention needs to be shifted to the other character, get the first character to move towards the second one in some way (a look, a point, a gesture), then have second character more animated

With two characters on screen at the same time, the audience needs to be looking at the right character at the right time.

When two characters are on screen at the same time having a conversation, the way they look at each other is very important.

than the first one. You have to get your audience looking at each character in the same way that a crowd would watch a tennis match, looking at each player in the turn as they hit the ball.

When characters look at each other they will behave in certain ways. In a conversation, a character talking will usually not look directly at another character, but will only occasionally give a quick look to check they are still listening. This allows the listener to look at the talking character directly without feeling uncomfortable.

When characters look directly into each other's eyes, it usually means one of two things – love or hate. (It is very uncomfortable to look directly into someone's eyes if you don't know them well.)

- Two lovers looking at each other will have a look where the pupils of the eyes are clicking from side to side, looking at the other character's eyes individually. This gives an open, loving or weak look.
- Two people who are looking at each other with hate in their eyes will stare directly at each other, the eyes not clicking from side to side. Think about two boxers, squaring up to their opponent before a prize fight.

With the two-character exercise, you have to make sure that the audience looks at the right character at the right time.

Exercise

Animate two characters on the screen at the same time.

- One person could sneeze; the other person sees this and hands the first person a handkerchief.
- One person could be reading a book and the other person tries to look at it.
- One person could be listening to headphones and the noise is annoying the second person. The second person could ask them to turn the music down and the first person ignores them and turns it up.

See if you can come up with any other simple situations to animate.

LIP-SYNC

When it comes to lip-sync, we need to give the illusion that your character is speaking. Ideally, you need to record the dialogue first, then break it down

If people are looking directly into each other's eyes, they either love or hate each other.

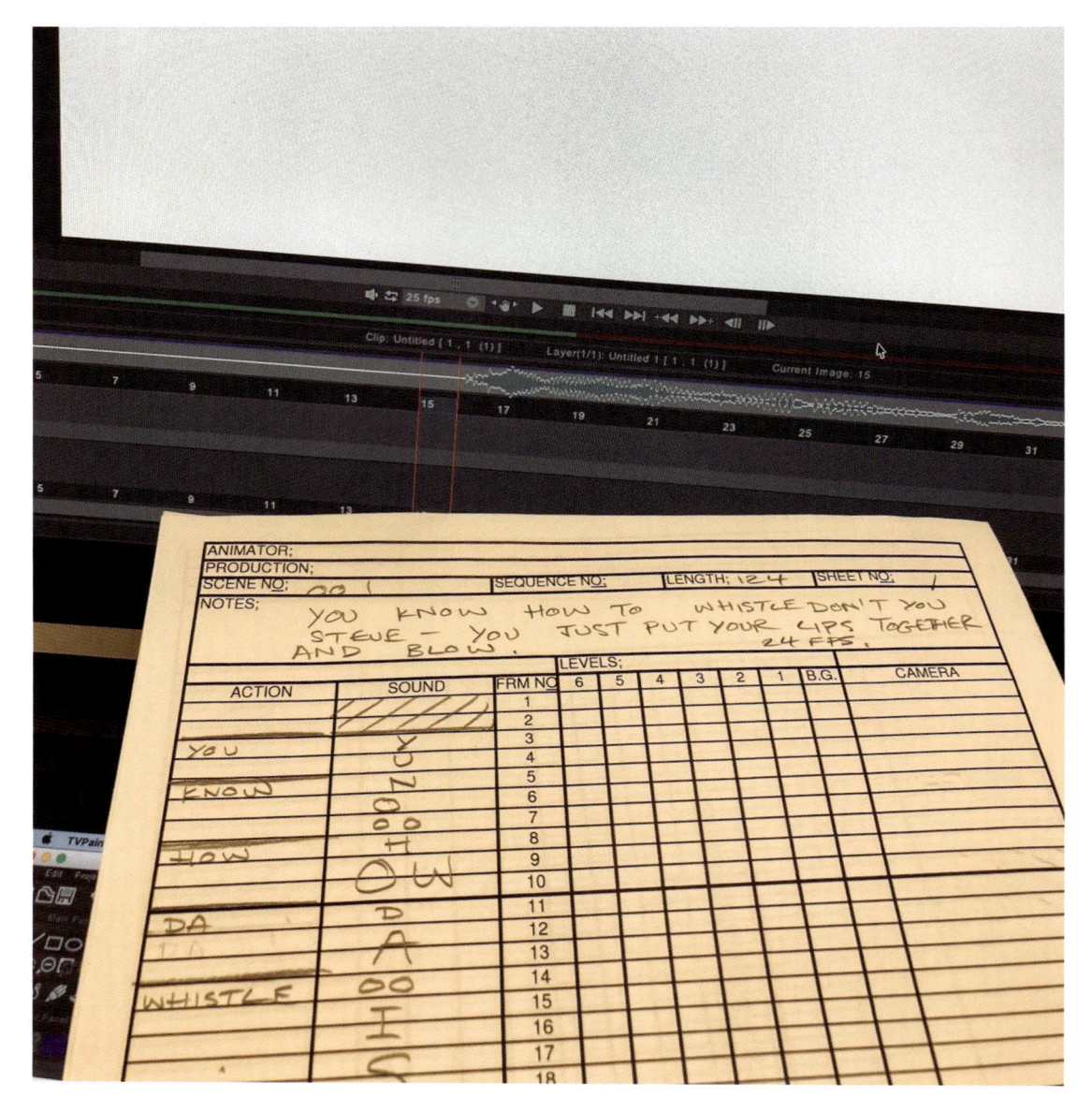

In order to do lip-sync, you need to break down a soundtrack and know when each major sound occurs, frame by frame.

so that you know what frames of a shot each sound corresponds to. You do this by taking the sound into a piece of software that can play it back frame by frame. You then 'scrub' through the soundtrack slowly, working out where the sounds are. Mark where these sounds occur on an x-sheet (or mark the sounds into the software, or just write down at what frame number a certain sound happens).

Phrasing

Once you know this, you can work out the phrasing. When a character speaks, they tend not to move around as much as when doing a piece of 'mute' (non-speaking acting). People tend to occupy poses that emphasize the major phrases of a piece of dialogue. The key is to keep this really

Basic Mouth Shapes

Strangely enough, the mouth shapes are the least important part of lip-sync; the acting needs to be sorted out first, via phrasing. Sound moves slower than light, so sometimes you can make the mouth shapes happen earlier than the sound to which they relate. To start with, stick with doing the mouth shapes exactly on the frame where they happen. Later on, you can experiment with making them earlier.

MOUTH-SHUT CONSONANTS

The most important mouth shapes are the mouth-shut consonants. These are, 'B', 'F', 'M', 'P' and 'V'. The reason these are so important is that it is impossible to utter these sounds without shutting your mouth (really, they are not sounds at all but a silent or quiet mouth shape that has to be done to get the following sound). An audience will notice these mouth shapes and whether they fit to the dialogue. Make them slightly longer (by a frame or so) than they are on the soundtrack.

'Ooo'

The second most important mouth shape is 'ooo'. It is difficult to do this sound without pushing the mouth into an 'ooo' shape with a small mouth and puckered lips. It also takes the mouth a while to get into this shape and out of it again, which is why it is really noticeable to an audience.

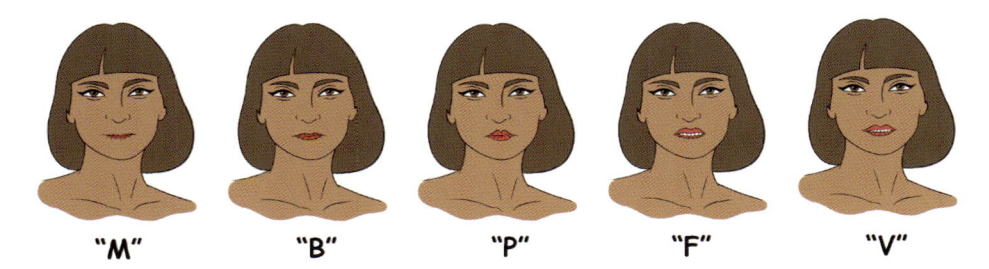

Phrasing is the breaking down of the basic postures adopted by a person when talking.

simple. In a four-second piece of dialogue, you will only need about three positions for your character to move into.

- For example, if somebody says 'I really … hate you,' the first phrase is 'I really …' and the second phrase is 'hate you!'
- So, have the character in one position for the phrase 'I really …' and then move forwards into the phrase, 'hate you!'

Once you have sorted out the phrasing, you need to in-between the animation. Finally, you can do the mouth shapes, unless you are doing straight-ahead animation, in which case the mouth shapes have to be done at the same time (puppet animation, for example).

The most visible mouth shapes demonstrated by someone talking are the mouth-shut consonants: 'B', 'F', 'M', 'P' and 'V'.

"ooo"

When a mouth produces the sound 'ooo', it takes a long time to get into the correct mouth shape and out of it again, so is very noticeable to an audience.

Large Mouth Shapes

The next most important mouth shapes are the big vowels: 'Ah', 'Eee', 'Eh' and 'O'. These involve having a large open mouth with the jaw open. Because these mouth shapes are so big, they are noticeable to an audience.

Linking Mouth Shapes

The least important mouth shapes are the basic consonants: 'C', 'D', 'K', 'N', 'S', 'T', 'Y', 'Z' and so on. Generally, you can make these sounds with

c, d, g, h, k, n, q, s, t, y

The basic consonants can be thought of as the in-between mouth shapes.

almost any mouth shape, so I always think of these positions as the in-betweens that come between the keys of the more important mouth shapes.

The following mouth shapes can influence the preceding mouth shapes. For example, if you say the word 'moment', the 'M' at the start will be a bit narrower (just before the 'O' mouth shape), while the 'M' in the middle will be wider because the following shape is 'ent', which is a wider mouth shape.

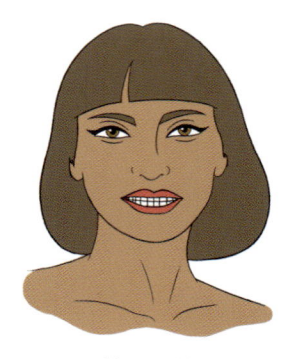

"oh"   **"ah"**   **"eh"**   **"ee"**

The big vowels involve the jaw opening and the mouth being wide open as well.

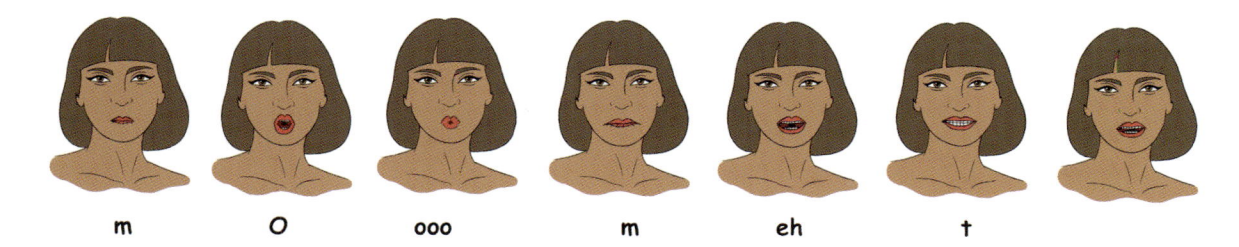

The word 'moment' being spoken.

Exercise

In this exercise, animate a short (less than five seconds) piece of dialogue in your chosen animation style.

Break down the lip-sync, so that you know where each of the mouth shapes comes. Act it out, so that you know where the major phrases are and work out the basic poses that your character will adopt during the sequence. With drawn animation and 3D animation, in-between the major poses, so that the animation is working without the mouth shapes.

Finally, add the mouth shapes to the face. With puppet animation, you will have to animate straight ahead, but note down at which frame each of the major phrases occurs and aim towards them as you are changing the mouth shapes.

"You know how to whistle don't 'cha Steve? You just put your lips together and blow!"

For the lip-sync exercise, take your favourite line from your favourite film and animate your character saying it.

4
2D ANIMATION

TRADITIONAL DRAWN ANIMATION

You will need the following items to do traditional drawn animation.

Peg Bar

With traditional drawn animation, the basic requirements are paper, a pencil and some way of registering the paper. Usually we use a *peg bar*, which is a flat piece of plastic or metal with pegs that engage in holes in the bottom of the sheets of paper on which you are going to animate. You can use a simple peg bar with two pegs that work with a standard hole punch, or a professional peg bar with three pegs and specially punched paper.

Peg bars are used to register your animation paper.

A peg bar is then taped on to a light box, or under your camera.

Pencils

With pencils, use a pencil that is not too hard and not too soft; an HB or 2B should be fine. You can also use Col-Erase pencils in either blue or red (coloured pencils that can be rubbed out). These can be used to rough out a drawing first. You can then *clean up* the drawing with an HB or 2B pencil, either on the same sheet of paper or on a fresh sheet.

Paper

Normal photocopy paper is okay, but a bit thick, which makes it difficult to see through. More translucent paper that is specifically designed for animation is preferable. The standard size for animation paper is called 12 field (or 12f). This means it is around 12in (300mm) wide. If you are likely to want to scan your work into a computer later on, it might be better to use A4-sized paper.

Light Box

The next thing you need is a light box. This makes it much easier to see your previous drawings when animating. You could use a simple, flat, plastic light box, the type used for tracing or viewing photo negatives. For the professional, a light box with a disc of perspex that can rotate makes it easier to draw at different angles.

Light boxes are used to see through the paper on which you are animating, so that you can see your previous drawing.

To start animating, place your paper on the peg bar that is taped to the light box. Do your first drawing. Place a second piece of paper on top of the first drawing and draw your next image, referring to the previous drawing underneath. You now have two drawings of your animation. If you are doing key to key animation, you should continue drawing one key drawing after the other until the action of the shot is finished. You then do the in-between drawings. Place your first key drawing on to the light box. Then place the second key drawing on top of the first key drawing. Place a blank sheet of paper on top of these two keys and sketch a drawing that is in-between these two key drawings.

If you are doing straight-ahead animation, just keep doing one drawing after another until you have finished your shot, using the light box to refer to your previous drawing.

You can buy peg bars, animation paper and Col-Erase pencils from an animation supplier such as https://www.chromacolour.co.uk.

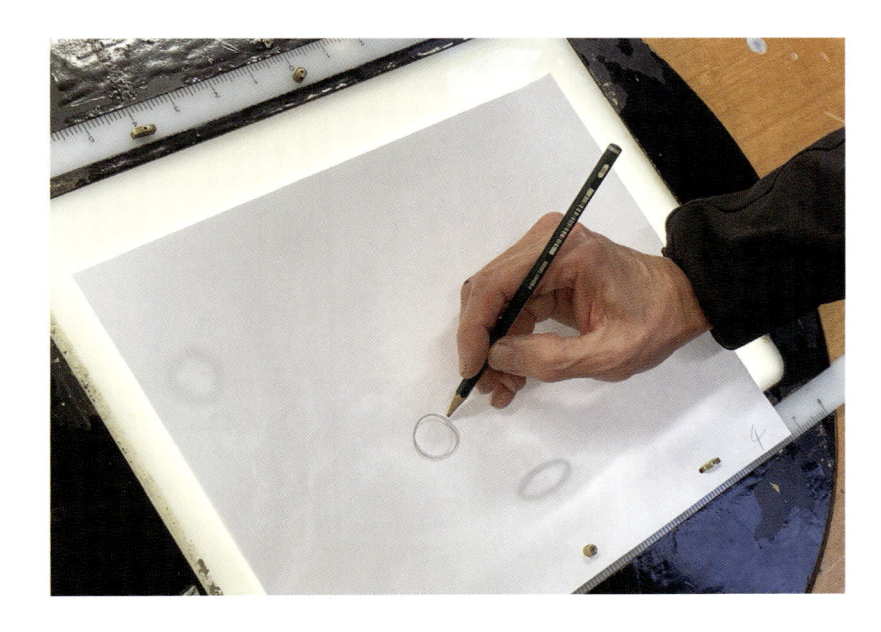

When you have animated the key positions of your shot, you will need to in-between the key positions on a light box.

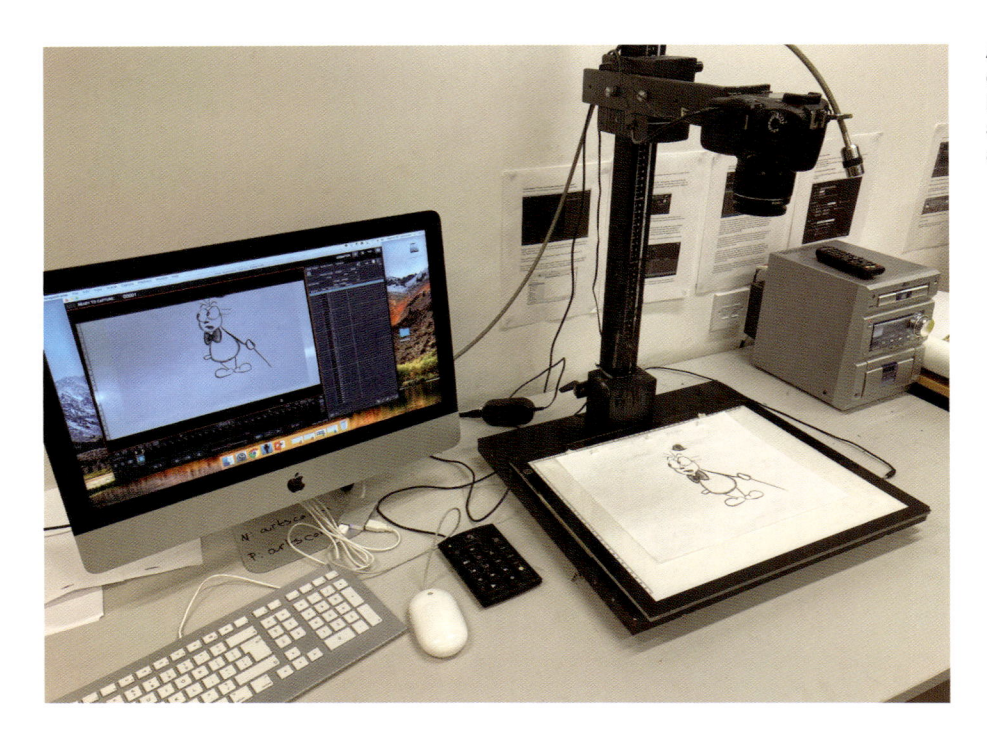

A line tester consists of a computer with a line testing or animation app, with a camera attached to it.

Line Tester

In the old days, we would shoot our rough drawn animation on a film rostrum camera and then have to wait until the film was developed. Once we got the film back from the processors, we would view the film on a projector or editor. This would take at least a day, maybe longer. Later on, video systems were developed, which meant that we could shoot our animation and play it back almost immediately.

Since the introduction of computers, it is now possible to shoot your animation with a digital camera, linked to a computer, and play the animation back straight away. Using a line-test program, you can vary the amount of frames that each drawing is shown for. (There are links to programs that can be used for this at the back of the book.)

The camera is mounted on a stand (or bolted to the wall) and the artwork is placed under the camera, with a peg bar to register it. You then shoot your animation, frame by frame. You could use an old photographic enlarger stand to mount your camera.

X-Sheets (or Dope Sheets)

When animating, there is always a lot of information to remember and the best way to store this is on an x-sheet. These are also referred to as dope sheets ('dope' is a New York slang word, dating for the early twentieth century, meaning information).

An x-sheet consists of a series of rows and vertical columns. Each row going down represents a frame; each column is for a layer of the animation, or for information about the camera position, the sound and the action. For example, if the animation is to be played back at twenty-five frames per second, one hundred frames will equal four seconds of animation. The columns on a x-sheet mean the following.

Sound Column

This contains the sounds that are relevant to the animation. Very often this is the dialogue spoken by the characters. For animation, the dialogue is recorded first. It is then broken down. You can use

ANIMATOR:										
PRODUCTION:										
SCENE NO:			SEQUENCE NO:			LENGTH:			SHEET NO:	
NOTES:										
					LEVELS:					
ACTION	SOUND	FRM NO	6	5	4	3	2	1	B.G.	CAMERA
		1–50								

An x-sheet is a way of storing information about your animation.

your line-test program to break down the sound by going over it slowly to work out where the sounds are, frame by frame.

ACTION COLUMN

This contains the instructions on when a given piece of animation will start and end (sometimes referred to as slugging out). An animator or director will fill out this part of the x-sheet before they start animating.

FRAME NUMBERS COLUMN

As the heading suggests, this is where the numbers of each frame are inserted. One of the main ways of 'cheating' in drawn animation is to do your animation on twos. This means that each of your drawings is shot for two frames, which saves a huge amount of work. For example, if you have to animate four seconds you only have to do fifty drawings, rather than one hundred drawings (assuming a rate of twenty-five frames per second).

At times, you may want to hold your animation. For example, at a given point in the action a character may move into a position where they stand still for a second or so. At this point, you could just have one drawing held for however many frames are needed.

There are two ways to number your drawings. The first way is to number them by the drawing. This means that drawing number one will be numbered '1', drawing number two will be numbered '2' and so on. The other way is to number them by the frame. This means that the drawing on frame one will be numbered '1'. The drawing on frame three (if the sequence is shot on twos, this would be the second drawing) will be numbered '3', the drawing on frame five would be numbered '5' and so on.

Each method has its advantages and disadvantages. It is probably better for the aspiring computer animator to number drawings by the frame so that when you look at your drawings in order to copy their position with your computer model it is clear exactly what frame that pose should be on. All the exercises done in this book will be numbered by the frame.

The columns show the order in which the levels are placed. The background is at the bottom level, the foreground at the top, with the character in the middle. Each drawing will have its own number. Each unit represents a frame. The drawing number is inserted to show where that frame of animation will be in the sequence. This varies depending on how many frames per second each drawing represents.

The illustration below shows a sequence that is shot on twos. When something is on twos, the first row has a number while the second is left blank. It is unnecessary to fill in every frame. At the end of the sequence, the last drawing is held for ten frames, that is, the drawing is shot for ten frames. This is indicated by the line that runs from the bottom of the drawing number to the last frame that the drawing is held for. If the drawing is held for more than two frames, it is necessary to insert a line to show how long the drawing is held for.

You can number your drawings with either odd or even numbering on an x-sheet.

Levels Column

When a sequence is animated, even if there is only one character, the drawing for one frame of animation may be on several levels of paper. If the body remains still during the sequence, but the head and arms are moving, there will be only one drawing of the body for the whole sequence. If the head is moving at a different rate to the arms, the head will be on a separate piece of paper and the arms on a further piece. It there is a background and the character is stood behind, for example, a tree, this will again be on a separate piece of paper. However accurate the final drawings are, if you have to retrace exactly the same drawing twenty times or more, there will be variations between the drawings that will show when the animation is played. It also is an unnecessary use of time.

Before the use of computers, the finished drawings were traced and coloured on to cel (cellulose acetate or clear plastic sheets). This allowed for a maximum of six levels before the thickness of the cell made the colours on the lower levels look muddy. Today, each of these levels would be painted and assembled together with programs such as DigiCel FlipBook or Toon Boom. This allows for infinite levels without any loss of quality.

Camera Column

Information in this column instructs the camera how you want the scene to be shot and pinpoints the area within the artwork. The most important piece of information is the field size. The most popular paper is 12 field, which means that the camera at its maximum setting will shoot an oblong area that is 12in (300mm) wide.

Traditional 2D animators use a field guide, also called a *graticule*, to work out the position of the shot. For example, shooting animation using the full size of the paper is marked on the top of the camera column as 12-field centre. A 3D-computer animator would not use field sizes, but it is worth understanding how they are worked out.

The field guide has north, south, east and west printed at the top, bottom, right and left. It consists of twenty-four columns and twenty-four rows in a grid. The columns are half an inch wide. By using these compass points and grid references, it is possible to specify any area on the paper to be shot.

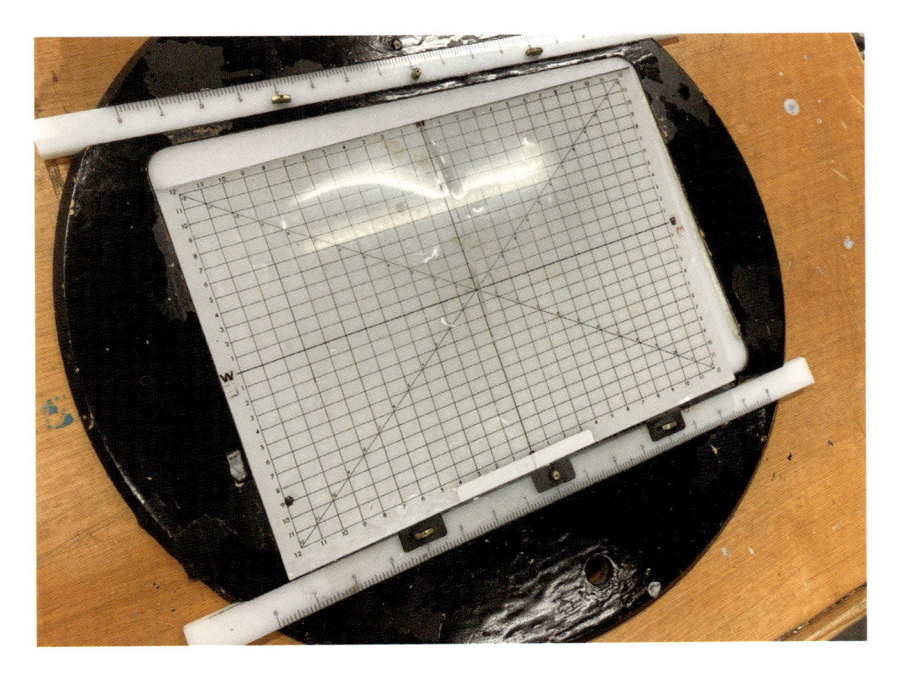

A field guide (also known as a graticule) is a way to position the camera on animation artwork.

Illustration of a 3 field on a piece of 12-field paper. An example of a close-up.

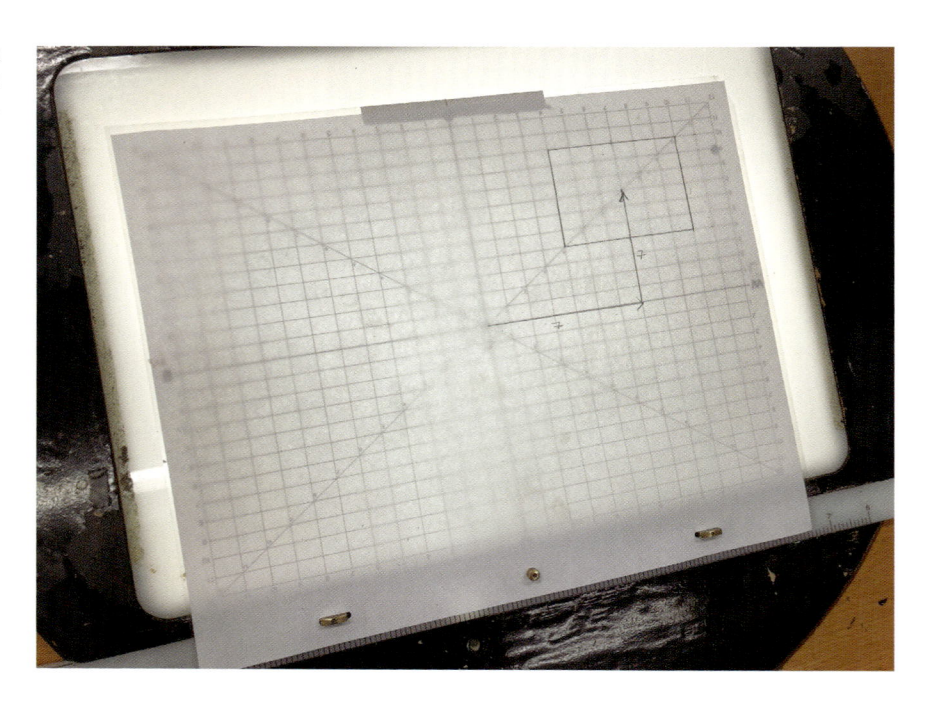

The illustration shows an oblong area at the top right of the paper that is 5in (127mm) wide. This

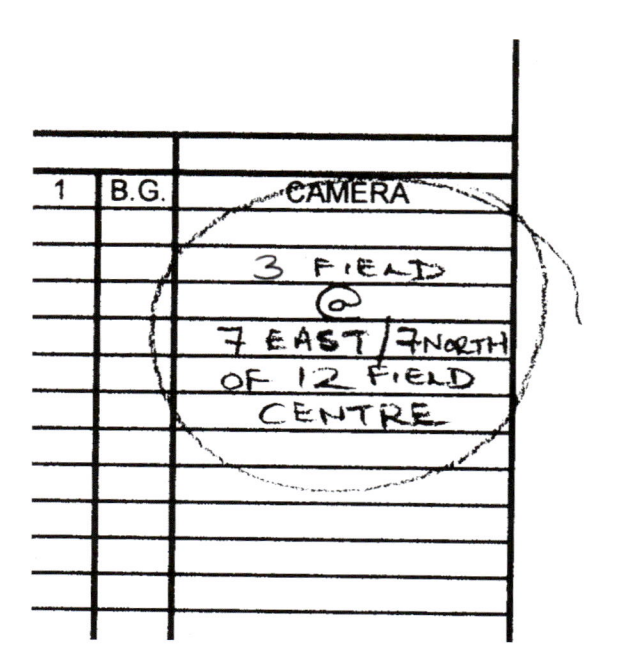

Illustration of a filled camera column on an x-sheet, at 3F @ 7E/7N of 12 F C.

would be 3 field @ 7 east/7 north of 12-field centre. Using the field guide, you work out where the centre of the oblong is in relation to 12-field centre (the centre of the field guide). To find the centre, count along seven lines east and seven lines north from the centre of the field guide (12-field centre). Using this method, you can place a field of any size in any area. An x-sheet is particularly good for pose to pose or key to key animation.

The way to approach doing a piece of animation is to work out the key positions first, then shoot them with a line tester. Give each key position an appropriate amount of frames (you basically guess how many frames each key frame needs). Play the animation back and it will jump forwards from key to key, giving the approximate timing that a piece of animation needs. Is it too quick or too slow? If parts are too quick, give more frames to that key position or positions. If it's too slow, take some frames out.

From this information, mark up the key positions on to the x-sheet. You can then renumber the drawings with the same number of the frame that it is on. You may have a key position on frame 1;

2D ANIMATION

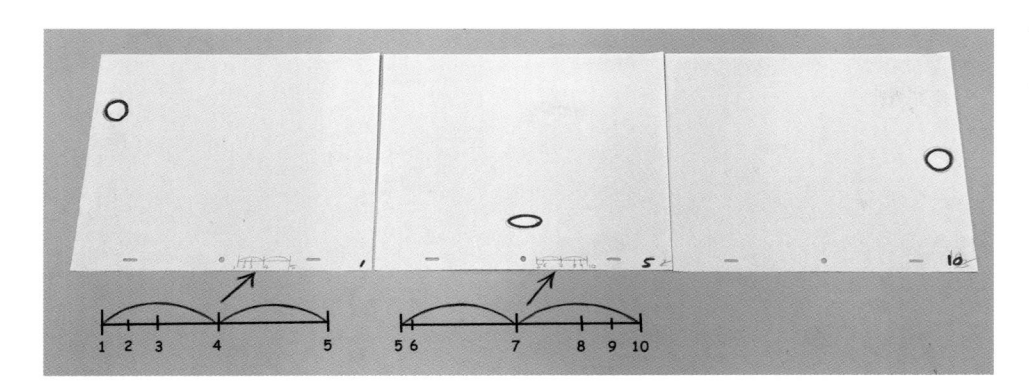

The key positions of a bouncy ball with timing charts.

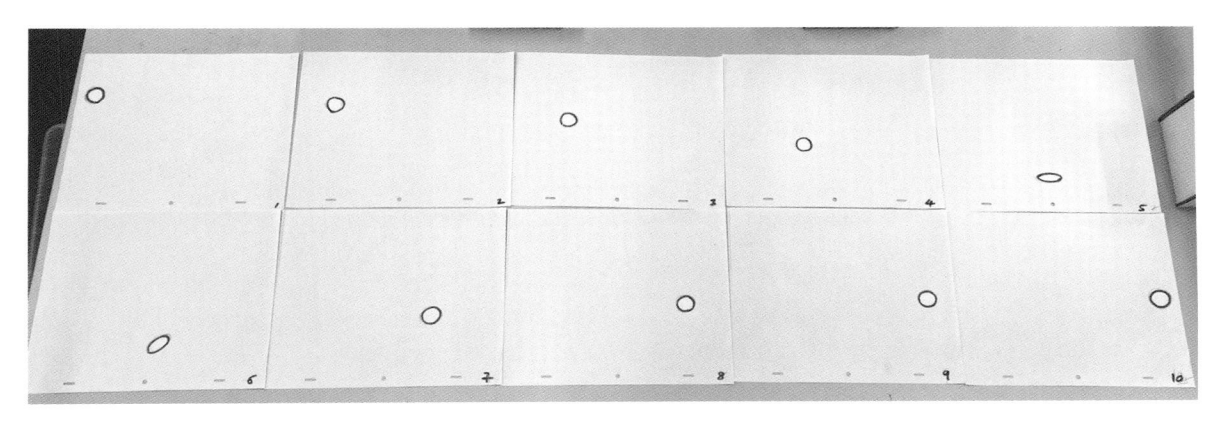

The same bouncy ball with all the in-between drawings.

this will now be numbered 1. If your second key position is on frame 9, this will now be called drawing number 9. If we are shooting our animation on twos, this means that there will be three drawings between key drawing number 1 and key drawing number 9. You can then do timing charts on the bottom of each drawing, showing where these in-between drawings are going to be placed.

The illustrations show an example of a ball bouncing across the screen. Each key position is at the top and bottom of each bounce. I have included the timing charts underneath each drawing. I have also shown the whole sequence, with the in-betweened drawings.

Once you have completed your animation, shoot it again. If it is okay, you can leave it as it is and render out a movie from your program. If you want to colour it in, there are several options (*see* below).

HOW TO ANIMATE TRADITIONAL DRAWN ANIMATION

Place your first sheet of paper on the peg bar, on the light box. Draw your first image on this sheet of paper. Then put another sheet of paper on top of the first sheet of paper and draw your second image. These could be done as key positions or one drawing after another as straight-ahead animation.

Flipping, Flicking and Rolling

Flipping, flicking and rolling are very useful techniques that will help you to look at your animation and how it is moving while you are still drawing it.

Flipping the animation drawings to create movement.

Flipping

Flipping is when you pick up your drawings, grasp them at the top with your left hand and flip the drawings, one after the other, with the thumb of your right hand, just like a flipbook. Watch the drawings and see how they move. Make sure that the drawings are in flipping order (first drawing at the bottom, last drawing at the top). If the collection of drawings is not thick enough for your thumb to get a grip of, stick some blank paper on top of the drawings to thicken them up. This is a good way to look at your animation and see how it's working. It also means you don't have to use any technology!

Flicking

Flicking is when you are doing an in-between drawing. Put the first key drawing on to the peg bar on the light box. Then put the second key drawing on top of that. Finally, put the blank piece of paper that you are going to use for your in-between drawing on top.

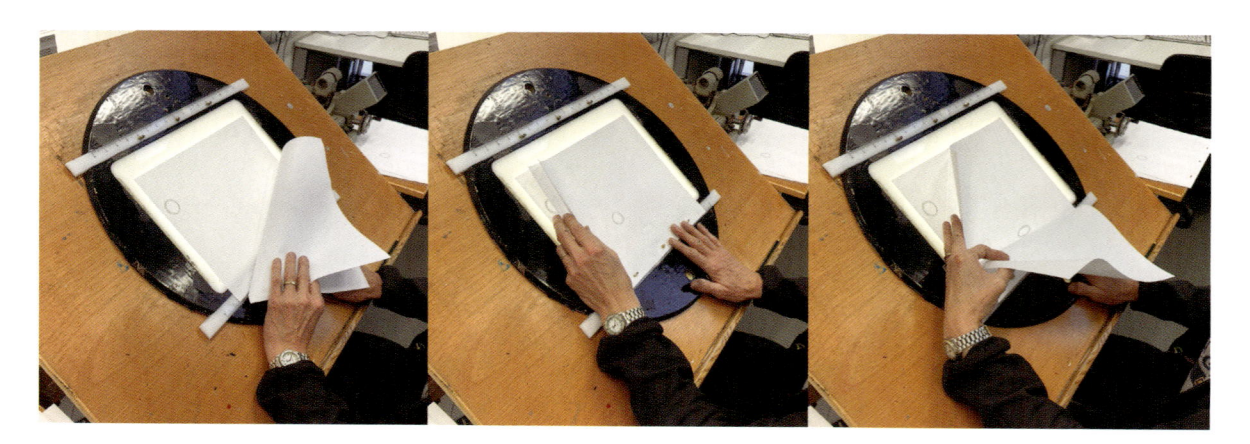

Flicking the animation drawings to create movement.

Place your index finger under the second key drawing and hold the blank piece of paper on top with the forefinger and thumb. Start your drawing. Then fold forwards both the second key drawing and the in-between drawing and look at the first key drawing. Fold back the papers to look at the in-between drawing. Then fold forwards the in-between drawing and look at the second key drawing. When this is done in fast succession, an impression of movement will be created. It helps to put a rubber band over the pegs of the peg bar to stop the paper slipping off.

ROLLING

Rolling is where you put five of your drawings on to the light box in flipping order (first drawing at the bottom and last drawing at the top). Insert the fingers of your left hand between each of the pieces of paper. Fold all of the pieces of paper up towards you, so that you can see the first drawing. Then let each of the drawings fall back, one by one, on to the light box. If this is done fast enough, an impression of movement will be created. Again, a rubber band on the peg bar will help to keep the drawings in place.

Rolling the animation drawings to create movement.

Colouring Animation

The traditional way to colour animation is to trace the animation on to sheets of acetate (also known as cel), then have a background underneath (if you want to have a complicated background with your animation). This can also be a way to produce really nice artwork that can be framed and displayed.

An example of a painted animation cel.

Trace on the top of the cel, then paint on its back.

The paint used is basically emulsion paint (the kind of paint used to decorate walls). You can buy professional cel paint, but it tends to be very expensive. Nowadays it is possible to get almost any colour mixed up at a local DIY centre. So choose your colours, get them mixed up into little match pots and fetch your brushes.

First, place your cel on top of your drawing. Next, trace the line on to the cel with an ink pen, using black (or any other colour) emulsion paint, thinned down with water so that it flows nicely from the pen. Make sure the paint is very well mixed.

Then turn the cel over and paint your fill colours on to the back of the cel. The paint should be thinned down with water to the consistency of single cream. It's best to paint the darkest colours first. Don't just paint the emulsion on like you would paint a picture. You need to 'pool' the paint on. Put a substantial blob of paint on to the area you want to colour and then drag the paint over the surface, trying not to touch the cel underneath. This will produce a thick layer of paint that will dry without any brush marks. Again, make sure the paint is very well mixed. You can also augment your cels with chinagraph or other types pencils that will stick to cel to soften areas.

There is nothing to stop you colouring your drawings straight on to the paper. This will produce something a bit more organic that will shimmer when the animation moves. The only problem is that you will find it difficult to see a background through the paper, so it is best not to have one. Next, shoot your animation with your line-test program (or scan the artwork in with a colour scanner), then render a movie, ready to be edited in an editing program.

Alternatively, you could scan the drawings into the computer and import them into a digital drawn animation program and colour them there. It is a lot quicker and ultimately cheaper that painting on cel.

Cut-Out Animation

Cut-out animation is where a character is made up of a series of shapes. The head, body, arms, legs, hands and feet are painted or drawn on thick cartridge paper, then cut out. When they have been cut out, take a black felt pen and make the cut card edges black.

Create a nice background and place your character on top of the background. Work out what it

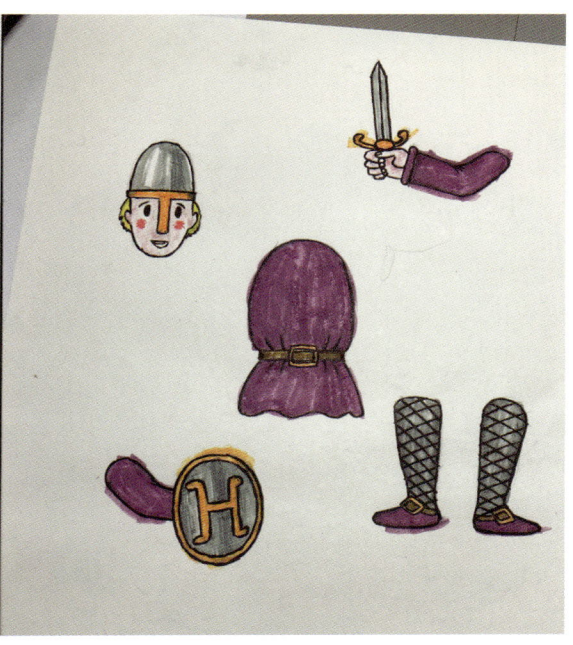

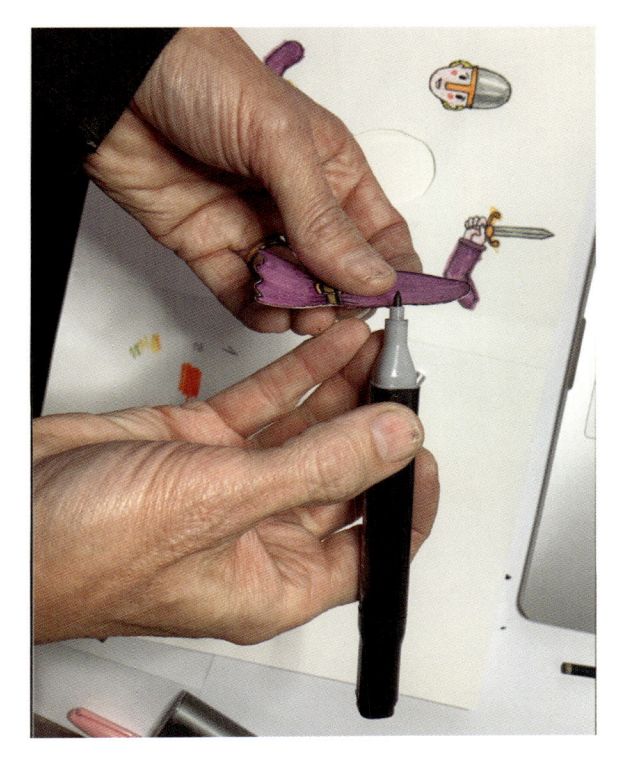

An example of a cut-out character.

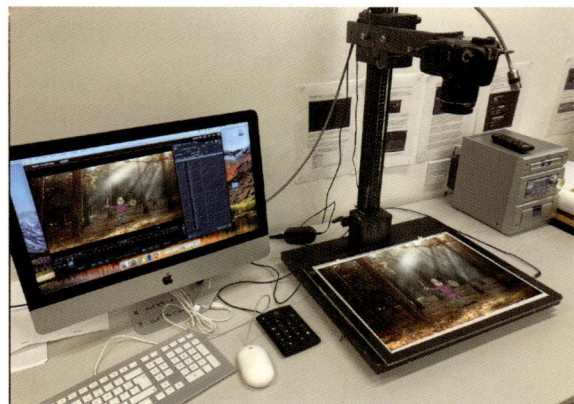

A cut-out character on a background, under the camera.

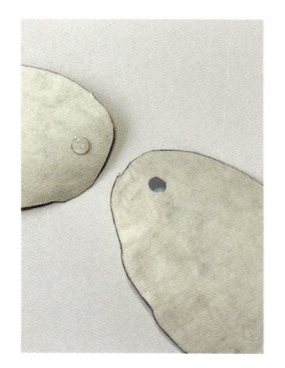

An example of a jointed cut-out character.

is that you want your character to do. I like to do a series of thumbnail sketches that show the action, like a series of key drawings. You then follow this as a reminder.

Move your character a small amount at a time and shoot a frame. Move them a little more and shoot another frame. Repeat this process until you have finished the shot. Play the movement back on your line-test program to see how it moves. If it's okay, go on to the next shot; if not, have another go. This is a fairly quick method compared to drawn animation and doing a shot several times is a good way to learn timing.

You can make even more sophisticated characters by joining them together. By punching holes into the lower parts of the body, for example, you can join together the sections of a neck of a dragon. Take the small disc that was punched out and stick it on to the bottom of the body, place the lower part of the neck on it, then cut a slightly larger piece of paper and stick it on top of that. You should end up with two parts of your character hinged together. Continue until you have a complete jointed character.

Fluid Animation

You can create animation by doing one image after another using a fluid material. These could be substances such as sand, tea, oil paint, acrylic paint, pastels, charcoal and so on.

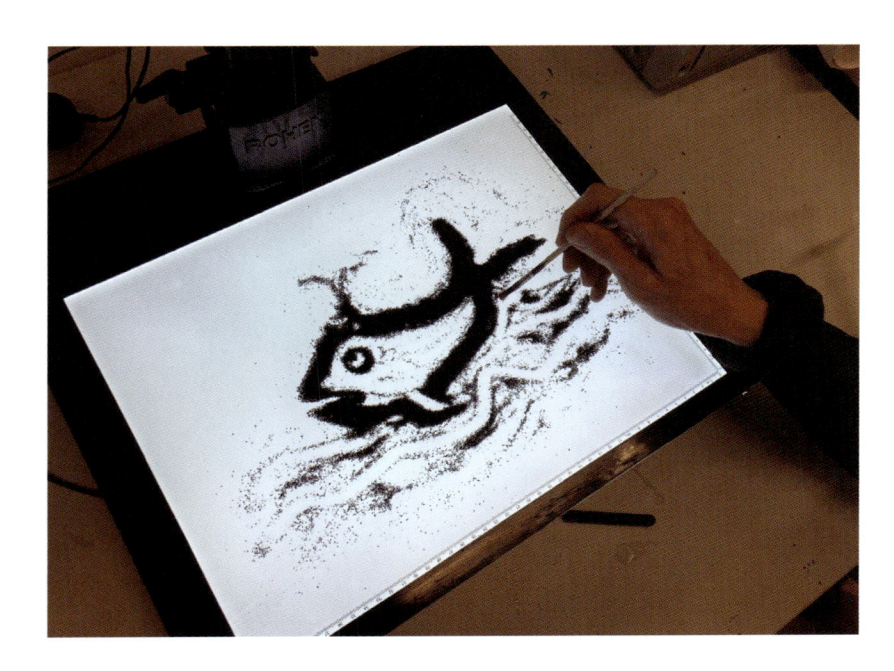

An example of tea/sand animation. A fluid substance can be moved frame by frame.

Animation with Sand or Tea

Set up a flat plastic light box under your camera. Build a small cardboard wall around the edge of the light box. Turn on the light. Take some sand or tea and create an image with your chosen material. Maybe arrange the sand or tea into a shape of a character. Take a shot with your line-test program. Move the sand or tea into a slightly different shape (for example, move the arm slightly). Take a shot. Move the sand or tea slightly more. Take another shot. Continue with the animation one frame at a time until you have finished it.

Make sure you cover your computer and keyboard with cling film to keep the material out of them. This technique will give a soft, silhouette-like look to your animation.

Animation with Wet Paint

For oil or acrylic paint (oil paint works best because it takes longer to dry), use a flat plastic light box and paint a picture of the animation you want to do. Take a shot with your line-test program. Then rub out part or all of your picture and do a slightly different image to create a small amount of movement. Take a shot. Rub out, do another image. Take another shot. Continue until your animation is complete.

This process can get very messy, so use rubber gloves and cover up your computer, keyboard and mouse with cling film. Put lots of newspaper down underneath. Also, if you are using turpentine or white spirit to thin your oil paint, make sure you

Wet paint can be moved, erased and manipulated frame by frame to produce animation.

Charcoal or pastels can be moved, erased and manipulated frame by frame to produce animation.

use a face mask and have the area well ventilated. (Oil paints that can be mixed with water are also available.)

ANIMATION WITH PASTELS AND CHARCOAL

For pastels or charcoal, set up a thick piece of paper under the camera. Paper with a texture to it works best. Do your first drawing, take a shot, then rub out and redraw to move the character slightly. Take a shot. Rub out and redraw and take another shot. Continue until your animation is complete.

You may need to change the paper a few times when it becomes too dirty. It is advisable to cover your computer, put down newspaper and wear a face mask to avoid breathing in dust.

Case Study – *No Body* by Haemin Ko

Ko's film is based on the journal she wrote when first moving to London. It is about her emotional experiences of loneliness and disconnection with the city and herself. She took extracts from these

Ko working on the city part of her project under the camera.

journals and arranged the sentences in a poem-like form.

Once the script was in order, Ko composed the music as an aural storyboard, with specific instruments, codes, techniques and rhythms to suit the mood and emotion of each part of the script. She would send these pieces of music to a composer to be orchestrated. About one-third of the production was spent composing the music.

Her fine-art background had involved emotional life drawing of the human body and she wanted to extend this artwork through her animation. She selected hundreds of her previous drawings and placed them in an emotional structure.

Ko did further life drawing, using these original drawings for inspiration and also as a guide to in-betweening these drawings.

Ko then animated all of the movie on paper under a digital camera connected to a computer. She would shoot each image as she manipulated the marks on the paper, rubbing out areas and redrawing in order to execute the movement. Most of the animation was done straight ahead, which gave the images spontaneity and energy.

The final film was edited to the musical score and the spoken dialogue. Ko's film has been accepted into over fifty film festivals, won numerous awards and been shown all over the world.

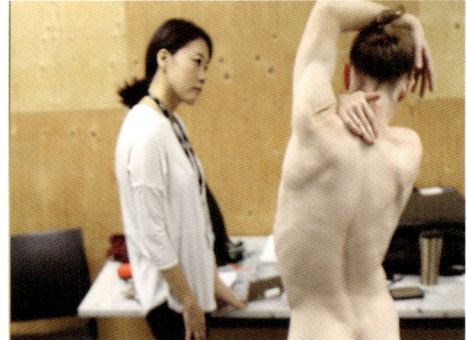

Ko directing her model, ready to be drawn for her project.

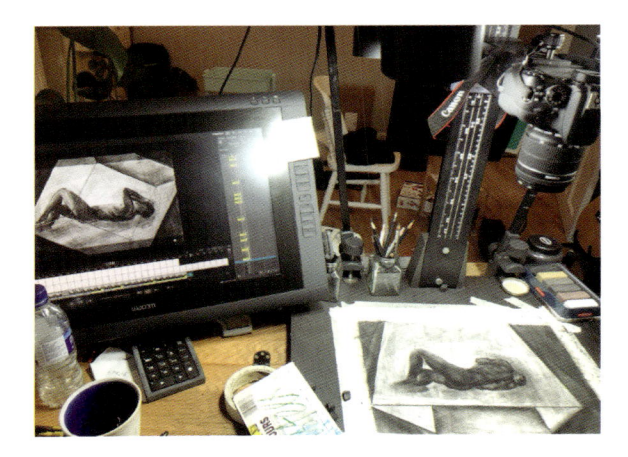

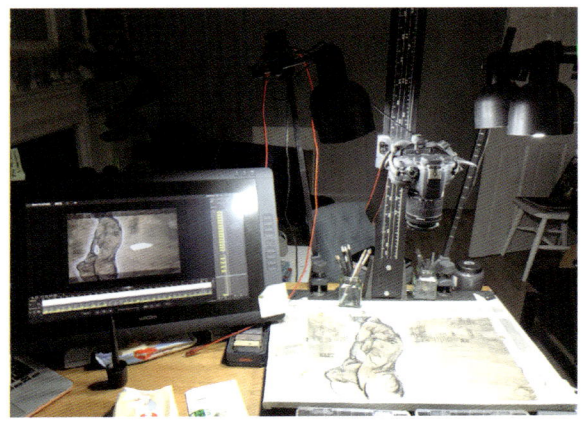

Ko working on the figurative part of her project under the camera.

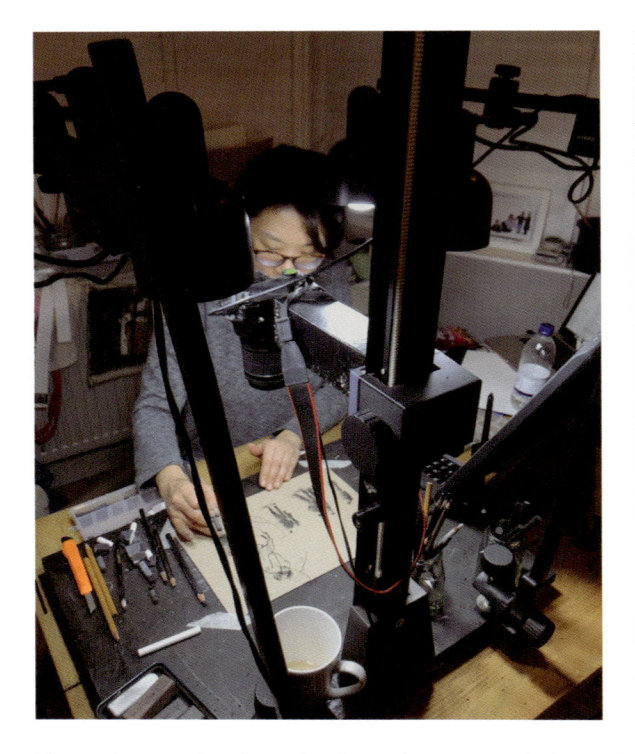

Ko spent many a long hour, drawing under a camera for her project.

2D DIGITAL ANIMATION

2D digital animation can be divided into two types: digital drawn animation and digital cut-out animation.

Digital Drawn Animation

In this technique, you either draw on to a drawing tablet connected to a computer, or draw on to the screen of a tablet computer. I mainly use TVPaint, but there are many programs that are great for drawn digital animation. You can also scan and import your paper drawings into most of these programs and colour them.

TVPaint (or any other digital drawing program) can be used just as you would animate on paper. Create the key frames first. Give each of the key frames an appropriate amount of frames to get the timing right. Work out how many in-between drawings are needed. Do timing charts to work out the spacing, then complete the in-between drawings to finish the sequence.

Once the animation is done, you can put a background on a lower layer and then colour in the animation drawings. There are lots of different brushes and pencils in any 2D digital program with which to colour in your characters.

Digital Cut-Out Animation

This is where your character is divided up into parts and you move the parts about with your mouse and set keys on the movements. It is a bit like moving a flat puppet. With all of these computer programs, you create a character that is jointed together like a flat puppet. The illustration here shows how to create a puppet in CelAction.

2D ANIMATION 99

The interface of TVPaint, a great drawn animation tool.

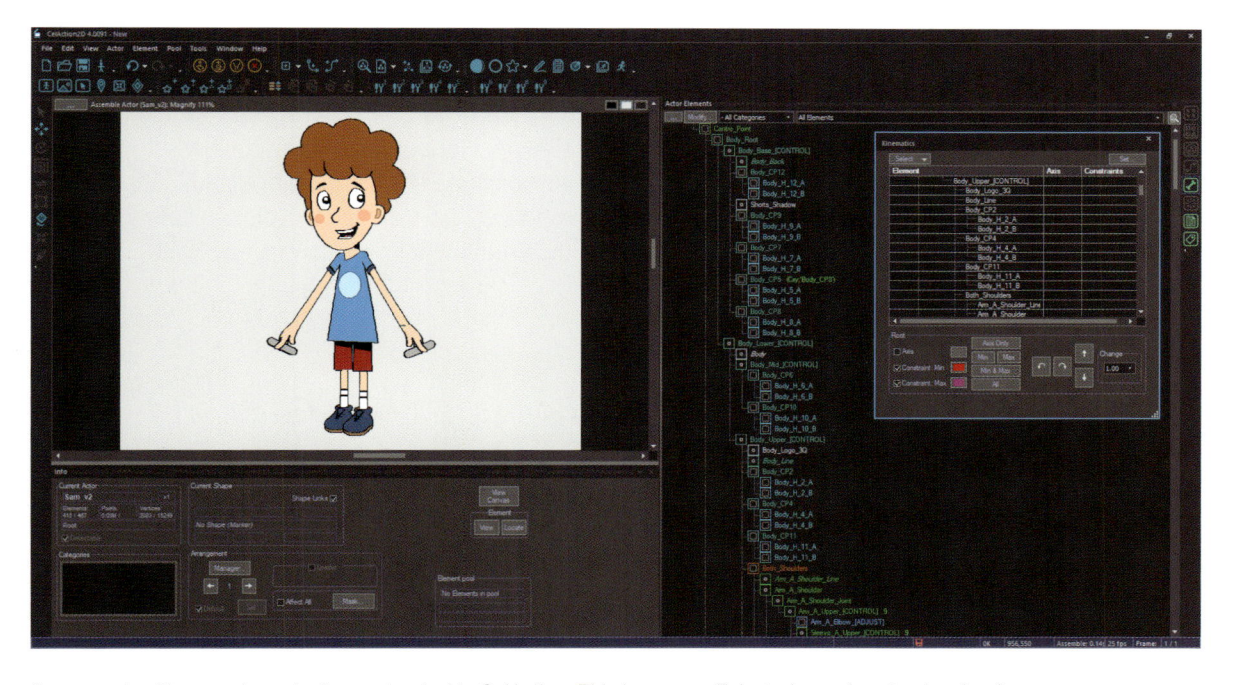

An example of how a character is constructed in CelAction. This is a very efficient piece of professional software.

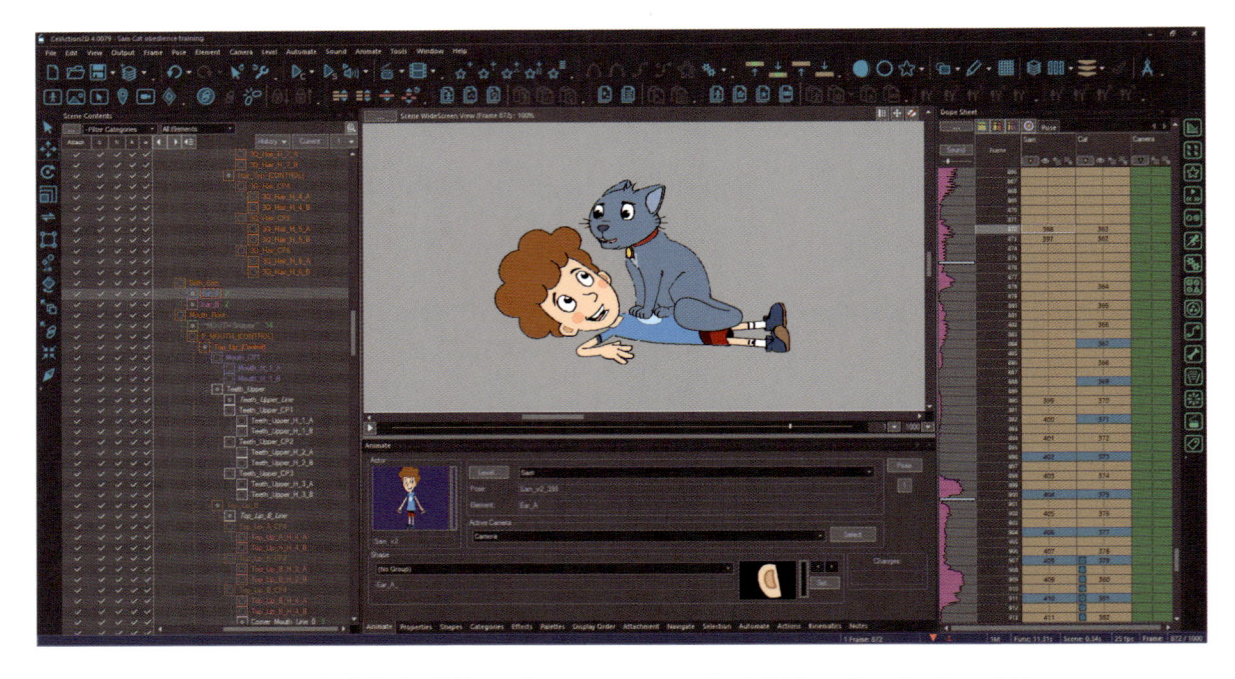

An example of how to animate in CelAction. This can be a great way to animate high-quality animation quickly.

You would have a background underneath and layers above. You then move the character and set key frames at the appropriate points. You can then get the computer program to do the in-betweens and control the movements. This method is particularly good for TV series work, where animation has to be produced quickly and efficiently.

Case Study – *J.K. Starley, The Man Who Put The World On Wheels* by Steve Roberts

I produced this animated film for an exhibition at the Vestry House Museum in Walthamstow, northeast London. The film is about J.K. Starley, the inventor of the modern bicycle, or safety bicycle.

J.K. Starley, the inventor of the modern bicycle.

In 2010, I discovered that J.K. Starley was born about 100m from where I lived. I had never heard of him and thought that he should be more well known. I am very keen on cycling and was fascinated to find out that such a significant invention was made by someone who was born in Walthamstow.

I made a very simple film about him, using still pictures and doing the voice-over myself. I showed the film during an art festival in my local area and it was seen by a curator at the Vestry House Museum in Walthamstow. She commissioned me to make a film for an exhibition held at the museum in late 2017 through to early 2018. The exhibition was called 'No Ordinary Bicycle'.

Having looked at J.K. Starley's history, it was not very interesting. He was born in Walthamstow, moved to Coventry to work for his uncle, set up his own company, invented the safety bicycle, then died. So I decided to bring in the important cultural influences of the bicycle over the last century. Bicycles were significant in the suffragette movement and for giving ordinary people the ability to travel long distances for the first time. They led to improvements in road infrastructure and the introduction of mass-production techniques in British industry. I also wanted to make the film fun for a family audience to watch. I decided to make it a musical-comedy film, influenced by Monty Python, Spike Milligan, Bob Godfrey and *Horrible Histories*.

Although the film looks like it was done with traditional drawn animation techniques, it was animated using the program TVPaint and drawn directly into the computer using a Wacom Cintiq tablet. I spent two weeks putting together an *animatic* (a movie made of a series of still pictures) that showed everything that would happen in the film. I drew the images for the animatic directly in TVPaint, then exported them into an editing program. From there, I gave each drawing a specific amount of frames, so that they fitted the dialogue. The images were very loosely drawn, but had a bit of energy to them. I also wrote four songs for the film. I recorded the initial voice-over for this stage of the film.

I presented this animatic to the client to see if it was okay. Some adjustments were made. I then had to find a voice-over artist, contacting many different actors. Jim Howick (who had worked on *Horrible Histories*) agreed to do the voice-over for a set fee. I booked a sound studio and recorded him for the film (he also sang one of the songs).

Next, I worked out what animation needed to be done and did the key positions. I used a lot of the original animatic drawings in the final project, because I liked their sketchiness (the film looks like an animated sketchbook). Next, I did the in-between drawings, followed by the colouring in. Several other animators helped me, most of them doing one or two shots each. I would give them the key positions to help with the animation. Once

Animatic drawings for *J.K. Starley, The Man Who Put The World On Wheels*.

A still from *J.K. Starley*. He was very influenced by steam locomotives.

The bicycle was a major part of the suffragette movement.

these had been completed, I coloured them as well. I engaged several composers to provide the backing music for the songs.

As each shot was finished, I inserted it into the animatic, so that, very gradually, the animatic turned into the final film. I would regularly send new versions of the animatic to the client, to make sure she was happy with what I was producing.

This thirteen-minute film was made in about eight weeks. It has been shown at many festivals around the world and won a couple of awards.

Exercise

Go through the animation exercises in Chapters 2 and 3 in order to practise your 2D animation.

5
PUPPET ANIMATION

WHAT IS NEEDED FOR A PUPPET ANIMATION STUDIO

In the following pages, I will discuss the things needed for a basic puppet animation studio.

A Computer and Camera Set-Up

You will need a computer with a puppet animation program and a suitable SLR digital camera connected to it. Details of these programs can be found at the back of the book.

A Puppet Stage

There are several ways to attach the feet of your puppets to a stage. You can pin the feet of lighter puppets to a stage made of a soft material, such as polystyrene sheet or a cork board, into which the pins can be inserted. If your puppets have magnetic feet, you can use a magnet to pin them to a stage. For larger puppets, it is best to bolt your puppets to a stage with nuts and bolts that go through the feet. This provides the most stable attachment. Drill a hole for each time the foot touches the ground and then fill the hole afterwards.

To make the stage, you need to create a frame with a thin piece of plywood or stiff steel mesh (for magnets or bolts), or a piece of polystyrene sheet (for pins) on top. For magnets and bolts you need access underneath to place the magnets or tighten up the bolts. You could even make a stage from a large plastic storage box, by cutting square holes in the side so as to gain access to the underside of the stage. Alternatively, you could buy a

The computer and camera set-up required for puppet animation.

stage from a company supplying them professionally (details at the back of the book).

Stage Lighting

A minimum of four lights are needed to light a stage correctly, but if you are just practising animation, ordinary room lighting will do. It is preferable to use LED lights. Professional photographic studio lights are best, but you could use LED work lights (the kind used on building sites), or cheap LED video camera lights.

Finally, we need a star!

MAKING AN ANIMATION PUPPET

There are many ways to construct a puppet for animation. The skeleton could be constructed of soft aluminium wire or steel rods with ball and socket joints. The skeleton could be covered with foam, cloth, clay, rubber or silicone. The head could be made of foam, modelling clay, latex rubber or balsa wood. The hands could consist of wire covered in silicone, bandage tape or hot glue. The mouth can be stuck on or a jaw constructed from the material the head is made of. The main thing to remember is to keep things as simple as possible and make sure that when the puppet breaks, it's easy to mend.

An example of a stage used for puppet animation.

Building a Basic Wire Puppet Body

To build a basic wire skeleton puppet, you will need the following materials:

- soft 2mm aluminium wire (for the basic skeleton)
- soft 1mm aluminium wire (for the hands)
- 30amp electrical connectors (preferably with steel internals so that they will work with magnets)
- 15amp electrical connectors, for connecting the hands to the arms
- foam rubber (the kind used for washing up can be used)
- wadding (the type of padding that is used inside jackets, but cotton wool would do)

Examples of the types of light you could use for puppet animation.

PUPPET ANIMATION

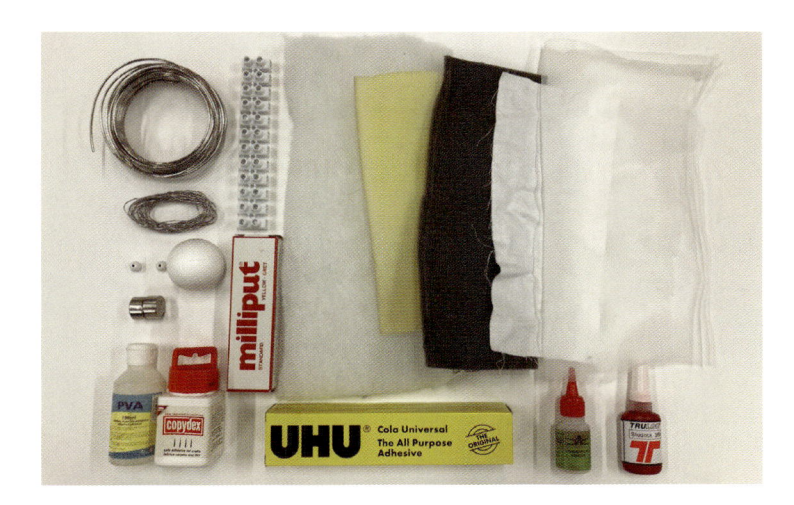

The materials required for making a puppet.

- thin nylon ribbon or cloth, cut into strips (the nylon material used for net curtains, but any very thin cloth would do)
- two strong magnets (these can be purchased form an animation supplier, or from eBay; they should be about 2cm wide and 1cm tall)
- superglue, contact adhesive, PVA glue or latex rubber glue like Copydex (or liquid latex rubber)
- thread lock (used to stop screws shaking loose; you can buy it from automotive retailers)
- cloth to make clothes (or some dolls' clothes); the weave of this cloth should be very fine
- polystyrene ball, solid foam, or a block of balsa wood to make the head
- acrylic paint
- wool for hair, if needed (the kind of wool used for felting, unspun wool that is dyed)
- beads for eyes or small dolls' eyes
- plasters or surgical tape
- epoxy putty, such as Milliput, but any epoxy putty will do.

The tools you will need are:

- large and small craft knives
- pair of pliers
- small screwdriver
- pair of scissors

The tools required for making a puppet.

- pair of rubber gloves
- pair of protective goggles
- old clothing (this can get very messy)
- pencil
- paper
- hot glue gun
- electric drill, small drill bits and a vice (not totally necessary, but very useful).

First, you need to design your character. Do as much research as possible and also do lots of character sketches. Once you have a good idea of what you want to make, you then need to sketch out a basic design on to a piece of paper. A4 paper should be okay. Try not to make your puppet more than 300mm (12in). The bigger the puppet, the bigger the sets you will have to build. However, do not build the puppet too small (less than 130mm (5in) tall).

Using the sketch as reference, trim the electrical connectors to either five or three sections (depending on the size of your puppet) with the large craft knife. Place at the shoulders and the waist. Draw on the sketch roughly where the arms, legs, neck and backbone will be placed.

Take the 2mm aluminium wire and twist three strands together (this will make the arms). This can be done by hand, or you can put one end of the wire into a vice and the other into the electric drill bit. Switch on the drill and it will twist the wire. Some model-makers say that it is better to twist the wire by hand, as this puts less stress on the aluminium wire and is then less likely to break while animating, but wire twisted in a drill tends to be neater and easier to insert into the electrical connectors. Then take three lengths of the 2mm aluminium wire and twist together for the legs, neck and backbone.

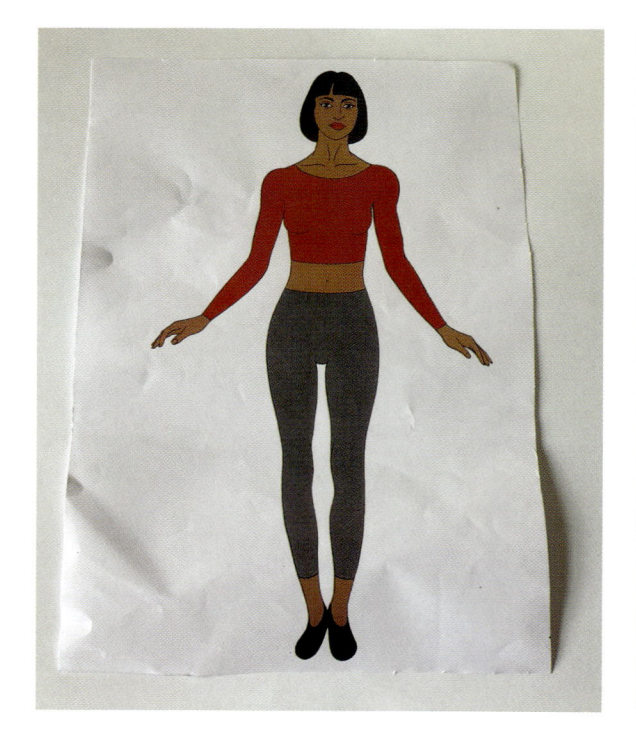

The design of the puppet on paper, ready to be interpreted into three dimensions.

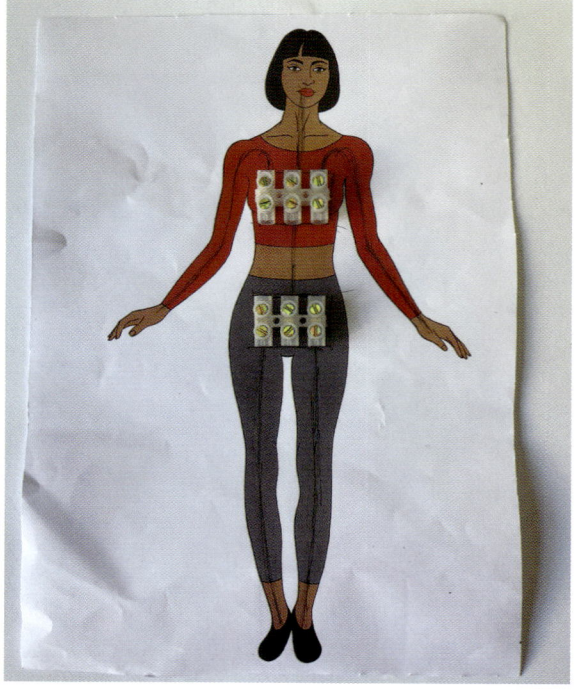

Electrical connectors are used to hold the wires of the puppet in place. Here they are on the sketch of the puppet.

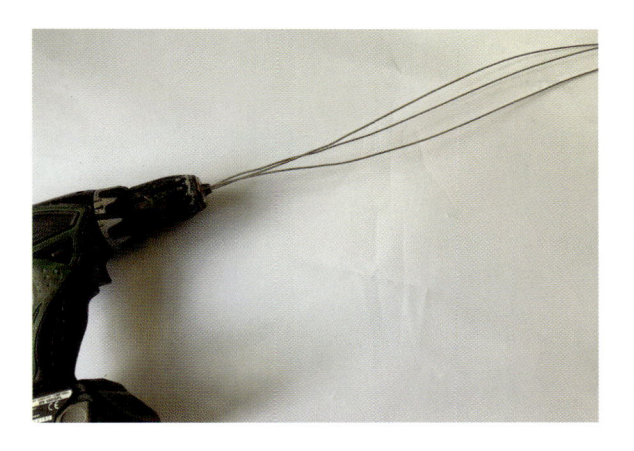

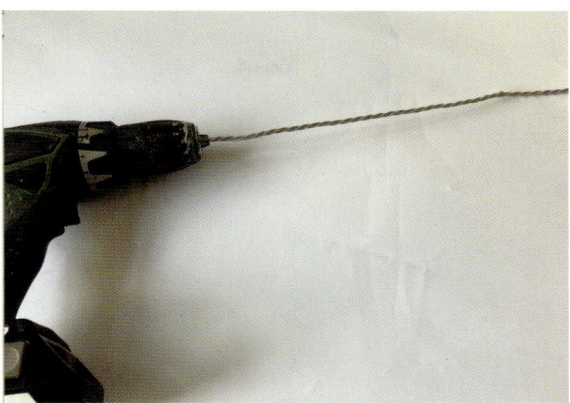

The wire for the backbone, arms, legs and neck can be twisted in an electric drill.

Using the sketch you have made for size, cut the three-strand twisted wire to length for the arms. Cut the three-strand twisted wire for the legs, neck and backbone. Next, unscrew the screws from the electrical connectors and put thread lock on to the screws. Insert the twisted wire into the holes of the electrical connectors and replace the screws tightly.

Put on your rubber gloves and take out your epoxy putty (epoxy putty is very sticky and can be difficult to wash off; it also has lots of nasty chemicals in it, so stay safe). Mix together a small amount thoroughly. We will make the arm and leg bones out of this. You only need a small amount and make sure that a lot of wire is between these bones (the wire will break more easily if the gap between the bones is too small).

Take two of the electrical connectors and trim to a single unit, then cut off the plastic covering (or take out the screws and push the metal part out). We will make the feet out of these. Attach the connectors to the end of the legs and bend 90 degrees. As long as the connectors are steel, they will fix to the stage with a large magnet. If they are not steel, the screws will be steel so they may attach to a magnet. If not, you could always glue a piece of steel or something that will attach to a magnet (a penny, for example) to the bottom of the feet. Shoes can be carved out of balsa or hard foam and glued on top of the electrical connector.

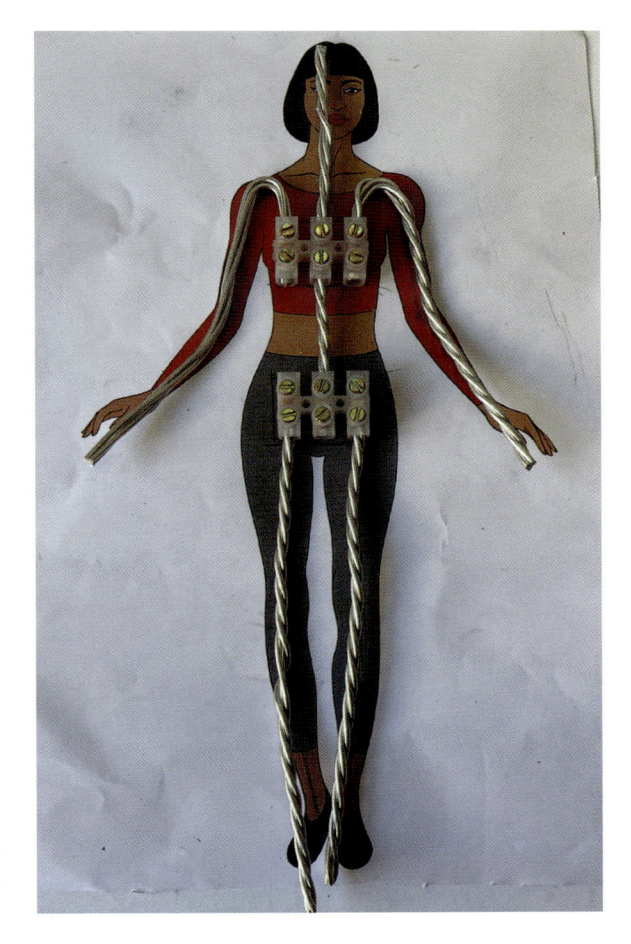

The wires mounted into the electrical connectors, on the sketch of the model.

Another method is to cover the feet with wadding and nylon material covered in glue.

For a much more solid connection to the stage, drill a hole through the electrical connector, so that a bolt can be threaded through the foot. You then drill a hole in the stage, push the bolt in the foot through the hole and screw a nut on to the bolt to hold the model tightly. Attach another pair of electrical connectors at the wrists. We will use these to attach the hands (you could cut off the plastic surrounding to make them a bit smaller).

You should now have the bare bones of your puppet. Make sure that the screws are facing towards the back of the puppet. Stick some soft foam to the body with contact adhesive, but make sure that you still have access to the screws, as you may need to unscrew them later to replace a broken limb. Do not glue the foam to the screws.

Once you have trimmed the foam to shape with scissors, cut the wadding into 10mm (0.4in) strips, coat one side of the strip with contact adhesive as well as one of the areas of the puppet. Wrap the strip of wadding around the area like a mummy. Keep gluing on strips like this till the puppet is completely covered. (Make sure that you can still gain access to the screws in the electrical connectors.)

Next, take the nylon ribbon (or nylon material cut into strips) and glue this on in the same way. Paint

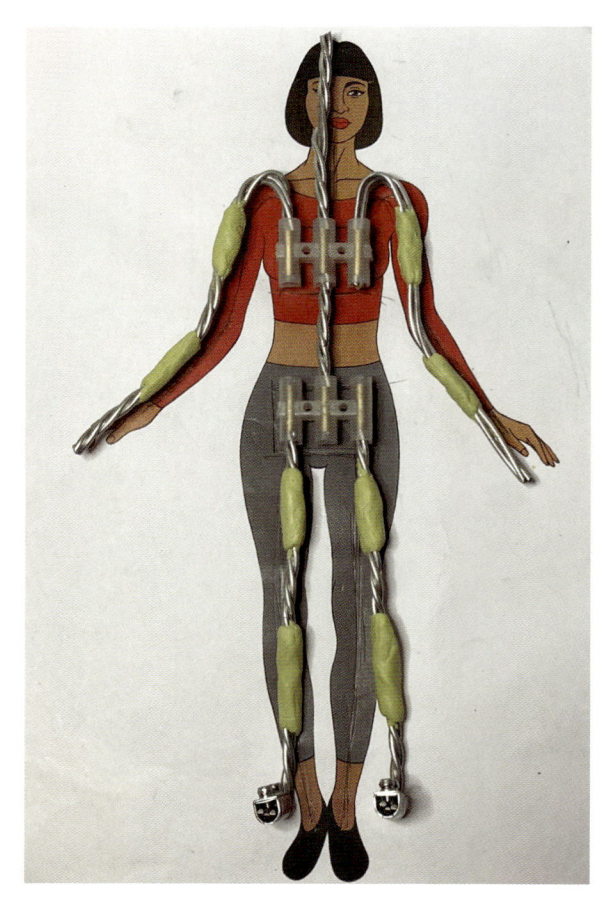

Epoxy putty is applied to the wires to create 'bones'.

Steel internals from the electrical connectors are used on the puppet's feet.

PUPPET ANIMATION 109

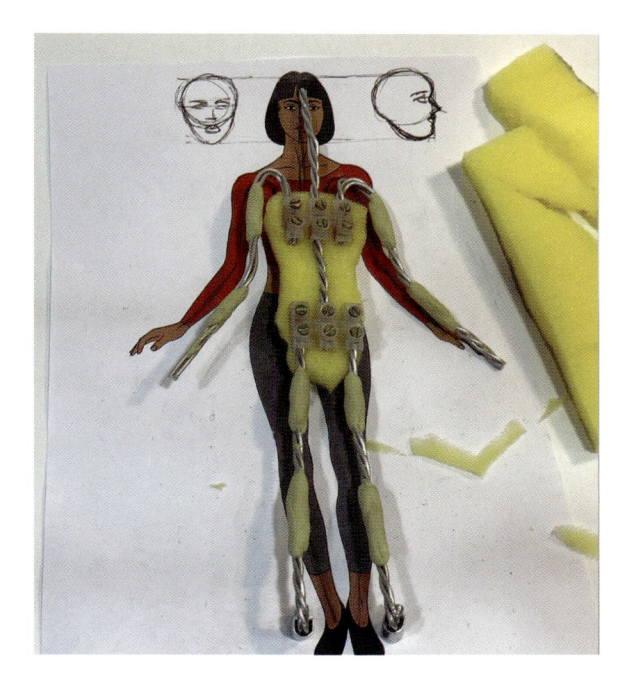

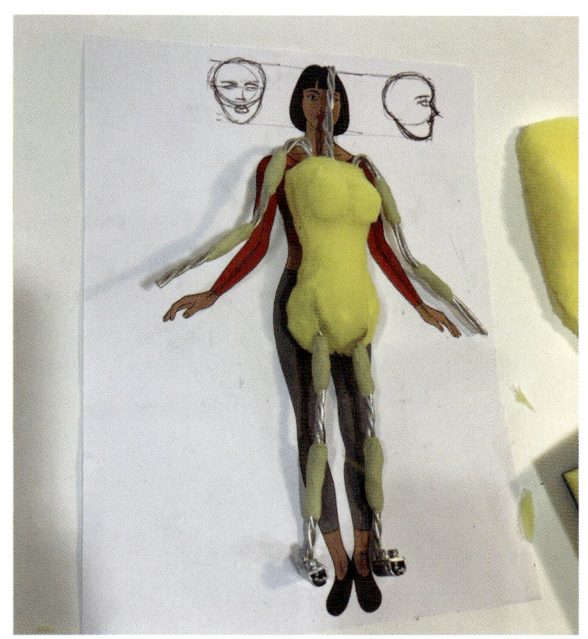

Soft foam is stuck to the torso of the puppet to build up the shape.

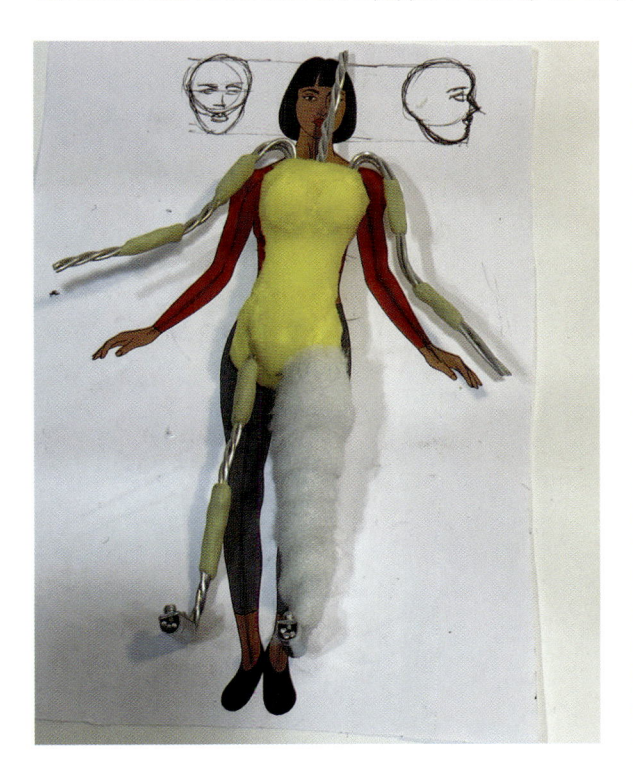

Wadding is wrapped around the limbs of the puppet to build up the volume of the arms and legs.

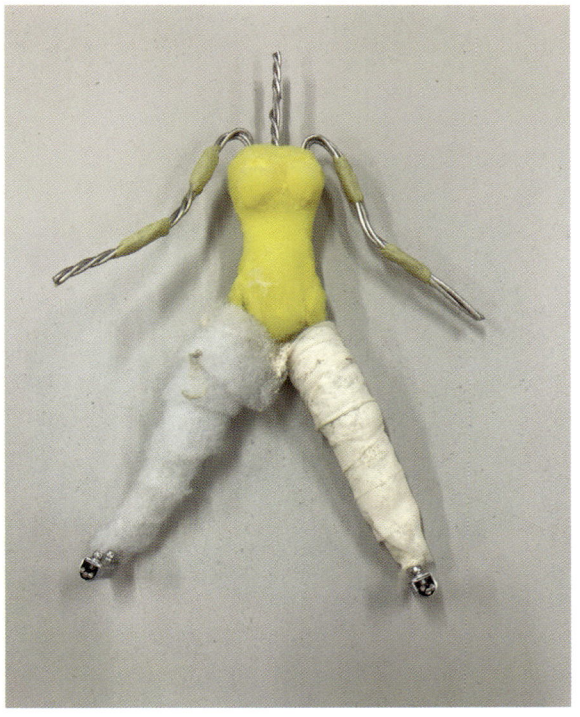

Nylon material, cut into strips, is wrapped around the arms and legs and painted with liquid latex rubber or Copydex.

the puppet all over with either PVA adhesive or latex rubber adhesive (such as Copydex), or liquid latex rubber. This should hold everything together.

Depending on how well you can sew, make clothes to fit the puppet or buy dolls' clothes and dress your puppet. Attach the hands after the puppet has been clothed. Start by making tubes of cloth that wrap around the arms. Glue them into place (but don't glue to the body). Then make a tunic-like piece of cloth with a hole in it for the head, wrap around the body and glue down the sides of the body (don't glue to the arms, as we need to be able to remove the arms if the wire inside breaks). The same procedure can be used for the legs.

If your character has some skin showing, the puppet body can also be covered with modelling clay, by forming the clay around the wrapped wires. These do tend to get rather dirty very quickly, so be prepared to clean the surface frequently with baby wipes. The body could be painted with liquid latex and coloured with paint. Build up several layers.

The feet can be covered with wadding, then painted with latex and nylon material, but make sure that the steel part of the electrical connector is exposed at the bottom. When placing your model on the stage, a magnet is fixed underneath to hold the feet in place.

You can cover your puppet with felting. This is where you tease wool over the surface of the

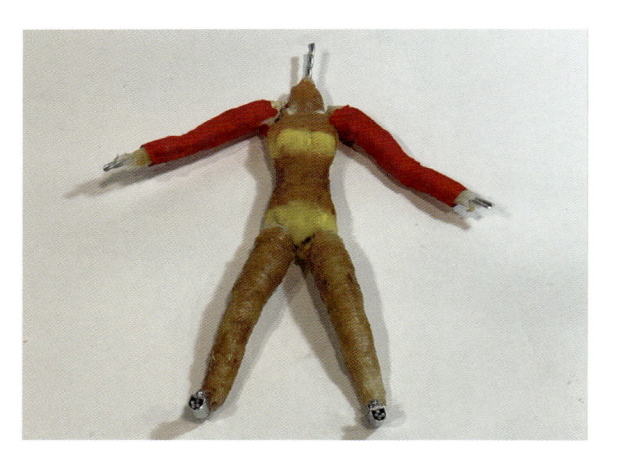

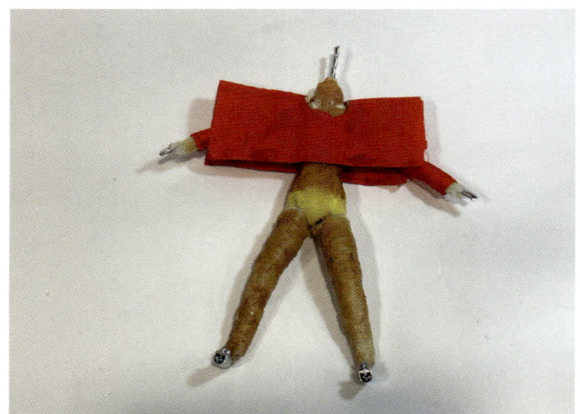

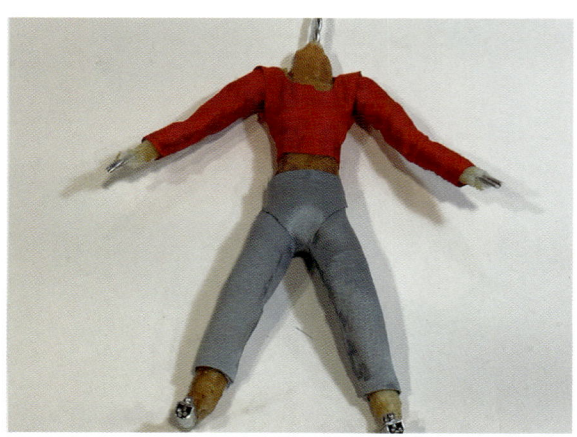

Puppet clothes are created from cloth that is either sewn or glued in place.

PUPPET ANIMATION **111**

model, then prick it with a felting needle. This pushes the end of the wool into the model and holds them in place.

You can make a four-legged character in a similar way and then either cover it in fake fur, or paint on lots of layers of latex for a smooth-skinned creature.

When they are finished, the feet of the puppet can be held in place on the stage with a strong magnet.

One way to cover a puppet is to use the technique of felting.

The same process used to make a human puppet can be used to make a four-legged character.

Making a Ball and Socket Puppet Body

Making a ball and socket skeleton from scratch would be a very complicated and expensive undertaking, so it's better to buy one of the kits available on the internet. These are still quite expensive compared to a wire skeleton, but will be a lot more reliable. Ball and socket puppets are much more robust than a wire one, but can sometimes come loose and need to be tightened up at the joints. So make sure you can get to these joints easily in order to maintain them. They can also be a much quicker way of making a puppet. They can be covered in the same way as the wire puppet.

A ball and socket joint puppet can be a lot more reliable than a wire puppet.

Making the Hands

To make the hands, take some of the 1mm wire and form it into a hand shape. (You could make a hand pattern by putting nails into a small piece of plywood, then wrapping the wire around the nails.) Make a central loop of wire and with epoxy glue stick a small nut into the middle of it. With this you can attach any props that your character needs to pick up (you can also pin things to your puppet's hands). Wrap with surgical bandage tape to cover the wires. The wires of the hands could be covered with thin nylon material and latex rubber or Copydex. The hands could also be covered with hot glue or silicone bath sealant. Attach the hands to the arms of your puppet with electrical connectors.

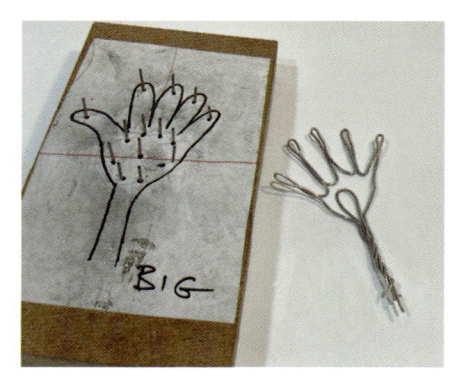

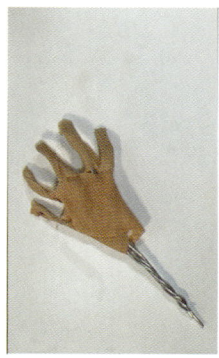

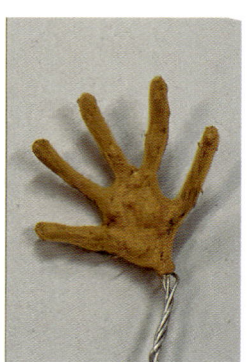

Puppet hands can be made with thin wire and surgical tape, hot glue or nylon fabric and liquid latex rubber or Copydex.

A polystyrene ball can be used as a simple way to make a head.

Making the Head

POLYSTYRENE BALL HEAD
The simplest way to make a head is to use a polystyrene ball. These can be bought from art shops in various sizes. Paint the ball with acrylic paint for the skin, eyes, mouth, eyebrows and hair (or make hair out of wool or artificial fur). When finished, push on to the wire at the neck of your puppet.

CARVED HEAD
Another way to make a head is to carve one out of hard foam or a block of balsa wood and push it on to the neck. Make a drawing of the front and side of the head, then redraw it on to the block. Start by carving away the edges and shaping it following the lines on the block. Work out where the cheekbones are and cut downward and upward from the cheekbone. You can stick a nose on afterwards if carving a nose is too awkward. The head could be painted with acrylic paint or latex rubber.

To make the eyes, take two beads or plastic dolls' eyes and carve two eye sockets in the head, slightly smaller than the eyes. Push the eyes into the sockets. With the beads, paint a pupil around the hole in the bead. You can then insert a pin,

A carved head made from hard foam can have a lot more character than a polystyrene ball.

piece of wire or a cocktail stick into the hole to move the eyes from side to side. With plastic dolls' eyes you will need to drill a small hole into the pupil with a tiny drill bit.

If you want the eyebrows to move, make some eyebrows out of the foam and pin them into the head. These can then be moved up and down and angled, by pulling them off and pinning them back on in a different position when animating.

114 PUPPET ANIMATION

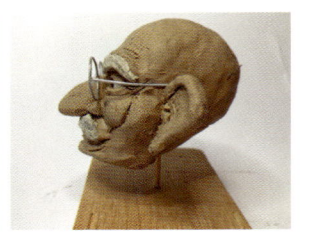

A head made from clay can be very detailed, but can be quite messy to animate.

CLAY HEAD

You can also make the head out of modelling clay (the best to use is Newclay Newplast). Start with a polystyrene ball and sculpt the head out of modelling clay. Using a polystyrene ball for a 'skull' will make the head much lighter. You can sculpt eye sockets to put the eyes in. The mouth and eyebrows can be sculpted as you animate to produce different mouth shapes.

Eyes

You can use either beads or dolls' eyes for the eyes. With dolls' eyes, you will have to drill a small hole in the front of the eye, so that you can insert a pin to make the eyes look from side to side (beads have a hole already).

For a blink, you can stick on a piece of paper or thin foam, painted the same colour as the face.

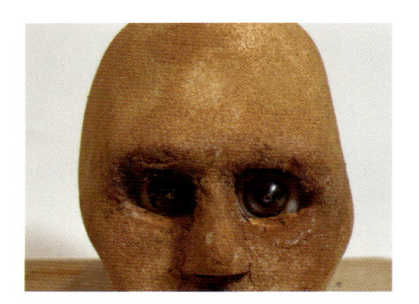

Eyes can be made from beads or from dolls' eyes. A hole in them makes it easier to move the eyes from side to side.

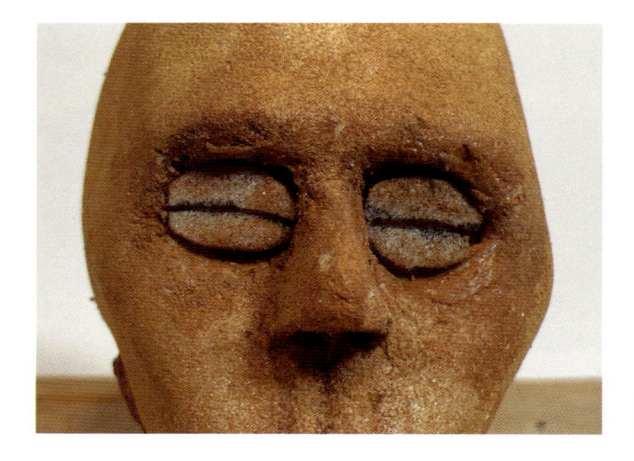

You can make your character blink by sticking either paper or foam eyelids over the eyes when needed.

PUPPET ANIMATION 115

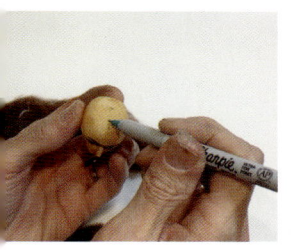

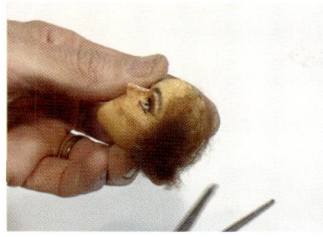

Hair can be made from wool or another suitable fibre.

Hair

You can use wool to make the hair. Dyed wool from an art shop is suitable.

Work out where the crown of the head is and then the parting of the hair. Then start adding the wool from the lower part of the head up, finishing with hair radiating from the crown of the head and from the parting.

Making the Mouth

STICK-ON MOUTH

The simplest method is to have stick-on mouths made of paper. Glue them on the face with a non-permanent glue like Pritt Stick. They could also be pinned on with sewing pins. This system is very suitable for a polystyrene ball or carved foam head.

Stick-on mouths can be made from paper, Newplast clay or thin, hard foam.

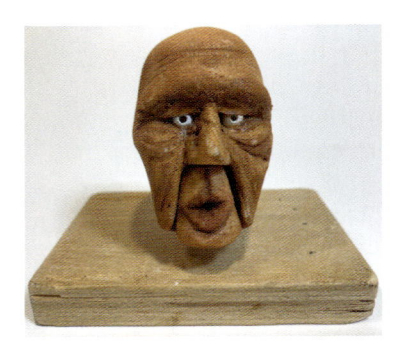

Carved mouths work well with older characters that have lots of wrinkles.

Stick-on mouths can also be made of hard foam, modelling clay (modelling clay mouths seem to stick in place without any glue) or even string! When animating, replace the mouths as and when needed.

CARVED MOUTH

Another way to make a mouth is to cut a box-like hole out of the head where the mouth should be. Then carve mouths out of hard foam or balsa wood. The rear part of the mouth should be a box-like shape that will fit into same-shaped hole in the puppet's head. You will need about eight shapes to achieve most mouth shapes and expressions required for basic animation. When animating, replace the mouths as and when needed.

HINGED-JAW MOUTH

A mouth can be made by hinging a jaw from the underside of a foam or balsa head. Cut out the top part of the mouth from the head, making sure there are jowls on either side of the hole to which to attach the jaw. Carve a lower jaw that fits into the mouth hole. Then push a pin or piece of wire through the jowls and through the rear part of the jaw, so that it can hinge up and down. This system is more suitable for animals where mouth expressions are less important than on a human face. A similar system can be used with modelling clay.

SCULPTED-CLAY MOUTH

Just like the carved mouths, make a box-like hole in the clay head and then construct clay mouths that can be put into the same-shaped hole. You can either choose to smooth over the join for each mouth shape, or leave as is.

Once your puppet is finished, it is ready to animate. Don't bend the limbs too much until you are animating with it. You don't want them to break too quickly.

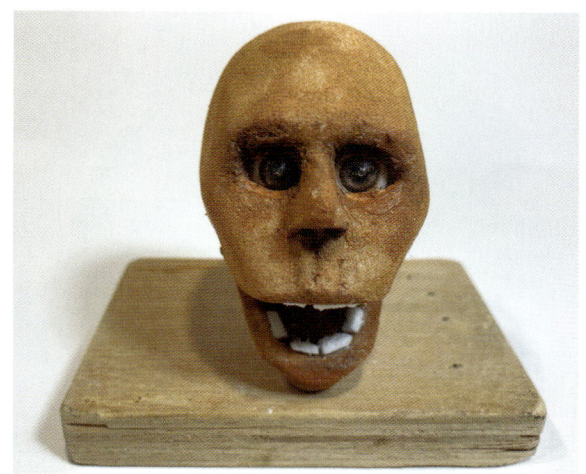

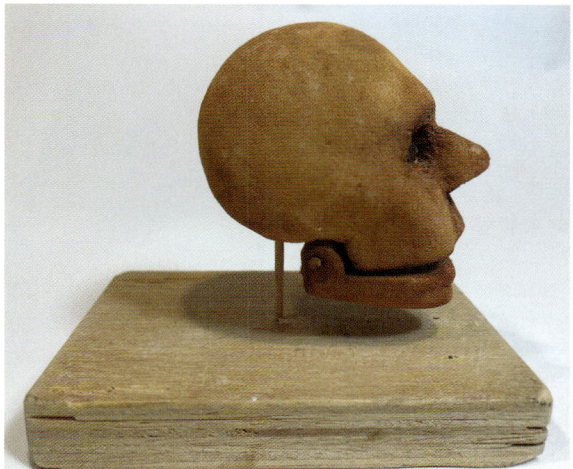

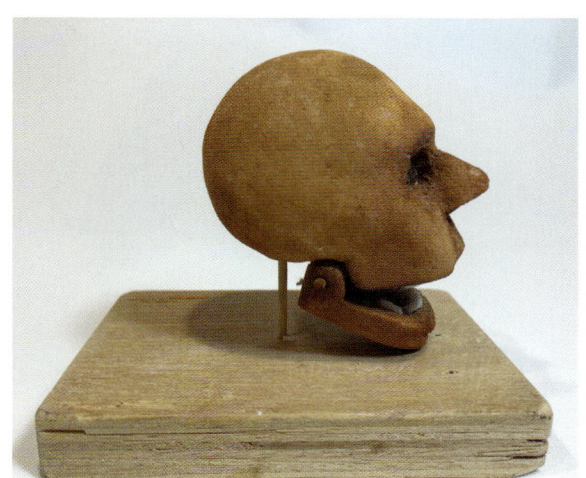

A hinged-jaw mouth works best with animals, robots or monsters (it is not very good for lip-sync).

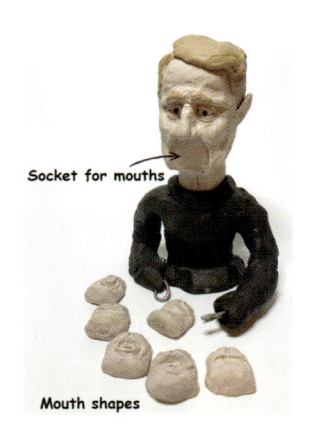

Sculpted-clay mouths can be placed into the socket of the puppet and smoothed over to give a professional look.

The finished puppet, in all her glory.

3D-Printed Head and Mouth

A lot of puppets for professional productions are designed on a computer, then 3D-printed. The head is 3D-printed, with gaps for the cheeks, eyes and forehead. Many thousands of mouths can be made that are then attached to the puppet head with small magnets. This can be a very costly process and is out of the scope of this book.

Making a Latex Rubber Head for a Puppet

You will need:

- modelling clay like Newplast
- natural clay
- casting plaster
- soft soap (or bar soap mixed with water)
- liquid latex rubber
- dolls' eyes (or beads)
- aluminium wire
- expanding foam (self-skinning flexible polyurethane foam)
- plastic piping (about 20mm in diameter)
- gaffer tape
- epoxy putty such as Milliput.

To make a head from latex rubber, you first need to sculpt a head out of modelling clay (such as Newplast). To do this, design your head on a piece of paper. Then build an armature out of wire and epoxy putty. Use one piece of twisted wire for the neck, two pieces of twisted wire for the upper and lower lip and two pieces of twisted wire for the eyebrows. Push these into the soft epoxy putty and allow to set.

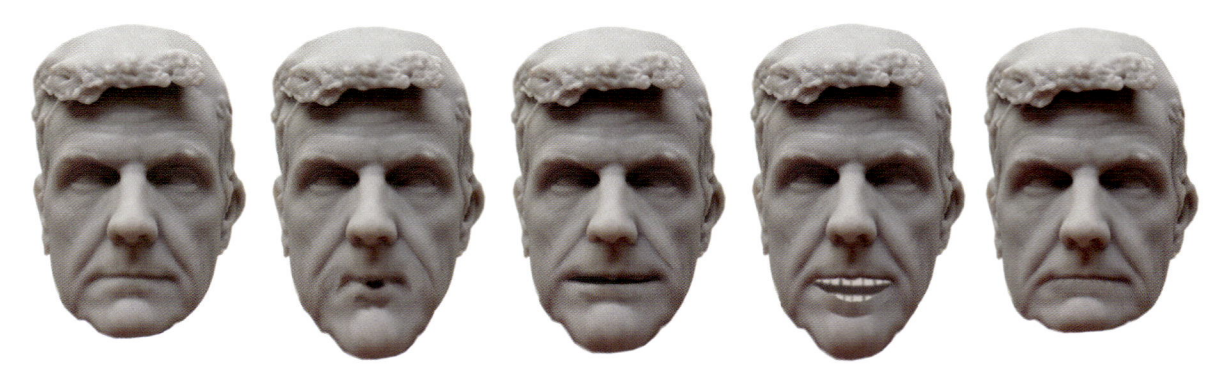

3D-printed head and mouths are the ultimate way to make mouths, but can be very expensive.

PUPPET ANIMATION 119

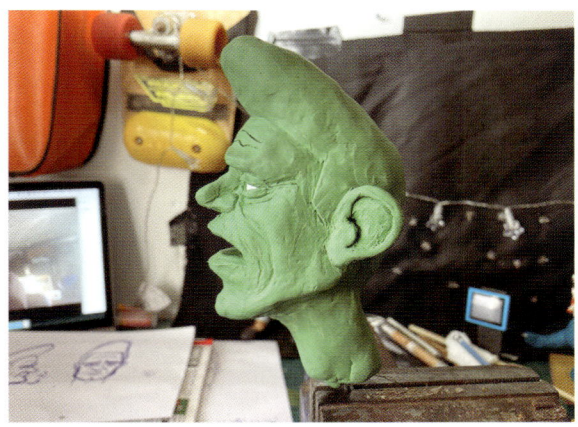

To make a latex rubber head you need to start with an armature and sculpt a head around it in clay.

Next, mount the wire of the neck on to the plastic piping. Build up the head out of modelling clay over the armature. Make sure that you put eyes with holes (or beads) into the clay head. Put a piece of wire into the holes of each eye. This will provide an eye socket in the latex head into which to push the eyes.

Now we need to cast the head. Build a base for the head to be supported on with some clay (this time use natural clay, rather than modelling clay). Make sure that the edge between the head and the natural clay is nice and neat. Build up some walls around the clay with further slabs of clay. Mix up some plaster and apply it to the head, making sure that it is well covered. Let it set.

Once the plaster is set, turn over the head and peel off the natural clay and liberally cover the underside of the plaster with soft soap (this could either be specific soft soap, or bar soap mixed with water). Mix up some more plaster and apply it to the back of the head. Allow to set. You then have to break apart the mould and dig out the original sculpted head. (You will use the head armature later.) Make sure that you place some beads on to the wire that was poking out of the eyes and should now be stuck into the interior of the mould.

Once the mould is clean inside, cover the inside of the mould with soft soap. Fix the two halves of the mould back together using gaffer tape, with

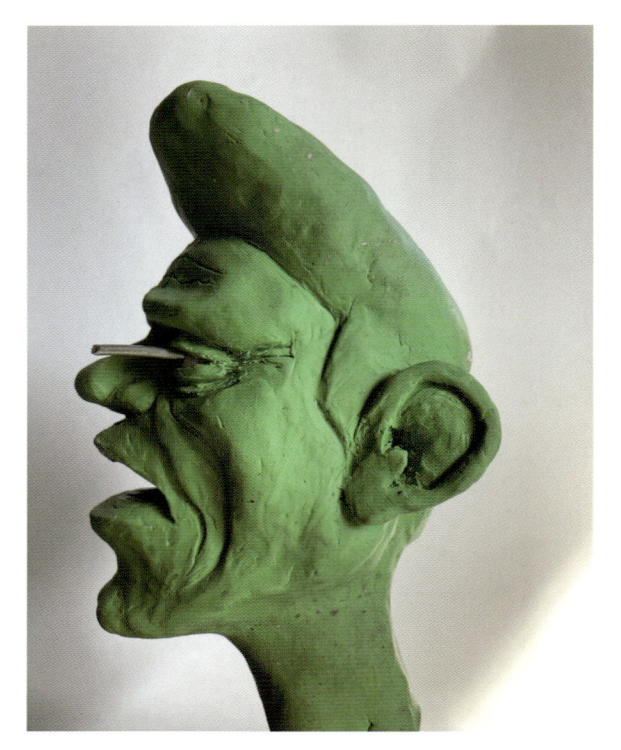

A piece of pipe needs to be placed at the base of the head and some aluminium wire placed into the eyes of your character.

The lower part of the mould is cast first.

The upper part of the mould is cast second.

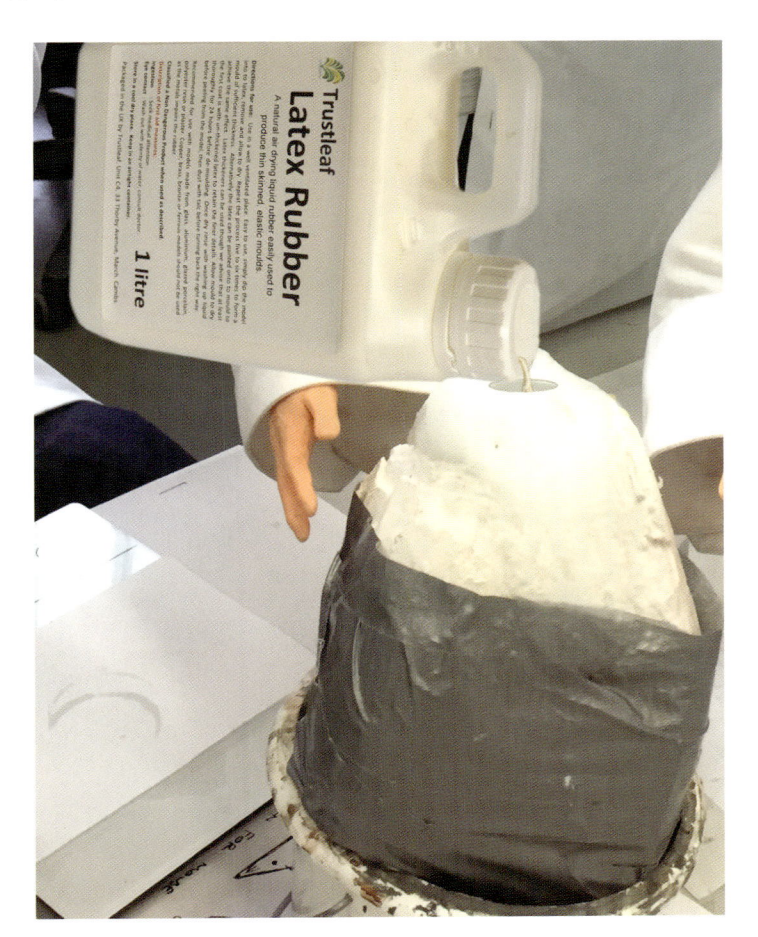

Latex is then poured into the mould.

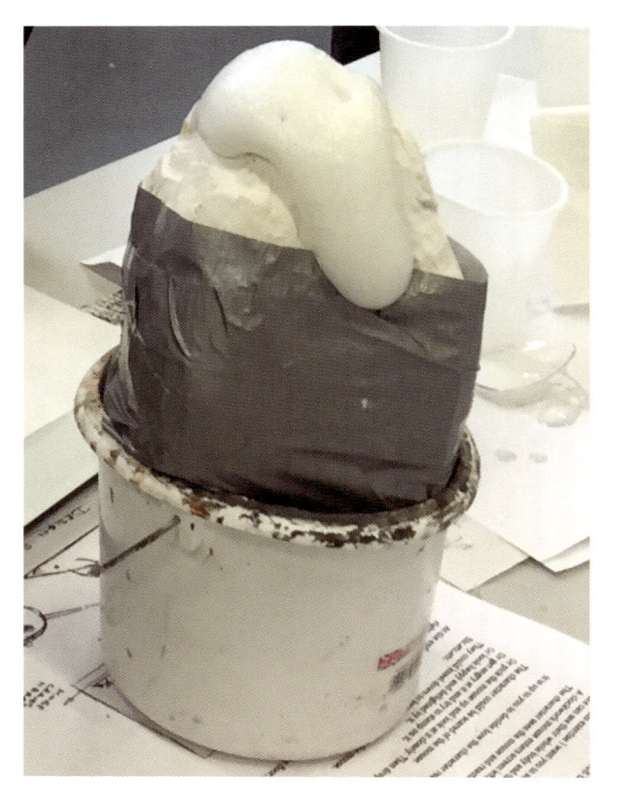

the head armature mounted inside. Pour in the liquid latex rubber and leave for a few minutes. Pour out the latex rubber back into its container and allow to dry for about eight hours. Repeat this process with the latex rubber three more times.

Next, fill the mould with self-skinning flexible polyurethane foam and allow to dry. Finally, pull the two parts of the mould apart and you should be left with a latex rubber head, with a mouth and eyebrows that can be moved by hand.

Once the self-skinning foam has set, gently pull the moulds apart and take out the head.

You can paint the head with acrylic paint mixed with Pros-Aide (a type of flexible adhesive), or mix some acrylic paint with latex rubber. Add hair if you wish. Push in the dolls' eyes, making sure they can swivel. Attach the head to your puppet's body and you are ready to animate.

A similar process can be followed to make latex rubber or silicone hands. You will need to mix two

The mould, with the latex skin on the inside of it, is filled with expanding self-skinning foam.

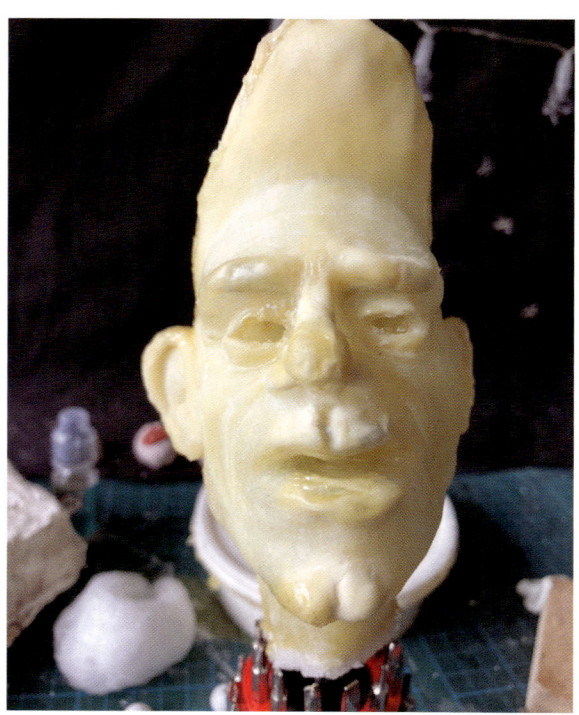

The raw rubber head is pulled out of the mould.

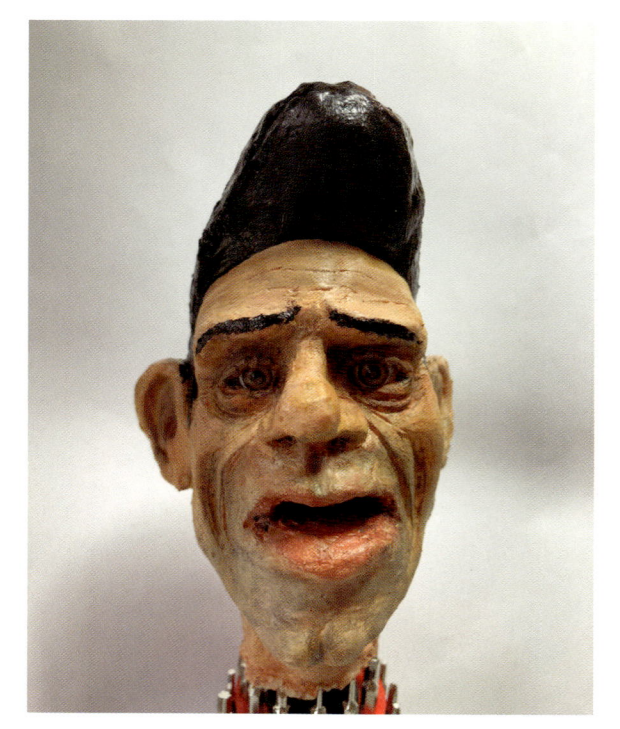

The latex head is then painted.

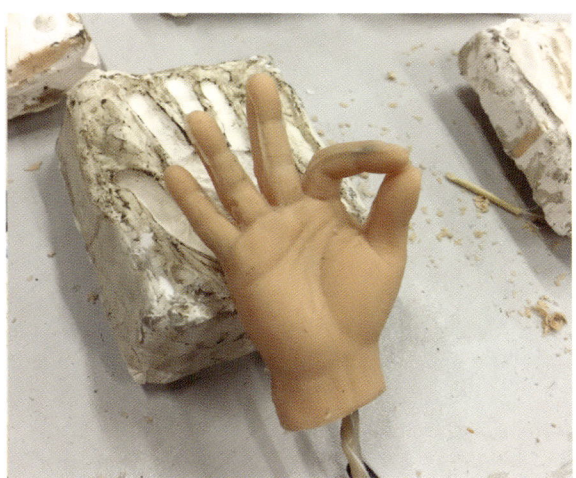

Hands can be made from two-part silicone rubber with wire internals.

parts of the silicone together (silicone and the activator, Transil 20 or Platsil 10 are great for this). Place a wire hand inside the mould, put the mould together, then pour the silicone solution into the mould. Leave to set.

BUILDING A SET

The simplest thing to do when it comes to building a set is to not have one at all! Just have a simple piece of white paper that is attached to your stage and then curved up on to the wall behind the stage. Another simple approach is to have a piece of green paper and in your editing program use this as a green screen, then place a photograph in its place to be the set.

Simple sets can be made of cardboard, foam board or any other material to construct props and other things needed for your production. Always keep your sets as minimal and simple as possible to start with and work up to making complicated sets. Make sure that each of the components of a set is securely tied down to the

A basic puppet green-screen set, with lights.

A full puppet animation set, with a backdrop, buildings and several puppets. These were created by Doreen Edemafaka.

stage. The last thing you want is to knock something out of place.

Lighting a Set

The basic lighting for a set will consist of four lights.

KEY LIGHT
The first light to put in place is the main light. Think about where the most light is coming from in your scene. If it is outdoors, the key light will come from the sky, so the light is positioned above. In an indoor set, where is the main light source coming from? A window, a light in the ceiling, a table lamp or from a fireplace? You should position your key light where the light is coming from. This can be a light directly pointed at the set, or pointed up at a white board that then reflects back down on the set.

BACKGROUND LIGHT
Set up a light to illuminate the background. This will be there to show the things in the background that are important. It should cast shadows that correspond with the key light, so should be aimed in roughly the same direction as the main light. Make sure the background is not too cluttered behind the area where your character is animating.

BACKLIGHT
The backlight is pointed at the back of your character. This is to give your character a three-dimensional quality. Usually, it is in the opposite direction to the main and background lights. Its purpose is to replicate the light bouncing off the background and to illuminate the rear of your character.

FILL LIGHT (SPOTLIGHT)
The fill light fills in the shadows on your character created by the key light. It creates the amount of contrast in a scene. It should be positioned near the camera and high up so that the shadows it creates are thrown down to the floor and kept as small as possible (unless you want long shadows, that is).

Lighting is very much trial and error. Certain parts of a set may require more lights to illuminate

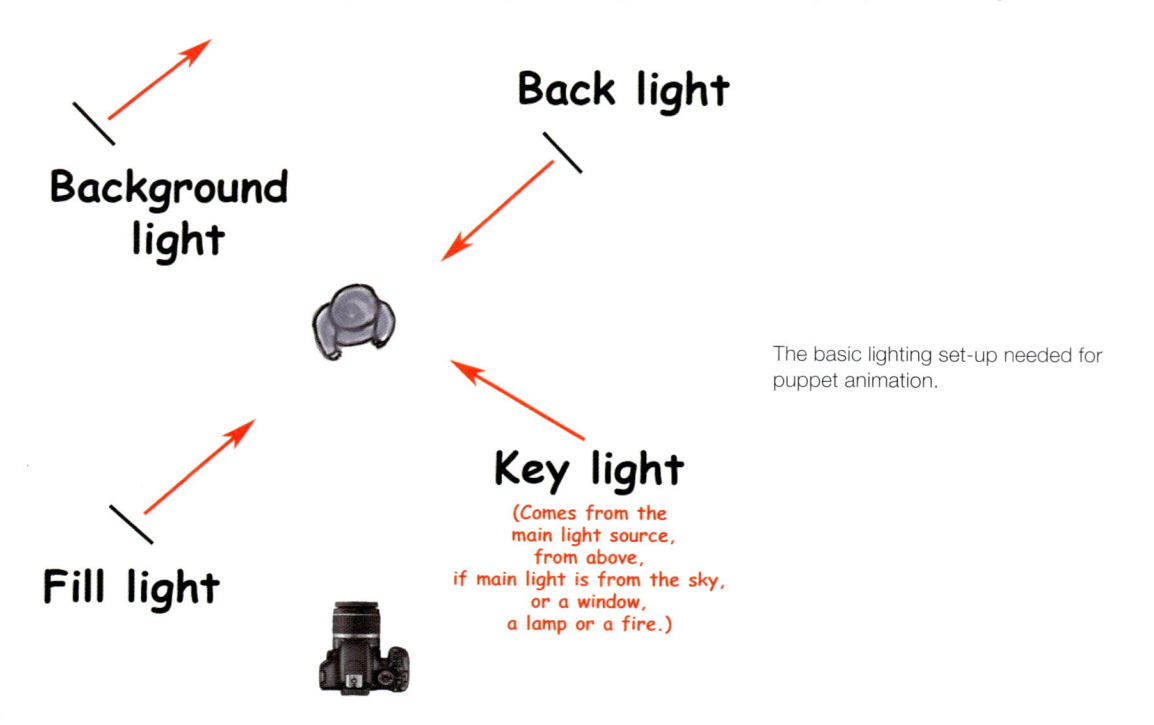

The basic lighting set-up needed for puppet animation.

the set properly. You may need to get some smaller LED lights to pick out small areas that are in shadow, or need to be highlighted. It is always best to start with as simple a set as possible.

HOW TO CREATE PUPPET ANIMATION

All puppet animation is done straight ahead. You can do something called a pop-through, which is a series of key positions to work out the basic movements. In your chosen program, give each of these key positions an appropriate amount of frames and make a note of where each of these key positions are (use an x-sheet). So if the second major key position happens on frame 25, when you do the animation proper you know it will take twenty-five frames to get from the first key position to the second one. The other thing that is really useful with puppet animation is to do a LAVS. Film yourself or someone else doing the action and use the timing from this video shoot to work out the animation you need to do.

To start with, animate each of the exercises in Chapters 2 and 3. Have a really simple set that just consists of a curved piece of paper, stretching from the stage to the rear wall. Once you have got the hang of animating with your character and lighting the set, you can start using props and making more complex sets.

If you have an object that needs to fly in the air, hang it from thin cord or build a rig that can be erased later in *post-production*. You can use an editing program such as Adobe After Effects or Premiere Pro to do this. Make sure that you have an image of the background without the character in it, place this on a layer below the animation layer and (as long as the characterless layer is in the same position), you can erase the cord or rig from the animation layer, showing the background layer underneath.

Case Study – *The Koala Brothers* by David Johnson

The Koala Brothers is an internationally successful and award-winning television series produced by Famous Flying Films. David Johnson first came up with the idea of a pair of koalas who fly around the Australian outback in a yellow plane, helping anyone in need.

David then made a short test film that illustrated the characters, the action that would happen and the look and atmosphere of the proposed television series. For this, he and his colleagues built puppets and sets and animated them to a short script, adding dialogue, music and sound effects. This was then shown to numerous television companies and other organizations as a way of raising money.

The cast of *The Koala Brothers*, a fantastic television series about the outback.

The koala brothers flying their yellow aeroplane.

Once the money for the show had been raised and a television company was on board, the puppets, sets and backdrops were remade. Scripts were written and storyboarded, character voices were recorded and a huge studio was rented to house the production. Many animators worked on the series, as well as lighting, camera, editing and model-making people.

Once each episode was completed, it was delivered to the television company for approval and screening. In all, seventy-eight episodes and one Christmas Special were made over a five-year period.

The *Koala Brothers'* set at night, with amazing lighting.

A *Koala Brothers'* set, showing how an area is cut out for the animators to get close to the puppets to animate them.

PUPPET ANIMATION **127**

A *Koala Brothers'* set showing how it can be accessed from all sides.

A *Koala Brothers'* set, showing how the camera is mounted on a rig and that as the character is animated, it has to be attached to the stage with bolts, drilled through and a nut screwed up underneath.

The cast of *The Koala Brothers*, demonstrating the beautiful lighting of this project.

6
3D COMPUTER ANIMATION

There are many different 3D animation computer programs – Blender, Maya, 3D Studio Max, LightWave, Cinema 4D, Houdini, Modo and many more. 3D computer animation is completely reliant on the software that you use. It is also very difficult and time-consuming to learn every single bit of each piece of software. Thankfully, you only need to learn a few basic things in order to animate in 3D.

This chapter is going to concentrate of the program Blender, because this piece of software is free to use, but is very powerful. The basic principles are, on the whole, similar with all 3D software. Before downloading and using any of these programs, please check the technical specification to make sure that your computer can run the software.

THE FIFTEEN BASIC THINGS YOU NEED TO KNOW ABOUT YOUR SOFTWARE

3D Animation Software Screen Basics

You will need to familiarize yourself with the interface of your software. Take some time to become familiar with what each button and menu does. Most 3D software will have four views of the space in which you are animating. There will also be buttons for how to create basic shapes and how to manipulate them. There will be a timeline that indicates where the

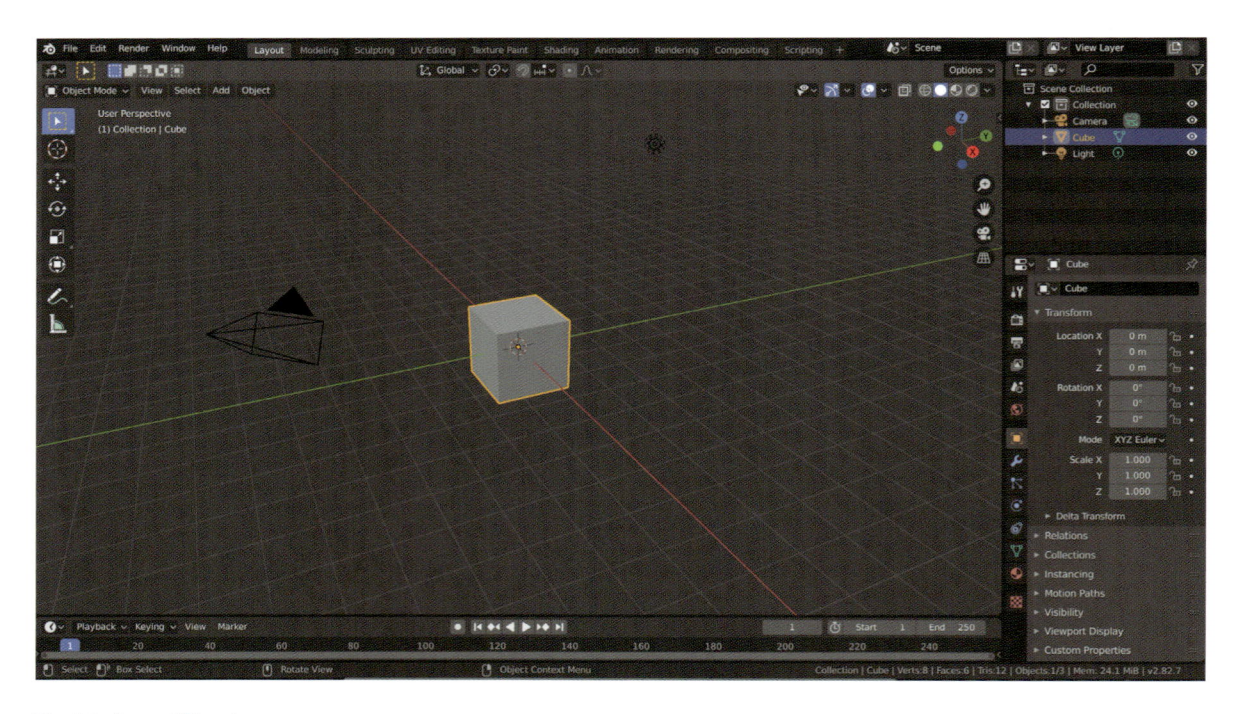

The interface of Blender.

key positions are placed and controls that allow you to play the animation back.

3D Animation Software Keyboard Shortcuts

Being able to use the keyboard shortcuts for your chosen piece of software can make modelling, animating, *rigging* and rendering much easier. Try to learn these basic keyboard shortcuts for your chosen piece of software. These are the basic shortcuts that will help your work to flow.

BLENDER KEYBOARD SHORTCUTS

View shortcuts:

- middle mouse button = tumble (only in perspective view)
- roll wheel of middle mouse button = track in and out
- shift + middle mouse button = *pan* from side to side
- number pad 0 = camera view
- number pad 5 = perspective view
- home key = frame all
- ctrl + alt Q = go from quad view to single view.

Animation/manipulation shortcuts:

- to select an object = left-click on it
- I = insert key frame
- shift + space bar + R = Rotate tool (to rotate your object)
- shift + space bar + S = Scale tool (to make your object bigger or smaller)
- shift + space bar + G = Move tool (to move your object).

Playback shortcuts:

- tap space bar = play back animation
- right arrow key = move one frame forwards
- left arrow key = move one frame back.

Saving:

- ctrl + S to Save
- shift + ctrl + S to Save As

Remember to create a new folder in which to save your 3D work by left-clicking the Create New Directory button at the top of the Save menu that comes up when you first Save or Save As.

Setting Up Animation Preferences

All pieces of software need to be set up, so that things like the frame rate and the screen size of the animation that you produce are correct.

SETTING UP ANIMATION PREFERENCES IN BLENDER

- Go to the Properties Editor Panel. Then select the Output Properties button.
- Make sure the resolution is X = 1920 and Y = 1080 (HD resolution).
- Then make the frame rate 24fps.

Fortunately, these are all default settings.

Creating Basic Objects

The basic objects created in a given piece of software are a sphere, a cube, a pyramid or a multifaceted object. These can then be manipulated into any shape you desire.

BUILDING A BASIC OBJECT IN BLENDER

- Make sure you are in Object mode.
- Go to the menu at the top of the view, left-click on Add.
- Choose Mesh, Curve, Surface or Metaball, then choose the type of object you want to create (plane, cube, circle, sphere and so on).
- In the Properties Editor Panel, left-click the Object Properties button and type in the size you want.

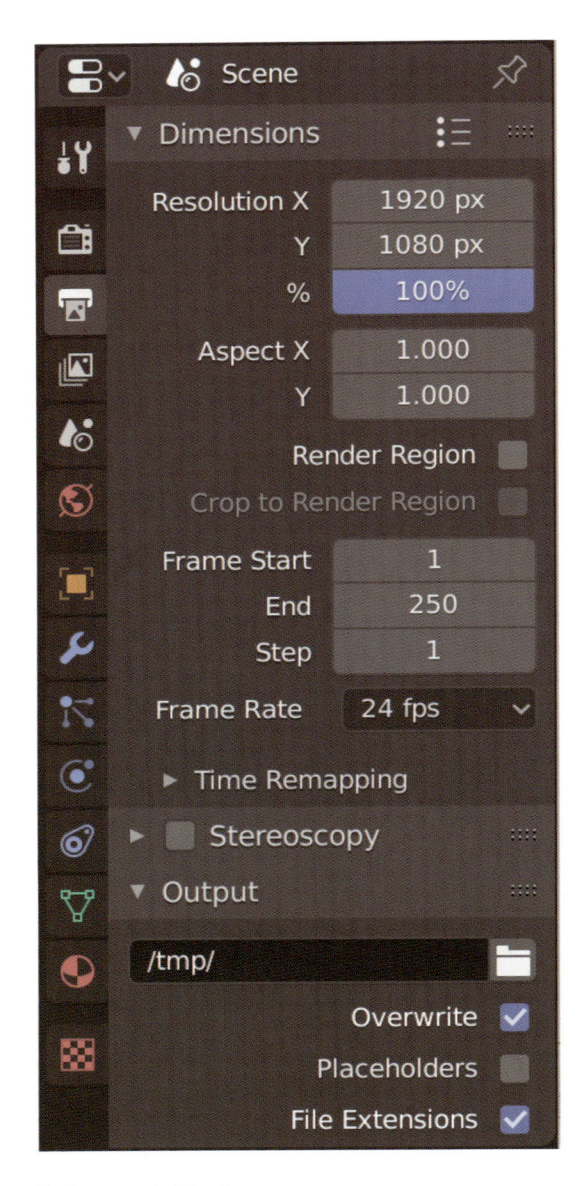

Preferences in Blender.

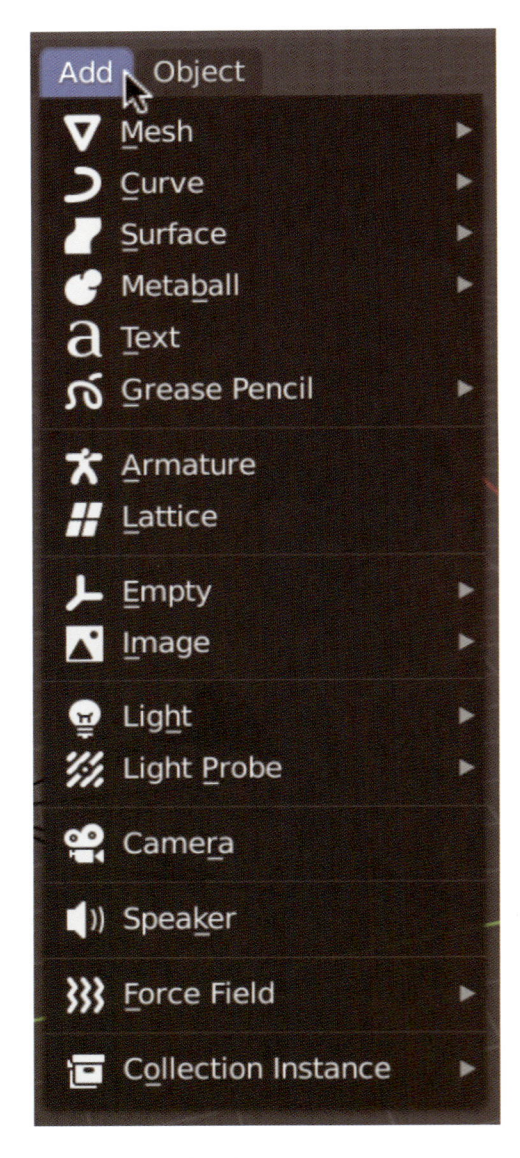

Basic objects in Blender.

Moving an Item

When it comes to creating your animations, you will need to move an object, rotate an object or scale an object.

MOVING THINGS IN BLENDER

- Select the Move Tool, Rotate Tool or the Scale Tool button on the left-hand side of the screen.
- Select the object in the View Panel and transform it by left-clicking and dragging.

Setting Keys

You will need to know how to set a key frame on the object that you have manipulated in order to save that key frame and then set another key frame.

Moving objects in Blender.

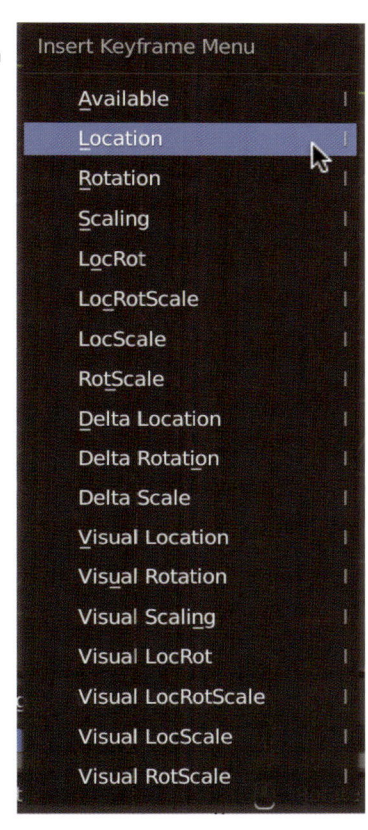

Setting keys in Blender.

Setting Keys in Blender

- Go to the Time Slider. Move the cursor to the frame you want to set a key on.
- Move your object to the position you want and press the 'i' key on your keyboard. A menu will come up, so select from this menu the type of movement you want to set a key frame on (Location [movement], Rotation or Scaling).
- Otherwise, you can select the Auto Keying button. To do this, left-click the Auto Key button next to the playback control buttons (small grey box with a white dot in it, which will turn blue when it is on). This means that whenever you move something it will set a key frame on that movement automatically. Once you are used to it, this can be a faster and more efficient way of working.

When you set a key frame, this will create a small diamond in the Time Slider that indicates where the key frame has been set. The computer can then do the in-betweens for you (but they may not be correct; if so, you will need to change them later).

You can delete the key frames by left-clicking to select the diamonds and then right-clicking on the diamonds and left-clicking Delete from the menu that comes up.

Using the Graph Editor in 3D Animation Software

Unfortunately, when a piece of computer software does the in-between movement, it is often not correct. You therefore need to know how to manipulate this movement to make it work correctly. Usually this is done by controlling the curves (a graph-like representation of the movement) in your chosen piece of software.

Using the Graph Editor in Blender

- To open Graph Editor in Blender, go to the Timeline at the bottom of your viewport.
- Go to the Editor Type button. A menu will come up; choose Graph Editor from it. The Graph Editor is just below the timeline, so move the timeline up by clicking and dragging up the top edge of the timeline.
- When you do some key animation, keys will appear in the Graph Editor. Make sure that the object you have moved is selected in the viewport.
- The curves between these keys can be manipulated in order to change the way the object moves in-between them. To do this, select the keys (black dots) on the curves and adjust by moving the arms attached to the dots.
- You can select different ways of manipulating these arms by clicking the Proportional Editing Falloff button.

Creating a Preview Movie in 3D Animation Software

At some point you are going to need to see what your animation looks like (when the animation plays back on the timeline, depending how complicated your characters are and the processing power of your computer, it may not be at the correct speed). You therefore need to learn how to render a quick movie in order to view your animation as a kind of line test (as you would with drawn animation).

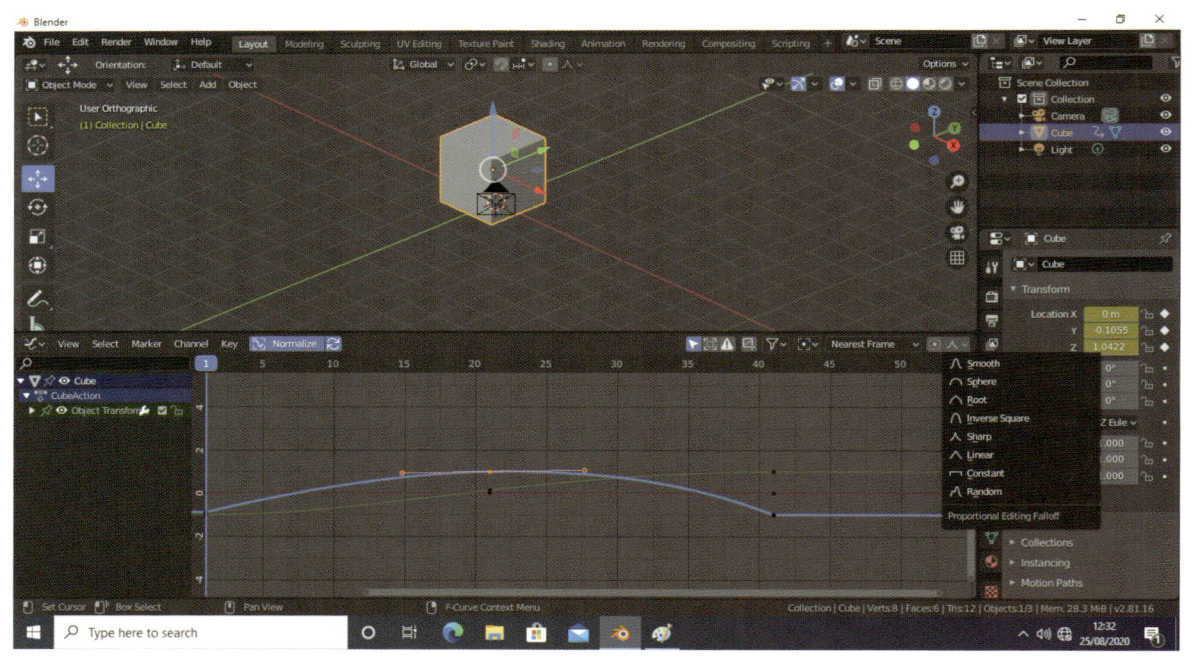

Graph Editor in Blender.

Creating a Preview Movie in Blender

- Go to the Properties Editor Panel. Select the Output Properties button. Go to the Frame Start box and choose the number of the first frame you want to render (probably 1).
- Then go to the End box and choose the last frame of your animation (if your animation is 100 frames long, you would choose 100).
- Look for the word Output and then go to the box below and click on the folder icon. You should now choose a place where your movies will be saved to (create a folder called 'Blender movies', for example).
- Next, go down the Properties Editor Panel and find the File Format box. Click on the little downward-pointing arrow and then choose a movie format, for example FFmpeg video. This will produce a small movie that will play back on your computer.
- Select a viewport and go to the View button at the top. A menu will appear. At the bottom of the menu, left-click Viewport Render Animation. Once it is done, go to the folder you created on your computer and the movie will be in there. Click on it to play it!

Hierarchies in 3D Animation Software

When creating a complicated model such as a human being in a piece of 3D software, you will need to build a hierarchy. For example, the fingers will be joined to the hand, the hand will be joined to the forearm, the forearm will be joined to the upper arm, the upper arm will be joined to the shoulder, the shoulder will be joined to the spine and the spine will be joined to the pelvis. These will form a hierarchy, the pelvis at the top and the fingers at the bottom.

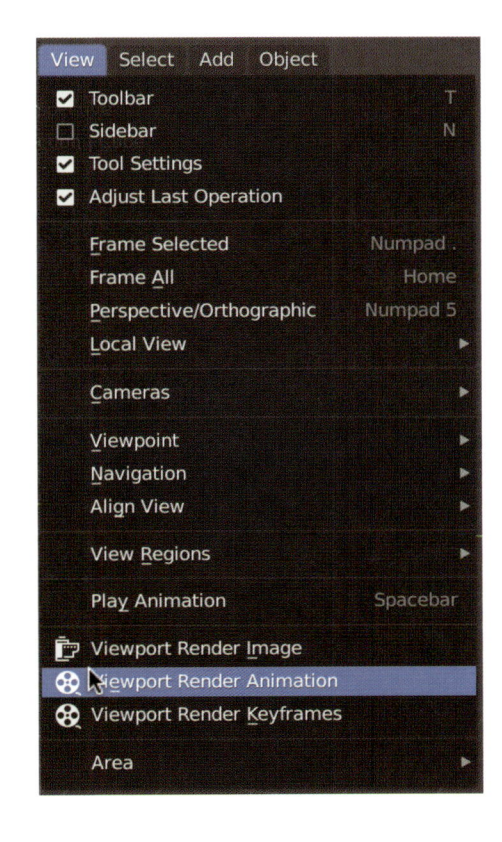

Previewing movies in Blender.

This is achieved by parenting. For example, the hand is the parent of the finger (the child). The arm is the parent of the hand and so on. When you move the arm, the hand and fingers will follow. When you move the hand, the fingers will follow, but the arm will stay in one place. When you move the fingers, the hand will stay in place.

HIERARCHIES IN BLENDER

- In Blender, left-click the object that is to be the child, press shift key on your keyboard and then left-click the object that is to be the parent.
- Press Ctrl + P keys on your keyboard (or you can right-click and from the Object Context Menu window left-click Parent, then Object). You should now have a parent and child.
- To un-parent, select Child then right-click and from the menu select Parent, then Clear Parent (or press Alt + P key on your keyboard). You will see the Hierarchy in the Outliner window.

Constraining an Object in 3D Animation Software

At some point you will need to constrain one object to another. For example, if making an eye for your character and you want to control where it looks, you can get the eye to always look at an object that won't be seen in your final animation. You can use an invisible object such as an Empty (in Blender). To create an Empty, left-click the Add button at the top of the viewport and from the menu, left-click Empty and then Plain Axes. This will create a cross-like object, which is your Empty.

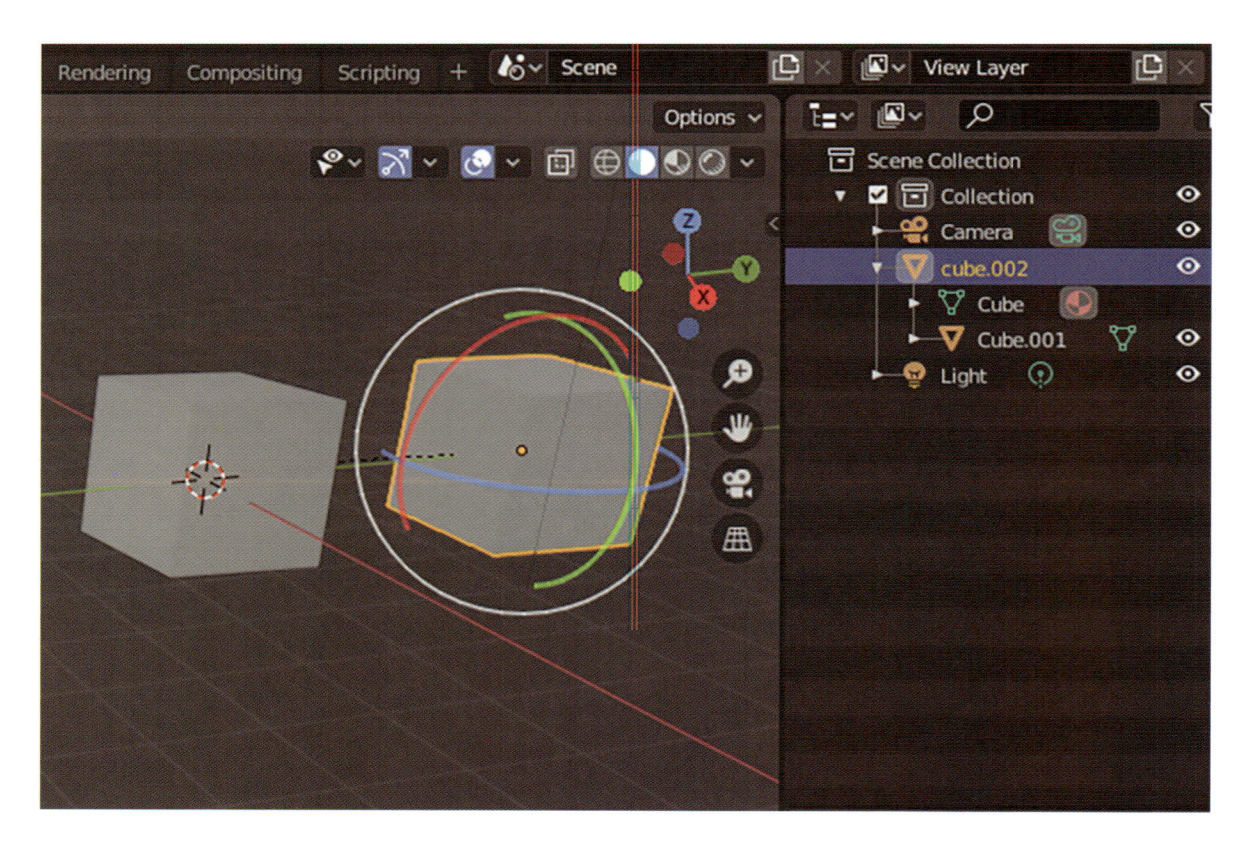

Hierarchies in Blender.

Constraining One Object to Another in Blender

- To constrain one object to another, left-click the object that needs to be constrained (the eyeball).
- Go to the Properties Editor Panel and left-click the Object Constraint Properties button.
- Left-click the words Add Object Constraint and from the menu left-click Track To.
- In the box next to the word Target, left-click the eye-dropper tool and left-click the Empty in the viewport.
- Your eyeball is now constrained to your Empty. If you select and move the Empty your eyeball should now always be looking at it.

Creating Objects and Putting Bones in Them

The basic way that you create a character in 3D is to build the body first, then put bones into it. These bones can be manipulated to move the character. Often the bones will have control handles on them.

Putting Bones into Objects in Blender

- Create a new file, by going to File > New > General in the main menu. This will create a new file with a default cube in the middle.
- Delete the cube by left-clicking it and then right-clicking to bring up a menu. Left-click Delete from the menu. Make sure you are in Object Mode (it should say Object Mode in the Object Interaction Mode button) at the top left of the viewport. If it doesn't, left-click the Object Interaction Mode button and choose Object Mode.
- Create a sphere by left-clicking the Add menu at the top of the viewport. Left-click Mesh and then UV Sphere.
- Scale the sphere into a cucumber-like shape by using the Scale tool. Move the cucumber up, so that the bottom of it is at the centre of the world.

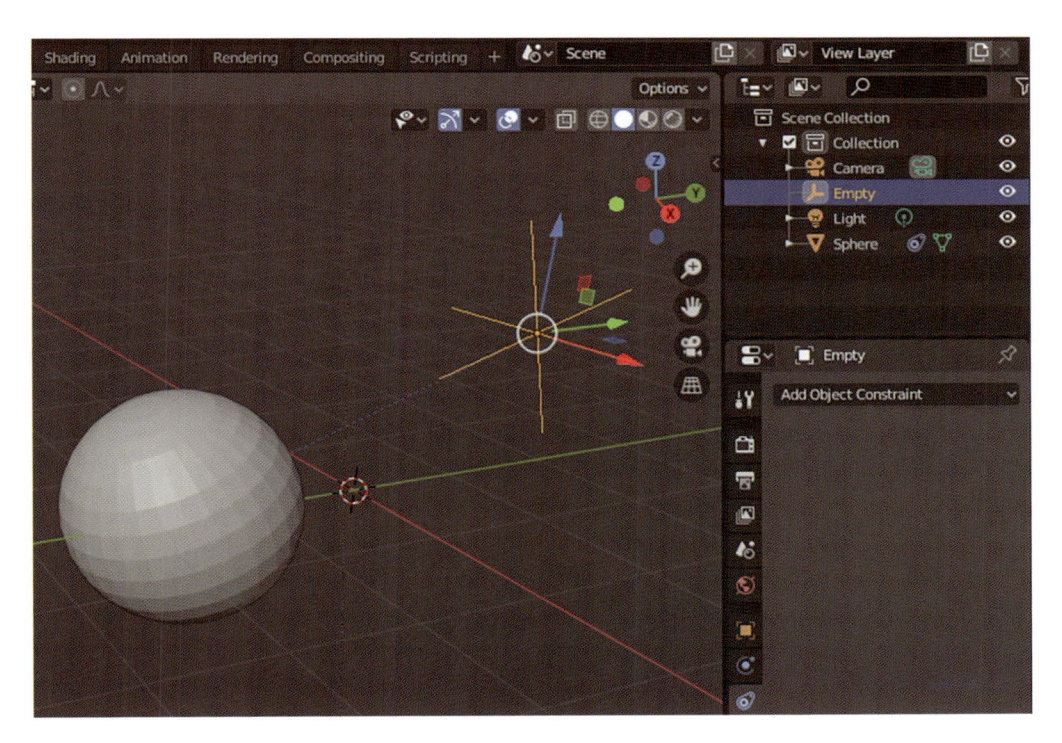

Constraining objects in Blender.

- To create a bone to put into the cucumber, go to the Add button at the top of the viewport, then from the menu select Armature. This will create a bone.
- To make it easier to see the bone, go to the Object Data Properties (little man running) button in the Properties Editor, select Viewpoint Display and then click on the box next to In Front. This will make the bone easier to see and select.
- At the moment we are in Object Mode. Go into Edit Mode by clicking on the arrow next to Object Mode at the top left of the viewport and select Edit Mode.
- With the Move tool selected, left-click on the top part of the bone and move it up the top of the cucumber. Left-click the middle of the bone and then right-click and select Subdivide from the menu. You now have two bones in your cucumber.
- To attach the cucumber to the bones, go back to Object Mode. Left-click the cucumber, then Shift and left-click the bones. Go to the Object button at the top of the viewport and select Parent, then With Automatic Weights.
- To test to see if it works, chose Pose Mode from the Object Interaction Mode button. Select each of the bones and rotate them with the Rotate tool. The cucumber should now bend with the bones.

Giving Your Characters Colour

There are lots of ways to colour your model. At its most simple, you can assign a colour to your model with the software. At its most complex, you

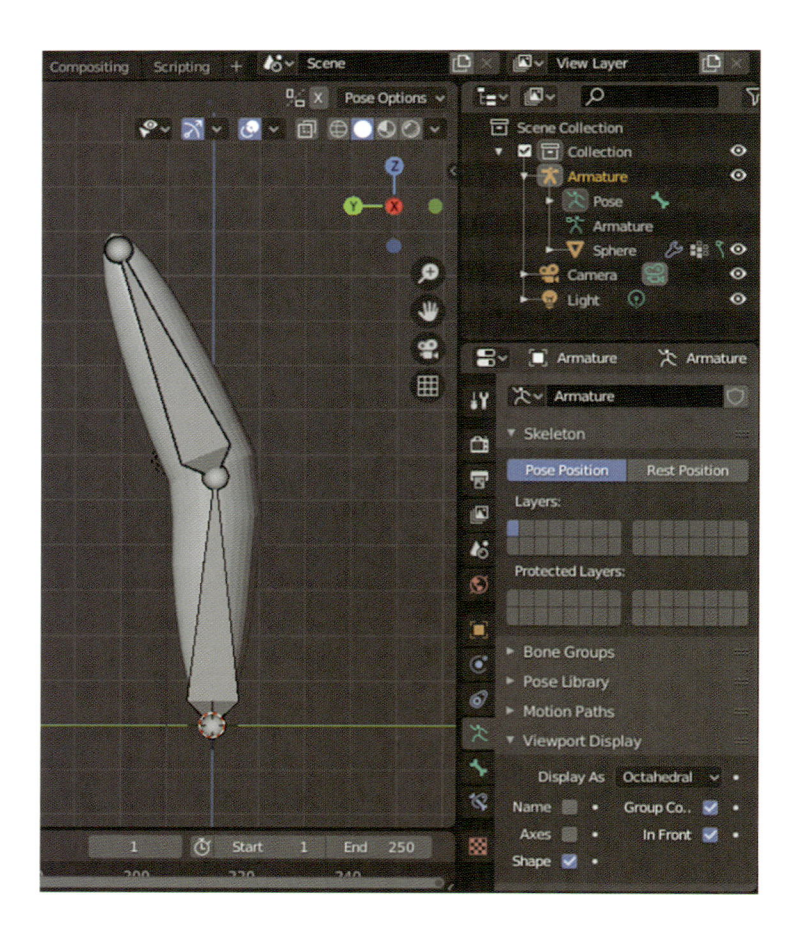

Placing bones within objects in Blender.

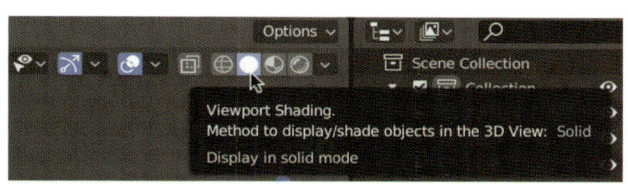

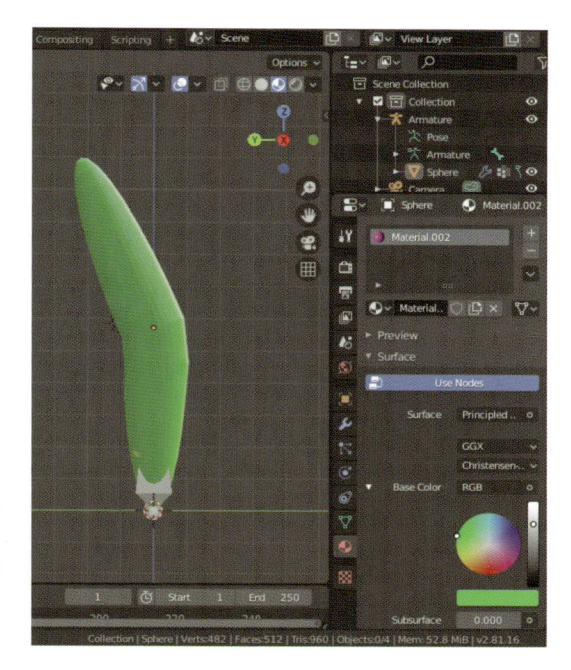

Colour in Blender.

can take the skin of your model and then colour the skin with different textures, or completely colour the skin with various tools.

Giving Your Objects Colour in Blender

- Select Object in the viewport, go to the Properties Editor Panel.
- Left-click the Material Properties button. Left-click the '+ New' button and a whole menu comes up.
- Go to the Base Colour box and left-click on the button with a circle on it. Choose RGB. In order to see the colour, left-click the Viewport Shading button at the top right of the viewport.

There are lots of other ways to colour and texture objects, but this is the simplest way to do it.

Importing Sound

When you need to animate to a piece of lip-sync, or if your character needs to dance to music, you will need to know how to import sound to the timeline and then animate to the sound.

Importing Sound into Blender

- Go to the Timeline, then left-click the Editor Type button. Left-click Video Sequencer. This will convert the Timeline to the Video Sequencer.
- In the Video Sequencer, left-click on the Add button and left-click Sound from the menu. Choose your piece of sound from your computer and left-click Add Sound Strip. This will bring the sound into the Video Sequencer.
- Hit the space bar on the keyboard to play the sound. The piece of sound (called the Sound Strip) can be moved backwards and forwards by left-clicking and dragging. Move it to the point where you want the sound to start in your shot.
- To see the Wave form on the Sound Strip, press N on your keyboard and a sidebar will come up. Tick the box next to Display Waveform.
- You can animate while the Video Sequencer is displayed, or you can go back to the Timeline

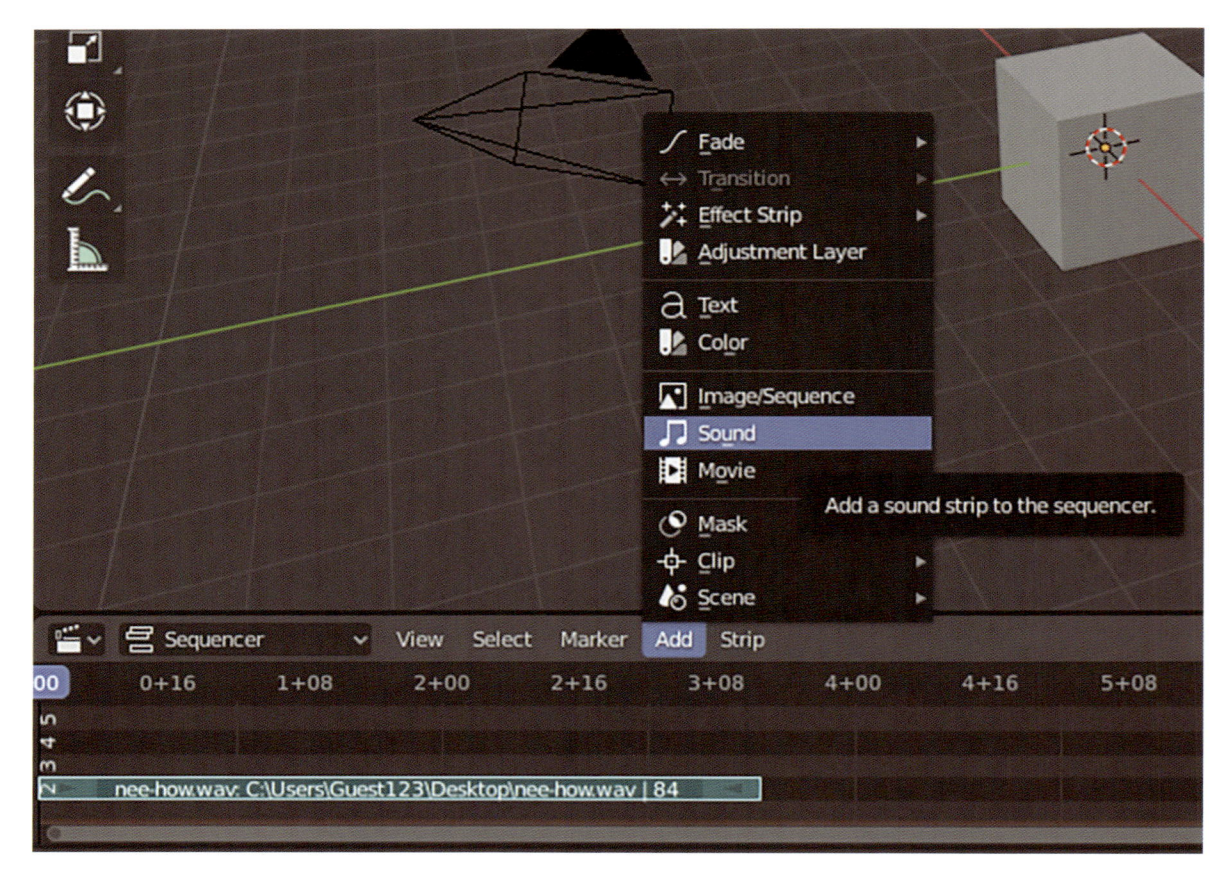

Sound in Blender.

by left-clicking the Editor Type button and left-clicking Timeline. The Sound Strip will not be visible in the Timeline.
- To 'scrub' through the sound to hear it while going from frame to frame, left-click the Playback button. Left-click the tick box next to Audio Scrubbing in the menu that comes up. You can't see the Sound Strip in the timeline.

Setting Up Lights

In many ways, 3D animation is similar to puppet animation. It needs to be lit correctly so that the audience can see characters and you can establish the mood of the scene with the lighting. In all 3D programs, when you open a new scene, there will be default lighting (basic lighting) present already. In order to light a scene correctly, you will need to set up at least four lights:

- a key light
- a fill light
- a backlight
- a background light (if there is a background).

SETTING UP LIGHTS IN BLENDER KEY LIGHT
Key Light

- When you open a scene in Blender you can use the default light that came with the scene as your key light. Left-click the Move Tool at the left side of the screen, then left-click the light and move it to the front, slightly to one side and above your model.

- To see what the lighting looks like, left-click the Rendered, Viewport Shading button (top of viewport at far right).
- To adjust the light, left-click the Object Properties button that looks like a lightbulb in the Properties Editor Panel. Here you can change the type of light it is, the power, size and so on.

Fill Light

- Left-click the Add button at the top of the viewport. Left-click Light, then left-click Spot from the menu. Move this to the correct position (front of the model, slightly to the other side of the key light and have it lower down) with the Move Tool.

Backlight

- Create your backlight in the same way and position it behind your model.

Background Light

- Create a Background light (if needed) in the same way and point it at the background. You may need to create extra lights to fill in areas. It all takes a lot of fiddling!
- To get a quick view of what the camera is seeing, left-click the Camera button at the left side of the viewport.

Rendering a Scene

Once you have done your animation, you need to know how to export it as a movie so that the particular shot you have animated can be cut into your film.

Rendering a Scene in Blender

- Left-click the Render Properties button in the Properties Editor Panel. Here you can adjust all the properties to get the look correct.
- If you left-click the Output Properties button in the Properties Editor Panel, you can adjust the start and end point of your animation. You can also adjust the size of your animation (1,920 × 1,080 is HD size).
- You can also select where to save your animation by clicking on the File Browser button (looks like a file).

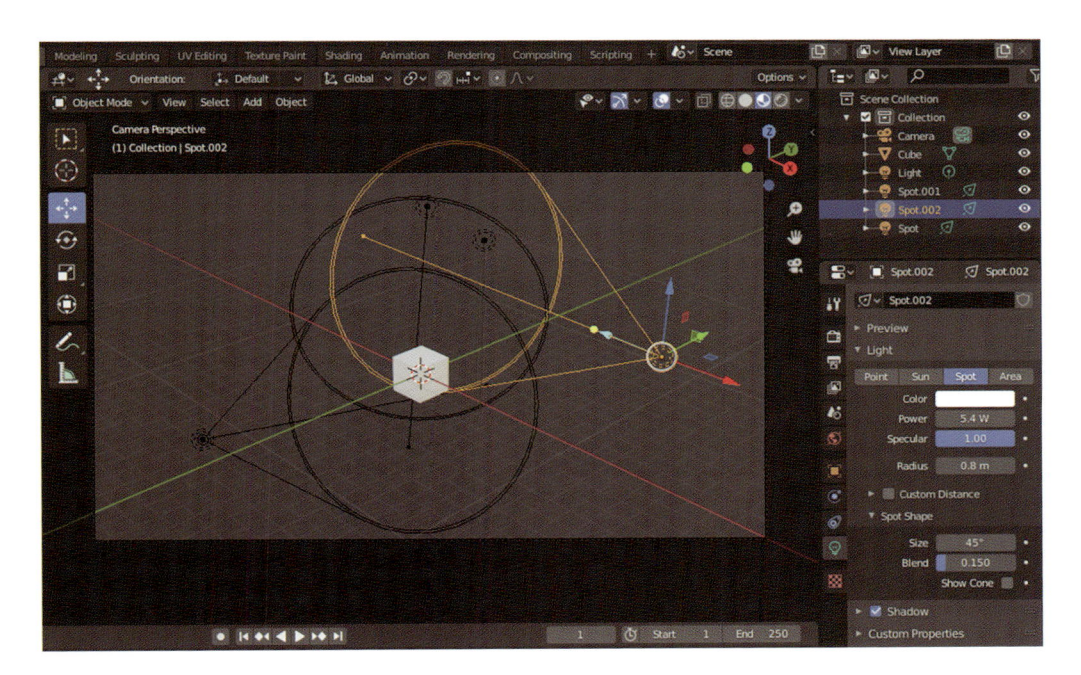

Lights in Blender.

- By left-clicking the arrow in the box next to File Format, you can select the type of file you want to produce, either a movie such as a FFmpeg video or an image sequence such as a .PNG sequence (an image sequence is much better quality than a movie and can be directly imported into editing software without any loss of clarity).
- To render an image, left-click on the word Render in the main menu at the top of the screen. Then left-click Render Image. This will render a single image of the frame on your timeline.
- To render your animation, left-click the word Render in the main menu at the top of the screen. Then left-click Render Animation. This will render the whole animation you have produced.

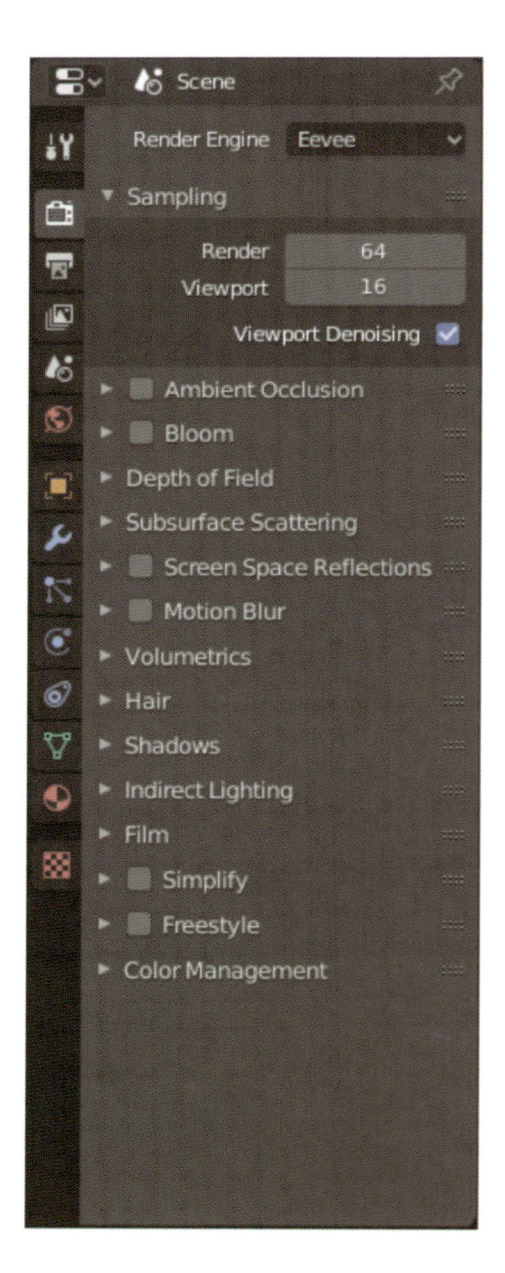

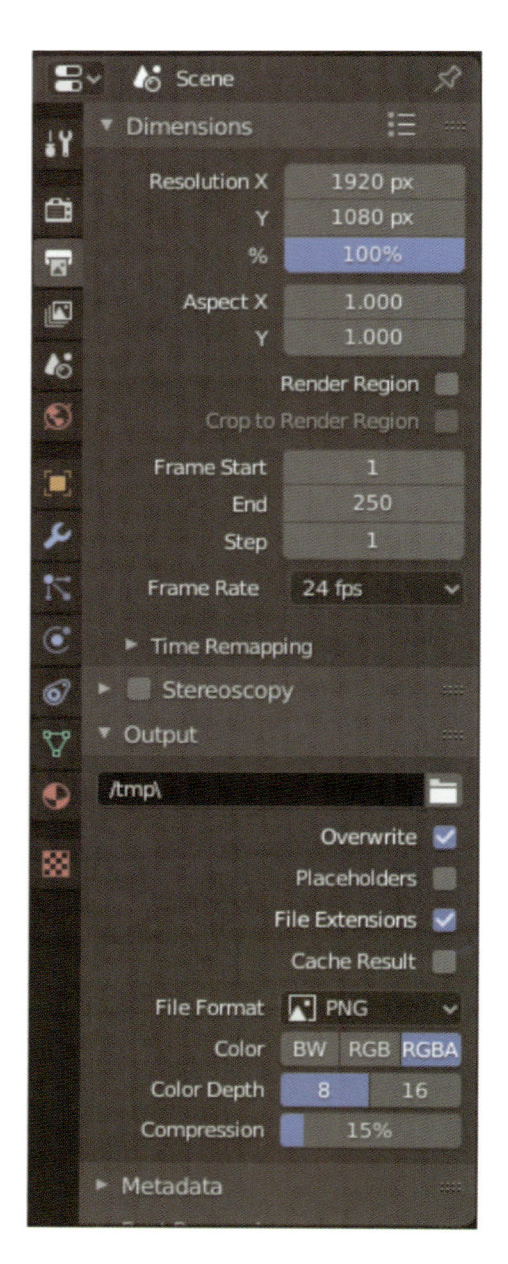

Rendering a scene in Blender.

BUILDING A BASIC CHARACTER IN 3D

Building a 3D model takes a lot of time and effort, so it may be better to miss this section out and download a model from the internet and start animating with that.

There are many models that can be downloaded for free from the internet for your specific piece of software.

If you really want to understand how a 3D model is made, it would be best to check YouTube or other websites, to see how to make a rigged character in your chosen software. Software does get updated quite regularly, so this will be the best place to learn the latest techniques.

HOW TO ANIMATE IN 3D

Firstly, 3D animation is no different to drawn, 2D digital or puppet animation. The same principles outlined in Chapters 2 and 3 are the same with all forms of animation. In the following section I will outline how to animate some of the exercises in Blender.

Animating a Bouncy Ball in Blender

- First, create a ball.
- In a side-view panel, select the Move tool and then select and move the ball to the top left of the view panel. Make sure the time slider is on frame 1.
- To set a key frame, press the I key on the keyboard and from the menu select Location. Move the time slider to frame 9.
- Then move the ball to the point where it touches the ground in the middle of the view panel. Set another key frame.
- Finally move the time slider to frame 17 and move the ball to the top right of the view panel.

Play back your animation. It will move in a rather strange way. In order to correct this, you will have to adjust the curves in the Graph Editor. Open up

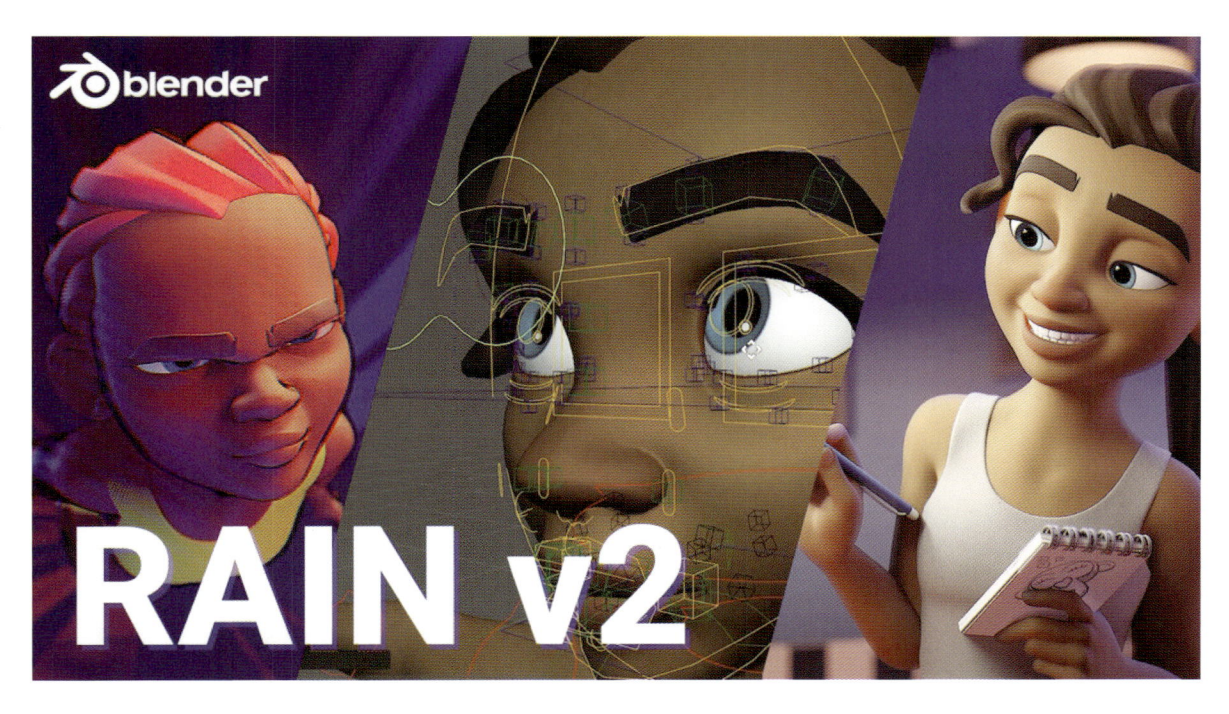

Downloaded model for Blender.

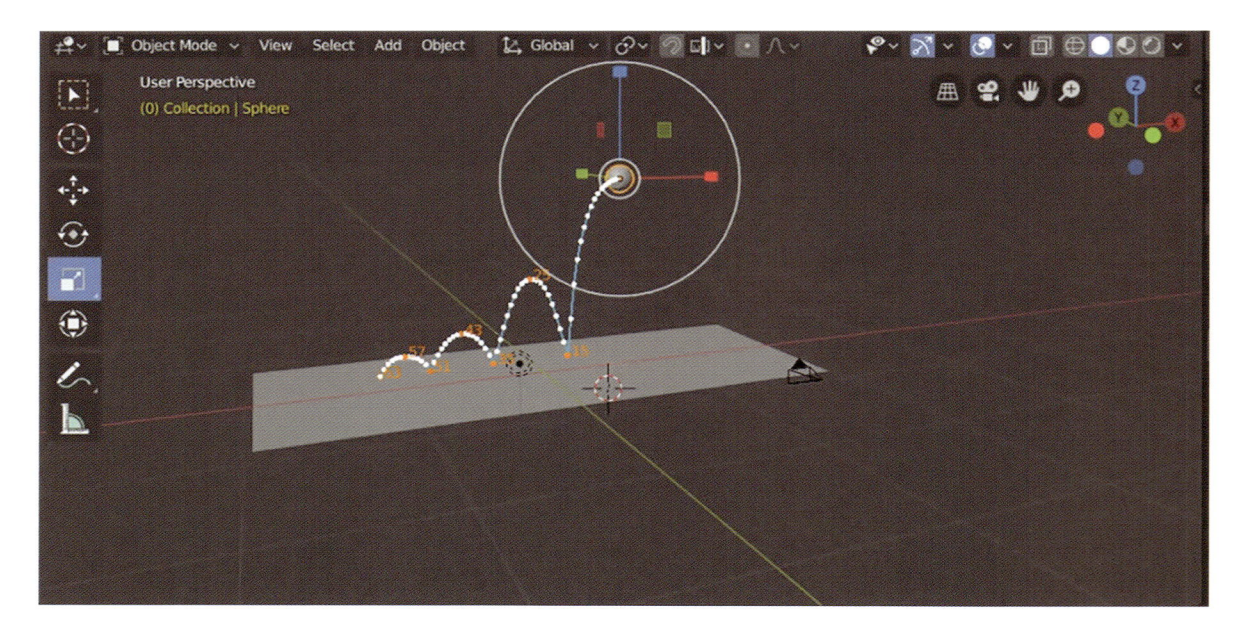

Bouncy ball in Blender.

the Graph Editor and you will be confronted with a curved line with dots on. Each of the dots are keys. Click on the dot in the middle at frame 9 and two handles will appear. 'Break' the handles so they move independently of each other and move them both upward. This will change the shape of the curve.

Play back the animation again and you will see that the movement will look much more like that of a ball.

If you want the ball to squash when it hits the ground, create a Scaling key frame on the frame before it touches the ground, then create a Scaling key frame on the frame after it leaves the ground.

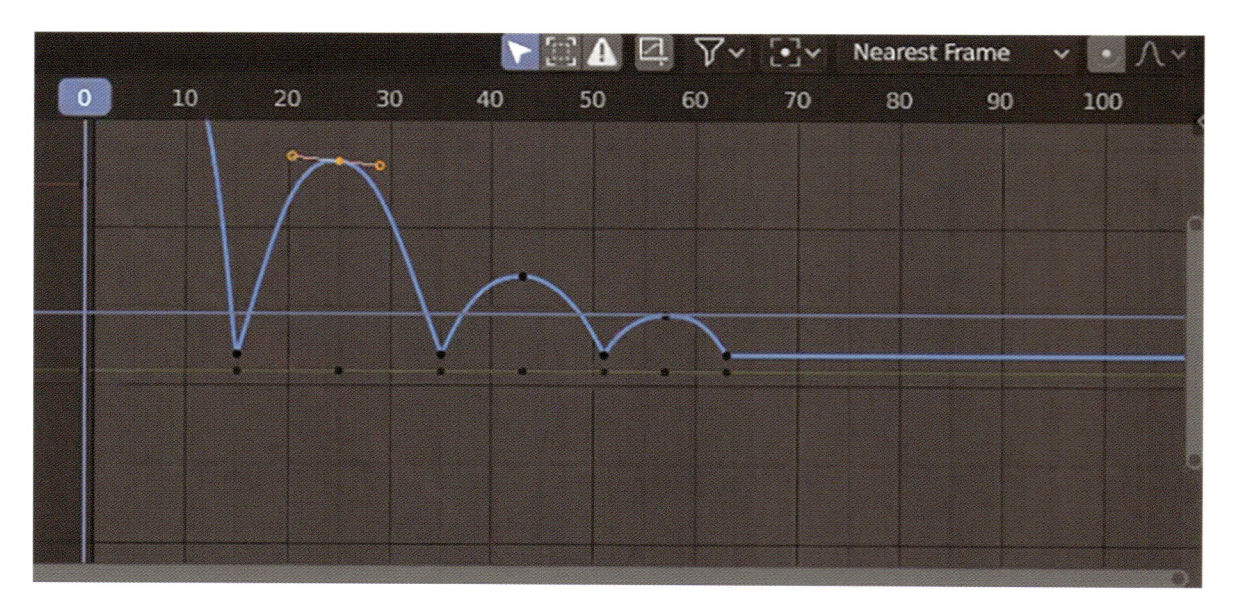

Curves in Blender for ball.

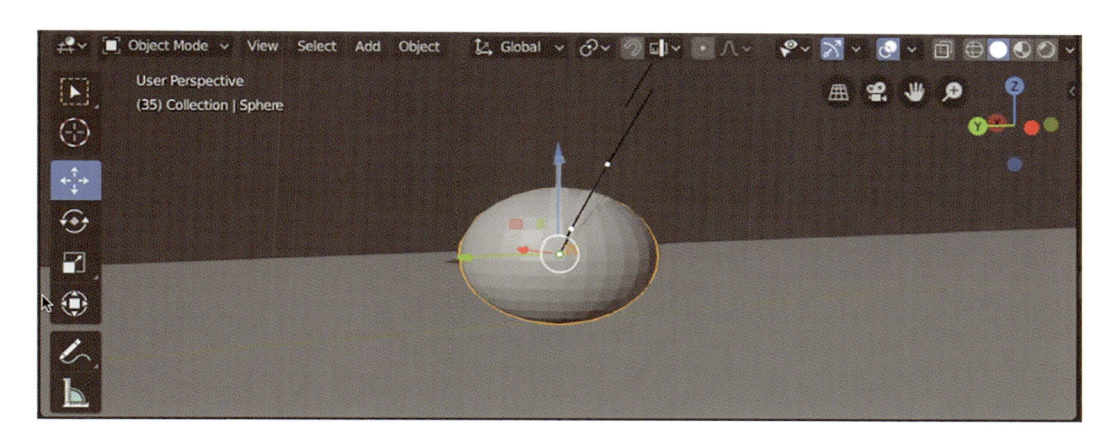

Squashing a ball in Blender.

Finally, go back to the frame where the ball has touched the ground and use the Scale Tool to distort the ball into a nice squashed shape. Set a Scaling key frame on that.

Animating a Character Picking Something Up in Blender

Make sure that you are familiar with all the controls on your downloaded character.

- To animate this character picking up a block, import them into a scene and create two blocks. Place one block at the feet of your character.

- The second block will be attached to the character's hand. The reason for this is that it is very difficult to animate something that a character is holding if it is not attached to the hand. What will happen is that the block in the hand will be invisible up to the point that the character grasps the ball on the ground. From that point, the ball on the ground will become invisible and the ball in the hand visible.
- Move the block so that it is against the palm of the hand. Attach it by left-clicking the ball that is to be the child, press shift key on your keyboard and then left-click the object that is to be parent (the hand). Press Ctrl + P keys on your keyboard (or you can right-click and from the

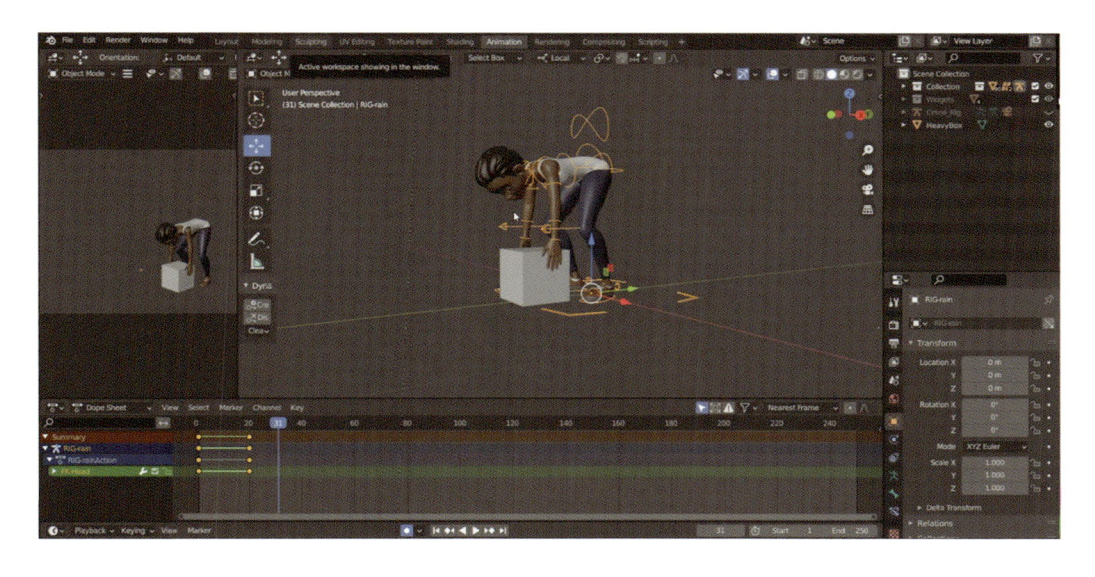

Character in a scene with a block in Blender.

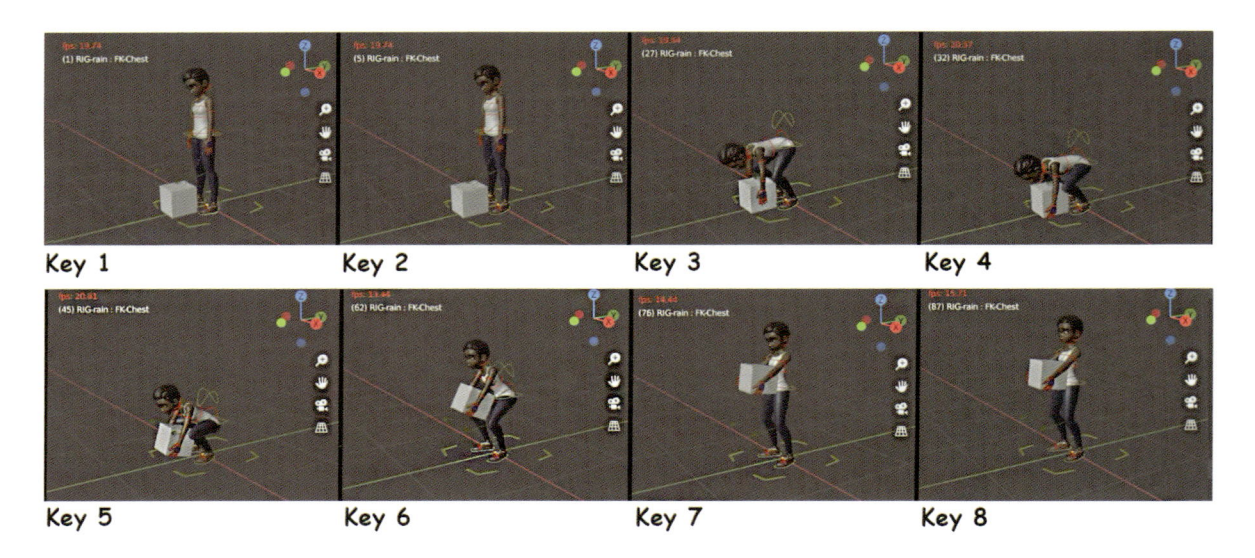

Picking up a block sequence in Blender.

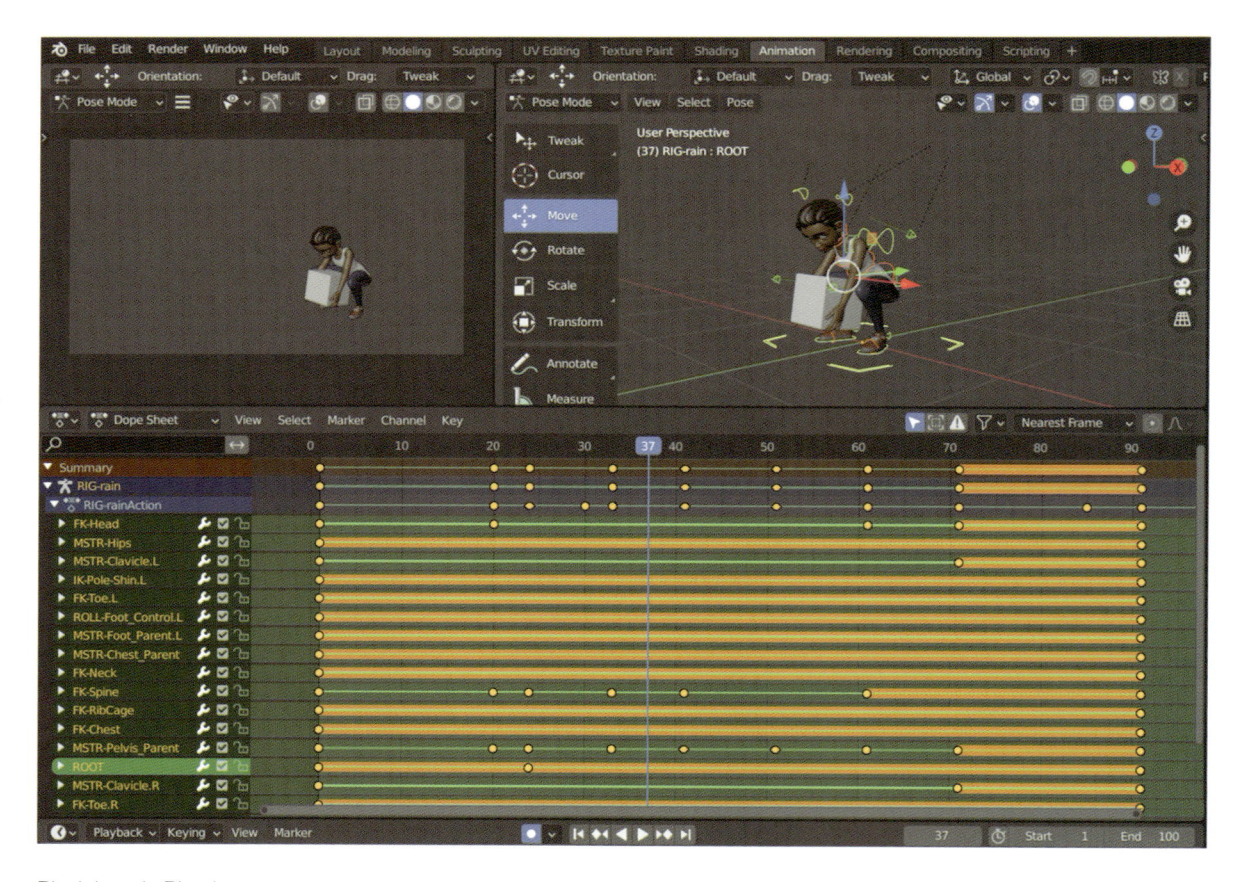

Block keys in Blender.

Object Context Menu window left-click Parent, then Object).
- Now we have to make it invisible. This is done by selecting the ball, right-clicking and choosing visibility from the menu.
- Animate the action of the character picking up a block, setting keys as you go along. Adjust the curves to make the movement more believable and don't forget about the visibility of the block.

Once the animation is done, you can look at the key positions of the movement in the dope sheet section of the timeline.

Case Study – *Unique* by Katie Chan

Katie created this short film as part of her animation course at university. She came up with the idea of an onion that is teased and bullied by a group of garlic bulbs. The onion feels depressed and lonely, but then discovers a hidden talent and is loved by all because of this.

Katie converted the script into a storyboard and then an animatic. Once this was done, she built and rigged the characters, created the backgrounds and worked out the textures and colours of the characters.

She then animated the film, shot by shot, adding each finished shot into the animatic.

Once all the shots were completed and the film edited, a composer and sound designer came up with a score and sound effects and these were mixed together with the movie.

The film is short and beautifully simple and shows what can be done with strong designs, great animation and a heart-warming story.

The main characters from the movie *Unique*.

The hero is laughed at by the other characters in the movie.

The characters of the film have a dance (shown as wireframe and fully coloured).

These are significant frames from the movie and show a huge amount of pathos and expression.

The hero of the movie discovers his superpowers.

7
HOW TO MAKE AN ANIMATED FILM

In this chapter, we will cover scripting, storyboarding, animatic making, animation production, editing, sound, music and post-production. When making your first short animated film, it is best to keep everything as simple as possible.

The first thing you need is an idea! To extend the old adage, 'We all have a novel in us', I believe that we all also have a short animated film in us. So the most important thing is to come up with an idea for a movie.

MOVIE STRUCTURE

Once you have come up with your basic idea, you will find that most short movies use a three-act structure – start, middle and end. These are essentially as follows:

- Act I: set-up
- Act II: confrontation
- Act III: resolution.

Another way of looking at this is that in the first act, you establish the situation and what the character is like. In the second act, you upset everything and give the character a problem. The character tries to solve the problem and towards the last part of Act II there is some kind of showdown/struggle/fight. Act III is where the film is finally resolved. The problem is solved, or the character does not solve the problem, but learns from it (or not). While this is incredibly simplistic, it is a good way of breaking down a story to its most basic parts.

In many ways, I think a short film is a bit like a pop song. There will be a verse and a chorus, a verse and a chorus, a verse and a chorus, a verse and a chorus, and about two-thirds of the way through the song there will be a guitar solo, a sax solo, a bridge, a key change or a rap. After that, there will be another verse and another chorus and then it will finish. Most pop songs are about three minutes long, and for your first movie I suggest sticking to something about three minutes long.

You will also find that most stories follow one of the eight basic plots.

THE EIGHT BASIC PLOTS

It is thought that there are seven basic plots, but I like to think that there are eight.

Cinderella or Rags to Riches

A character who is downtrodden, through hard work or luck, gets all that they desire. You follow the journey of the character. Examples of this type of story are: *My Fair Lady*; *Jane Eyre*; *Pinocchio*.

Achilles

The main character has a fatal flaw. This could be a disability, a character flaw, a regret, or a problem that the character has. It is the groundwork for practically all classical tragedy and comedy films. Examples of this type of story are: *Vertigo* (lead character has a fear of heights); and *A Christmas Carol* (lead character hates everybody).

Faust

The debt that must be repaid. Faust sold his soul to the devil in return for earthly happiness, but when he died he went to hell. Examples of this type of story are: *Citizen Kane* (Kane creates an enormous news empire, but pays the price with loneliness); *Frankenstein* (man creates monster, but has to live with the consequences); *Jurassic Park* (man creates theme park that goes wrong); *The Fly* (man creates a new way to travel, but pays the price with a mistake).

Tristan

The standard triangular plot that involves three people. Tristan and Isolde is the story of a knight (Tristan) who has to collect a Princess (Isolde) who is betrothed to his King (Mark). During the journey, Tristan and Isolde fall in love, but there is the little problem of the fact that she needs to marry King Mark. Examples of this type of story are: *GoodFellas* (husband, wife the mob); *Brief Encounter* (husband, wife, lover); *Casablanca* (husband, wife, lover).

Circe – The Spider and The Fly

Put a group of people in a dark place and bump them off one by one. Finally, one character defeats the thing that is bumping them off – the basis of any horror film. Examples of this type of story are: *Alien* (alien kills off crew of spaceship, one by one), *The Blair Witch Project* (unknown thing kills off film crew, one by one), *Jaws* (shark kills off people, one by one).

Romeo and Juliet

Boy meets girl, they may hate each other at first, then they fall in love, they fall out of love, they get back together and through various trials and tribulations either end up with each other or not. Most romantic comedies fit this plot. It can also include 'buddy movies', where two men or two women find a love of deep friendship for each other. Examples of this type of story are: *West Side Story* (a man and a woman fall in love, in spite of being from warring gangs); *Pretty Woman* (a prostitute and a rich businessman find love); *Toy Story* (two toys, Woody and Buzz, dislike each other to start with, but when thrown together in adversity find friendship).

Orpheus – The Gift Taken Away

A character who has it all has an accident and loses something, whether it is a person that they love, a special thing, or part of themselves. Examples of this type of story are: *Brideshead Revisited* (aristocratic family loses home); *Love Story* (husband loses wife); *Trading Places* (successful businessman loses everything).

The Hero Who Cannot be Kept Down

Create a heroic character, put them in a bad situation that they need to escape from or deal with, and they (amazingly) escape or solve the problem. Then stick them into another situation where they have to deal with a problem, and so on. Examples of this type of story are: *Raiders of the Lost Ark*, *John Wick* and any James Bond Film.

Of course, most feature films will twist several plots together during their duration. A television series or soap opera will have several plots running at the same time. But for a short movie, just stick to one.

HOW TO MAKE A SIMPLE MOVIE

All of these plots seem pretty elaborate. So, the simplest movie you can make is to give a character a difficult thing to do. For example, have a character try to build a house of cards:

- Show a long shot of the character sat at a table that has a pile of cards on it (shot 1; frame 001).
- The character picks up the pile of cards and looks at them (still shot 1; frame 002).
- Cut into medium shot of character holding cards, thinking (shot 2; frame 003).
- Character takes two cards off pack and places pack on table (still shot 2; frame 004).
- Cut back to long shot; the character then places two cards together on the table, propped against each other (shot 3; frame 005).
- Cut to close-up of face with a look of concentration (shot 4; frame 006).
- Cut to medium shot; a second pair of cards are arranged next to them (shot 5; frame 007).
- A card is then placed between the tops of the two piles of cards. Close-up of cards (shot 6; frame 008).
- Cut to a close-up of character's face as they delicately place this card on to the other cards (shot 7; frame 009).
- Cut to medium shot; a further pair of cards are propped up on top of the lower cards (shot 8; frame 010).
- Another close-up of character's face as they delicately place the cards (shot 9; frame 011).
- Cut to medium shot, as the character leans back and looks at the house of cards with satisfaction (shot 10; frame 012).
- The character twitches their nose, almost sneezes, stops, but then suddenly, uncontrollably, sneezes and blows all the cards over (still shot 10; frames 013, 014, 015, 016, 017).
- Cut to a close-up of character looking annoyed (shot 11; frame 18).

You will notice that I have basically put a plot together using a list. Doing a list of what will happen during the movie can be really useful, as it reduces the story down to its basic elements.

Once you have sorted out what is going to happen, you need to do a storyboard. It is best to do

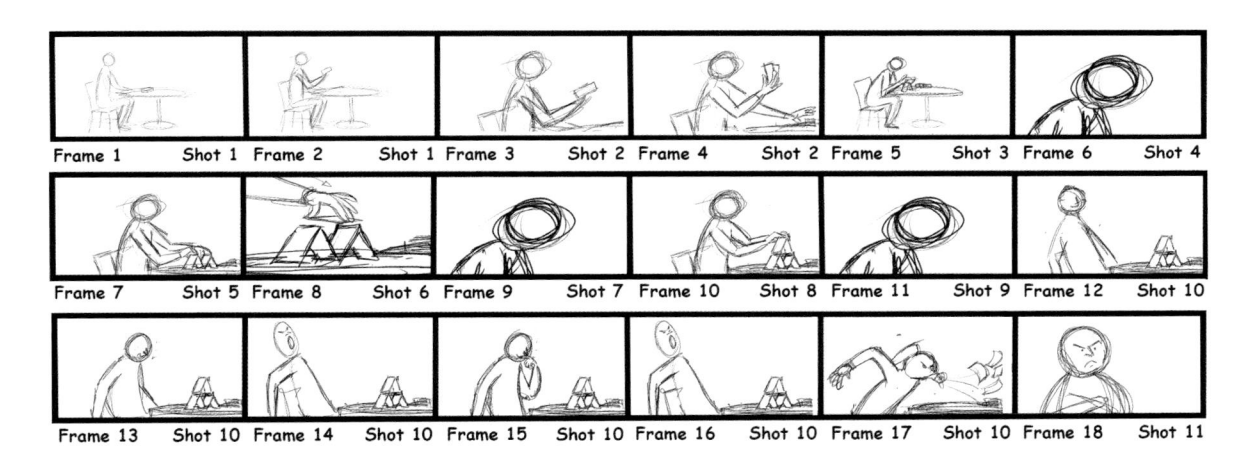

An example of a rough storyboard that would be part of the script writing process.

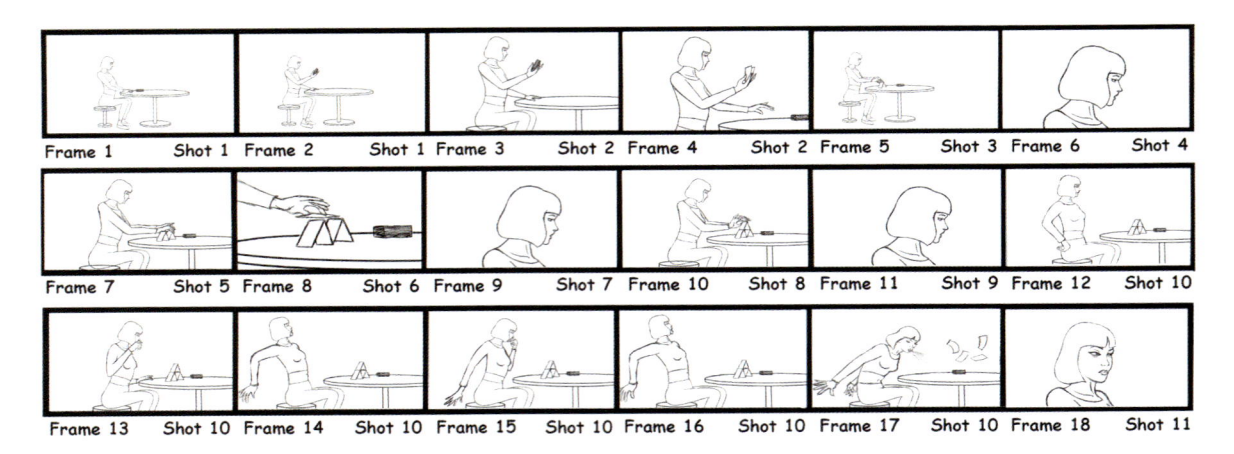

A tighter storyboard that gives an idea of how the film will be put together.

a really rough storyboard first, just to sort out all the story problems. This could be done on Post-it Notes or scraps of paper. Once the basic problems are sorted out, you can then do a tighter storyboard with better drawings.

HOW TO MAKE A STORYBOARD

A storyboard is a series of images that sum up the action of a film – a bit like a comic strip. Storyboards are usually drawn artwork, even if the final project will be produced as puppet animation, or as 3D computer animation.

A storyboard should show all the major composition changes that happen during a film. A film will usually consist of a series of scenes (places where the action takes place, for example the kitchen scene). It could have several scenes, or just one. Each scene will consist of a series of shots (different camera angles) that will explain the story.

BASIC SHOTS IN A MOVIE

Establishing Shot

It is important to have an establishing shot. This is a shot that shows where everything is. Without this establishing shot, it is difficult for an audience to know where everything is and they could end up getting confused.

So, for our house of cards building movie, we need an establishing shot of the character sat at the table. We need to see them sat in a chair. We need to see the table and the pile of cards on the table.

Long Shots

Long shots are where the camera is a long way from the characters and background, but we can

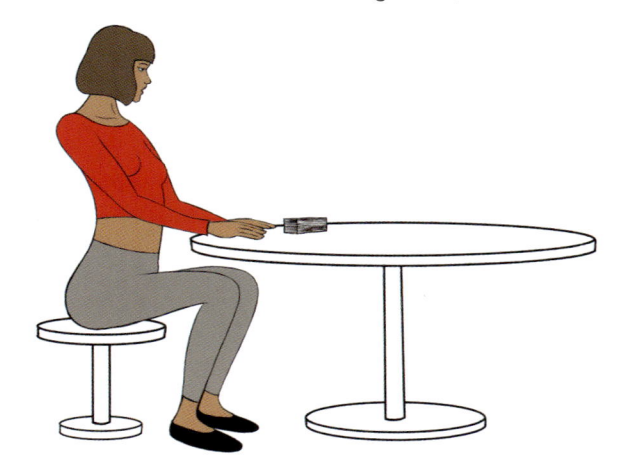

An establishing shot contains all that is needed for the scene that will take place.

HOW TO MAKE AN ANIMATED FILM 151

A long shot is a view from a long way off and can also be an establishing shot.

A medium shot gives an idea of where the character is and what props are near to them.

see where everything is (this is usually how you construct an establishing shot).

Medium Shots

Medium shots are where we are closer to the action, but can still see the props that a character might be dealing with (the character holding a pack of cards), or where there are two characters in the scene at the same time.

Close-Up Shots

Close up shots are either where we see the expression on a character's face, or we see what the character is interested in or looking at (the pack of cards in the hand).

A close-up shot gives a lot more information about the emotions of the character.

When composing a shot, it is better to set everything up following the rule of thirds.

Composing a Shot

The Rule of Thirds

The simplest way to put together a shot is to have the most important thing in the middle of the screen. This would make sure that the audience is looking at the thing you want it to. Unfortunately, this would be really boring. It is best to arrange your character to occupy an area that is one-third closer to one side of the screen and two-thirds away from the other side of the screen. This gives an asymmetrical composition.

You can use the background to guide the audience to look at the most important part by using perspective lines. Make sure that the area of the background is less cluttered behind the character, so that the performance is easy to watch.

Do Not Cross the Line

You must make a movie that works with the establishing shot. Once you have done the establishing shot, all the camera angles must relate to this.

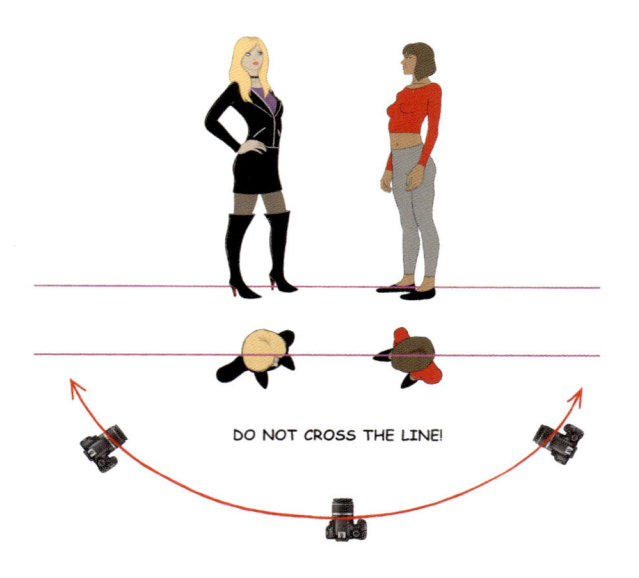

Crossing the line in film-making is a very bad thing to do, unless you want to confuse your audience.

Think of your establishing shot as being a stage and the camera must always stay where the audience is. Imagine that there is a line between two people on screen or one person and the object that they are looking at. So, when you do a close-up of either character, they must be facing in the correct direction relating to the establishing shot.

Close-ups should work with the establishing shot and should not cross the line.

The camera must never be pointed from the back of the stage at the characters on it. (The camera can be in any position on the correct side of the line.) Doing this is called crossing the line. If you cross the line, the audience will become confused.

Direction of the Movie

Generally, most movies have a direction to them. If someone is going on a quest, they will usually travel from the left-hand side of the screen to the right-hand side. Each shot will show a character entering a shot from the left and leaving to the right to give a feeling of continuity. The reason for this is that we read from left to right. (In Arabic or Japanese, one reads from right to left, therefore Arabic and Japanese films tend to have a direction that goes from right to left.)

You may also find that the direction of a shot is related to geography. For example, a ship leaving Southampton on its way to New York will exit from left to right and arrive in New York entering from left to right. An aeroplane taking off at Heathrow Airport, London, and flying to Beijing will take off

Most movies have general direction to them. Try to keep the direction of a movie consistent.

Ship leaves UK

arrives in New York

A ship travelling to a location should relate to a map of the world.

Takes off in London

Lands in Beijing

An aeroplane flying to a location should relate to a map of the world.

from left to right and land from left to right. It does not matter what direction you use, keep it consistent from shot to shot.

HOW TO MAKE AN ANIMATIC USING AN EDITING PROGRAM

An animatic is a movie where the storyboard pictures are shown, one after the other, as a series of stills. Each image should be shown for a certain amount of time that will allow for the action to take place. This can initially be very difficult to work out. As a basic guide, make each storyboard image last on screen at least one-third longer than you think it should. The reason for this is that it is much easier (and quicker) for an audience to work out what is happening from a series of still images than from moving images. When you start animating things, you have to slow everything down. You could think of each of the images for a storyboard as being like key positions, but loosely drawn.

You will need to use an editing program to do this. There are many to choose from, such as Adobe Premiere Pro, Avid, Final Cut Pro and DaVinci Resolve (which is free). Take each of the images into the program, place them on the timeline, give them a certain amount of frames for each image and keep playing it back to see how it is working.

HOW TO MAKE AN ANIMATED FILM 155

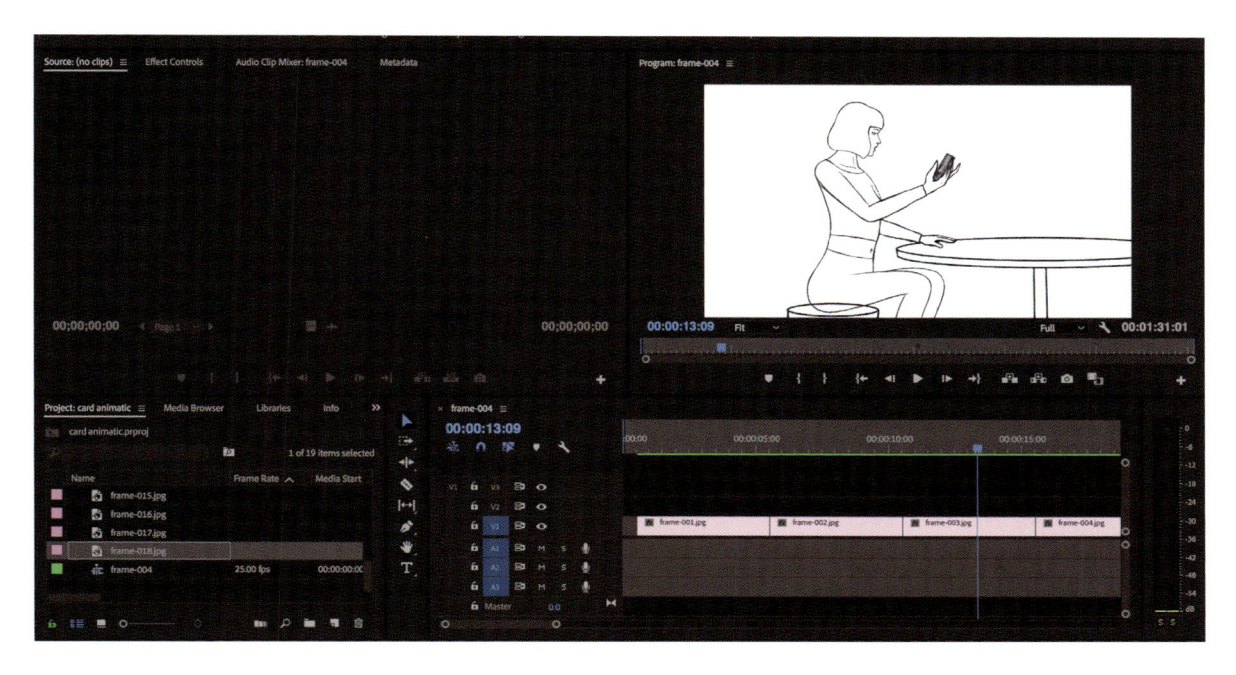

An animatic is assembled in an editing program.

LAYOUT AND PRE-VIS

Once you have done the animatic, it is time to provide more accurate artwork for your project. If your production is a 2D project, this is the time to draw up the backgrounds accurately and also (on another level) draw the basic positions of your character during a shot. When these are done, insert them into your animatic by replacing the animatic images with your *layouts*. Very gradually, your animatic will change from a series of storyboard drawings to a series of layouts.

With puppet animation, this is the time to build your sets and create your puppets. Set up the camera and position your puppet in the sets as a series of still pictures, so that you can make sure

Layout for 2D animation setting up everything ready for a professional production.

Layout for puppet animation, making sure that the composition is correct and the audience can see everything.

the design of the camera angles works well. When these are done, insert them into your animatic by replacing the animatic images with photographs of your sets and puppets.

For 3D animation, build the sets and also have a basic character that can be positioned in the sets for the key positions they need to do during the movie. As with puppet animation, this will ensure that the design of the camera angles looks correct. This process is often called Pre-Vis (Pre-Visual). When these are done, insert them into your animatic by replacing the animatic images with the images of your backgrounds and characters in position.

ANIMATE THE FILM

Once the layouts (or Pre-Vis) have been done, you can get on with the animation. With 2D and 3D animation, do the key positions first. As you do each shot, insert it into your animatic by replacing the layout shots with the key animation in your editing program.

It is at this point that you will find out how long a piece of action takes to do. Sometimes you may need to make a shot longer in order to fit in the movement. Sometimes you may need to make a shot shorter. You may also have to insert another shot to make things clearer, or take out shots, or

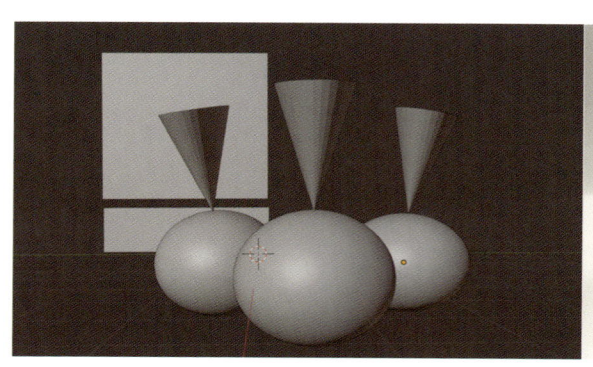

Pre-Vis for 3D animation works out all the problems that might come up with the full production of the project.

change them completely. A movie is constantly changing at this stage.

With puppet animation, you have to animate straight ahead, so you animate the shot completely. You may need to have several goes at getting a shot right. Once the shots are animated, insert them into your movie using your editing program, replacing the layout shots. As you cut them together, you may find that you need to change the shots by making them longer or shorter, or by adding extra shots to make the movie work better.

DO THE IN-BETWEENS

Once all the key positions have been established in 2D and 3D animation, start doing the movements between the key positions. This is done by in-between drawings in drawn animation, or by adjusting the curves in digital 2D or 3D animation (or inserting more key positions into the animation).

As you finish each shot, insert it into your movie in your editing program to see how it is working. If shots need to be made longer or shorter, change them.

This is not relevant for puppet animation, because you are working straight ahead.

COLOUR YOUR ANIMATION

With drawn animation, it is at this stage that you colour everything in. If working on paper or cel, you will need to get your colours out and start colouring. If using a drawn digital program like TVPaint, you will need to colour each drawing on the computer. If you are using a 2D cut-out type program, a 3D computer program, or puppet animation, your characters will be coloured already, so you can skip this stage.

Insert each of the coloured shots into your movie, replacing the uncoloured shots. You should now almost have a completed movie. But what about sound?

SOUND

About 50 per cent of what you take in from an animated movie is sound. Sound is therefore very important in establishing the atmosphere and feel of a film. All editing programs have the capacity to add several layers of sound. The first thing is to work out the atmosphere of each scene.

If the scene is outdoors, where is it set? If it is on a busy road, you need the sound of traffic. If it is in the countryside, you need the sound of birds and

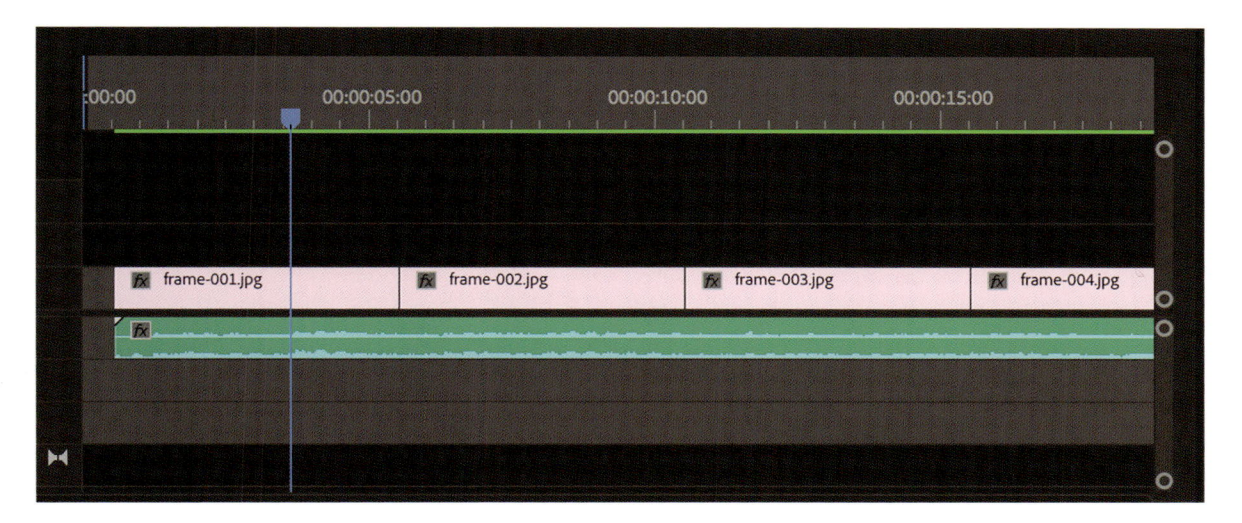

Sound is so important in an animated movie – here are the sound layers in an editing program.

wind. If it is set at a beach, you need the sound of waves crashing on the shore. There must be something to describe where the situation is.

If the scene is indoors, you could have the sound of distant traffic if it is a house in a city, or the sound of a television, or the hum of air-conditioning. If it is in a kitchen, the hum of a fridge can work well. Try to think what sound sums up the place in which your movie is set.

Once the atmosphere for each scene has been established, you will need to work out the main sound effects – sounds such as doors opening, dropping a glass, shutting a lid all need to be put in place. If there is dialogue, that will need to be added too. This needs to be louder than the atmosphere and the sound effects.

MUSIC

Music can really add to the mood of a movie. But be careful not to just stick in a piece of existing music to a film for the entire duration. A properly scored film will have music that changes as the feel of the movie changes. Happy sequences have joyful music and scary sequences have sinister music. All of this adds up to the overall mood and effect of the movie.

VFX AND POST-PRODUCTION

If your project needs explosions, smoke, sparkles, fog, water or something to give it some depth, this is usually the last thing you do. Special effects can either be animated or done digitally with a program like Adobe After Effects. They can add that finishing touch to a movie, which sets it apart.

FINAL RENDERING

Once all of these elements have been put together in your editing program, you can now render a final movie. An .mpg4 is perfectly adequate to produce a movie to upload to any video site like YouTube or Vimeo, but if you want to show your film at a cinema you may have to produce a DCP (Digital Cinema Package) file so that it can be shown at very high quality. You can do this yourself with an editing program, but often it is better to get a professional company to do it for you.

DOCUMENT THE PROCESS OF MAKING YOUR MOVIE

While making your movie, it is a good idea to document the process by taking photos and sketches and publishing these to a social media platform, such as Instagram, Tumblr or Facebook. This way, you can generate some interest in your movie – which brings us to the last chapter!

Documenting your film is very important.

8
PROMOTING YOUR ANIMATION AND WORKING IN ANIMATION

Once you have made your animation masterpiece, what do you do with it? Get it seen! You could just show it to your friends, family and loved ones, or you could try to get the whole world to see it. One of the best ways to get recognition for your film is to enter animation and film festivals.

FILM FESTIVALS

Every week of the year, there will be a film festival happening somewhere in the world. These are places where film and animation fans can see the latest movies in a cinema setting. You need to enter your film into these festivals and can find out about them by doing a quick internet search. There are websites dedicated to giving you information about all the latest festivals happening around the world.

Some film festivals are tiny and may just be a few films being shown in an arts centre or the back of a bar. Other festivals are huge and very prestigious. If you get accepted into the competition of a festival, the organizers may pay for you to visit (or at least pay for some accommodation and living expenses). Even if you're not accepted, it can be really great visiting a film or animation festival, because you get to meet other animators and film-makers and can learn a huge amount from them.

What You Need to Enter an Animation Festival

In order to enter an animation or film festival, you will need your film and an Electronic Press Kit (EPK). An Electronic Press Kit will consist of:

- a biography of yourself
- a picture of yourself
- a selection of stills from your film (three or more)
- a synopsis of your film
- a list of credits for your film
- a list of your contact details.

Nothing beats seeing your film projected in a cinema.

160 PROMOTING YOUR ANIMATION AND WORKING IN ANIMATION

Credits
Director; Stephen Roberts
Writer; Stephen Roberts
Producer; Stephen Roberts
Key Cast; Jim Howick,
Stephen Roberts

Contact details;
xxxxxxxxxxxxxxxxxxxxx
xxxxxxxxxxxxxxxxxxxxx
xxxxxxxxxxxxxxxxxxxxx
xxxxxxxxxxxxxxxxxxxxx

Biography
Steve has been doing animation for over 35 years. He's painted cels, traced, cleaned up, inbetweened and animated. He's even used a computer on occasion. He's had films shown at festivals all over the world and won an award or 2 as well. He currently teaches at Central St Martins (animation of course).
He also has a motorbike and sidecar, several old bicycles and likes to fly model aeroplanes.

Synopsis
In 1885, John Kemp Starley invented the modern bicycle. This piece of transport revolutionised the world.

"J K Starley, The Man Who Put the World On Wheels". Charts the life of Starley and the effect his invention had on the world. How ordinary people could explore the world for the first time. How it led to a huge diversification of the gene pool. How it led to women's liberation and the modern feminist movement and how it also caused one of the first banking crises.
The film has 4 songs and is a bit of a tribute to the 1975 film "Great" by Bob Godfrey.

An EPK (or Electronic Press Kit) is a vital part of entering your film into film festivals.

Remember to take postcards of your film and give them to as many people as possible.

Enter your film into as many film festivals as possible. Some festivals are for animation only; others will have a specific section for animation. Some are free to enter; others cost money. Definitely enter your film into all of the free festivals and then be selective about the ones that cost money. There are websites to which you can upload your film and all of this information, then send it to many festivals without having to do this for every single festival that you find. A good example is FilmFreeway at filmfreeway.com.

Animation festivals are great places to meet other people who work in animation and a fantastic place to network and learn new ideas. They not only show films, but offer workshops, lectures and exhibitions that can inspire you and help with your animation career and practice.

Make sure that you have either postcards or business cards to hand out to people when you meet them. These should have artwork from your movie and details of your website, Instagram, Tumblr or Facebook page, YouTube or Vimeo site, telephone number and email, just in case they need to contact you at some point. And don't just limit yourself to animation festivals, as many film festivals have animation sections and also will accept animated films into their programme.

LOCAL OPPORTUNITIES

There is a good chance that someone living near you is also making animation or short films. See if there are any groups near you who organize film shows and events. In London, there is the London Animation Club and also Bring Your Own Animation, who organize events in the upstairs rooms of pubs once a month. These are great places to meet people and exchange ideas and information, as well as seeing films you would not normally see. If there is nothing like this near you, you could have a go at setting something up – you never know whom you might meet!

ONLINE PROMOTION

Another way to show your movie off to the world is to put it on to video-sharing platforms like YouTube, Vimeo or Daily Motion (there are lots of other video-sharing websites; find the best one for your country). Having a personal website is also a good way to promote your movie, as it can contain artwork and images as well as your film or a trailer. Use a name for your website that is simple and easy to communicate to other people. For example, 'yourname.com' will be easy for people to remember you and what you do.

Set up an art-based image-sharing platform like Instagram, Tumblr, DeviantArt or Facebook, to which you can post the production details of your film. Make sure that you link to your Video channels and website. The more you share, the more followers you get and the more people will be interested in watching your work.

Join online communities on the web that are involved in animation, follow blogs of animators and set up a blog of your own. Try to get as much feedback on your work as possible and develop as many contacts as you can. There are lots of people out there that would love to help you.

HOW TO GET A JOB IN ANIMATION

Animation studios, graphic design studios, television companies and arts organizations are always looking for new animators to work for them. If they don't know you exist, they are not likely to employ you, so you need to contact them and send them a link to a showreel. Do an internet search and find any animation studios near you. Find out the name of the person to whom you should send a showreel and then send them an email, requesting that they have a look at your reel (provide a link to it on Vimeo, YouTube or other sites).

How to Make a Showreel

A showreel is a short movie that shows the animation you can do and how brilliant you are. It should be between thirty seconds and a minute long. It should consist of short clips of your animation cut together with a piece of music (try to get a copyright-free piece of music). Make sure that you put your best bits of animation into the showreel and always start with something particularly good. When you have sorted out a reel, show it to people, get feedback, add things, take things away, keep improving it.

When you feel ready, contact animation studios and find out to whom you should send a showreel (look on their website or ring them up). Email the person in question and send them a link to your showreel and include a CV. Don't ask for a job directly; ask for feedback on your reel. Start trying to build up a relationship with different studios. One of them might just spot something in what you do and give you some work.

WORKING IN ANIMATION

When working on an animated film of your own, you can do everything (or you have to do everything!), but a lot of studios have a certain *pipeline* system in the way that they work. That is, they have particular ways of giving you the work and where you should save it when it is done.

When given a piece of work to do, try to get as much input from the director as possible before you start animating. Then, either video yourself doing the action, or do a series of thumbnail sketches and show them to the director. Do they like your idea for the shot? If yes, great, you can get on with it. If not, redo the video or sketches until you get the thumbs up.

Then do the key positions. Show them to the director as a movie, timed out. If it is drawn animation, this would be in the form of a line test. If it is 2D digital, you would show a series of key positions. If it is puppet animation, you could do a pop-through (a series of key positions of your puppet doing the basic move, with each image given an appropriate number of frames). You would then have to reanimate it all the way through later, using the information for timing from the pop-through to help your animation. If it is in 3D, show your key positions, but set the curves to Linear or Stepped, so that they play back without any of the animation done by the computer (it distracts from the animation you are trying to do).

Once this is approved, you can go on to the in-betweening. With drawn animation, you may be lucky enough to have an assistant animator or in-betweener. You must provide them with timing charts, so that they know how to do the in-between drawings. If it is digital 2D, you may also need to pass it on to an assistant, or, if it is a cut-out type program, you can adjust the in-betweens done by the computer with the Curve Editor. With puppet animation, you are on your own! You will have to animate the whole thing yourself, using your pop-through as a guide. With 3D animation, you can put in extra key positions and also adjust the in-betweens provided by your software, by manipulating the curves in the Curve Editor.

Show this to the director. You may need to fiddle with things a bit to make it work better, or have to redo parts of the animation to keep the director happy. Be prepared to redo your animation quite a few times in order to keep the director and the ultimate clients happy. In feature films, some shots may be re-animated twenty or thirty times before being eventually approved.

In the professional world of animation, the jobs are divided up among lots of different specialists. This can be the most efficient way to produce an animated film on time and on budget.

The Different Jobs in Animation

Some jobs in the animation industry are common to all animation techniques. They are as follows.

Producer A producer liaises with all the people involved in making an animated film, such as the clients (or 'money people'), the director and the writer. They have to keep everything on track. They will also be in charge of *pitching* projects to a client.

Director The director oversees the creative side of things. They will guide the storyboard artists, character designers and animators. They may also be involved in the script.

Animation director An animation director will be in charge of the animation on the project. They are the people you will be dealing with as an animator. They are more concerned with the movement than the overall project.

Scriptwriter The scriptwriter will come up with the story and flesh out the characters. They need to write for animation. Animation tends to need longer scripts to achieve the same effect as a live-action film, because you can fit so much more into an animated film than its live-action equivalent. With live action, if you need a new set or exterior shot, these have to be either built or arranged at great expense. A new location in animation can be made much more cheaply and quickly by just creating a new background. Consequently, animation can cover a lot more ground in a shorter space of time than a live-action film.

Storyboard artist The storyboard artist takes the script and turns it into a series of pictures that sum up the story. They are also responsible for the camera angles, timing and *pacing* of the film.

First, a *beat board* is put together. This is a series of illustrations that sums up the feel and colour of the film. It is what you show the client to give them an idea of what the final film might look like.

Then you produce a rough storyboard to work out the basics of what will happen. This will often be done in conjunction with, or by, the scriptwriter. The drawings will be really rough, so as to iron out all the initial problems (you would not show these drawings to the client). After this, you can produce a more detailed storyboard that can be turned into an animatic. The animatic would include a voice track and basic sound effects so as to make the story progress.

Character designer The character designer will do concept work for the characters, then turn them into model sheets for the animators, the puppet-makers or the 3D modellers to work from.

VFX A visual-effects animator will animate any effects, such as smoke, water, mist, flames or explosions. These could be done using either traditional techniques or digital methods. They would then be superimposed over the character animation.

Compositor All of the various elements have to be put together using a *compositing* program such as After Effects, Shake or Nuke. In the old days, this was the kind of job done by a rostrum camera person. They would shoot all the elements together (effects levels, characters and backgrounds) under a camera. Elements could also be combined by reshooting film with the effects levels in place (for example, the shadows of the animated characters in *Who Framed Roger Rabbit*, which would leave certain parts of the character underexposed to produce a shadow).

Editor Although most of the editing of an animated film is done at the storyboard stage, an editor would be in charge of the dynamics of the film-making in an animated film. They should be involved in the storyboarding process to advise on the flow of the film, but also can make suggestions at a later point in order to make the film more expressive. An editor could ask for additional shots to be animated to complete the film. In the past, an editor would have filled out the sound column in the x-sheet to show where the dialogue would be.

Sound designer Because nothing is real in an animated film, a sound designer can really add to its depth. They would start with an atmosphere track for each shot (for example, if the shot is in the countryside, it would need the sound of a breeze, birds singing, leaves rustling), then add sound effects and foley in order to give a sound dimension to the film. (Foley sounds are the reproduction of everyday sound effects, such as a squeaking door, footsteps or the sound of cloth when it moves.) Spot sound effects without an atmosphere can sound very artificial.

Composer Animation is very reliant on music to carry it along. A composer should create music that helps with the mood of each scene. Animation came into its own with the invention of synchronized sound, whereas the introduction of sound into live-action movies limited the scope of film-making until microphones could be made smaller and more manoeuvrable.

Jobs Specific to 2D Drawn Animation

Layout artist The layout artist takes the storyboards and turns them into an exact plan of the backgrounds and also composes where the characters will be during the shot. These are then given to an animator, with an x-sheet that has been 'slugged out' (directions added into the action column) and the dialogue (if any) placed into the sound column.

2D animator The animator takes the layouts and does the key positions. They will also give a guide, in the form of a timing chart, to the assistant animator about how many drawings need to be done between each key position. The key drawings may only be done in rough with a blue pencil, or perhaps the first drawing of the sequence will be cleaned up, to show how the rest of the shot should look.

Assistant animator The assistant animator will often redraw the key positions to make sure that they look like the characters and will clean the keys up for the final line. They will do the major in-betweens (the breakdowns) and clean those up as well. (The assistant needs to be a better draftsperson than the animator.)

In-betweener The in-betweener will take the drawings done by the assistant and do the in-between drawings and clean them up.

Background artist The background artist takes the layouts and produces the backgrounds from them.

Cel tracer and painter In the past, the drawings would have been traced by a cel tracer. Their job was to provide the line that would be seen by the audience. A good cel tracer could improve the animation no end, while a bad tracer could destroy the look of a character. A cel painter would paint the cels with cel paint on the back of the cel.

In the 1960s, the Xerox process was introduced, in which the drawings were copied on to the cels. This was quite a crude process to start with, but the animators loved it because their drawings were shown directly on screen. Later technology allowed drawings to be scanned into a computer to be coloured with a digital colouring program. As a result, these roles are considered a little old-fashioned but are still used in the animation industry for certain projects.

Jobs Specific to 2D Digital Animation

The jobs associated with a drawn animation program such as TVPaint are similar to traditional drawn animation, with the exception of a colourist. Today, a colourist will take the digital drawings and colour each of them by just touching and filling the area to be coloured with a computer tablet and pen.

Jobs Specific to Puppet Animation

Puppet builder The puppet builder will build the puppets. This job could be divided up into armature maker, sculptor, casting, costume maker and even people who do the hair styling!

Set builder Set builders will build the sets and could also make props, furniture and anything else needed for the production. Often sets have to be designed so that an animator can get near to the puppets in order to animate them.

Lighting person The lighting person will set up the lights and camera, consulting the director and storyboards to get as close to the director's vision as possible. This could involve lighting for effects as well as making the character look three-dimensional.

Puppet animator The puppet animator animates the puppets, one frame at a time. They would have to act out the shot first as LAVS, show this to the director to make sure it is what they want and then animate a pop-through (if needed) and finally animate the whole shot.

Jobs Specific to 3D Computer Animation

Pre-Vis Pre-Vis artists put together the movie as a simplified 3D version in order to work out the camera moves in 3D, as well as the positions of the characters and backgrounds in a shot. This has become a very important part of big Hollywood effects movies, where a lot of different elements have to be put together. The whole structure and editing of the movie can be arranged at this point.

Modeller The modeller will model the characters in a 3D program such as ZBrush. They have to be able to construct a 3D character so that it deforms correctly at the joints, as well as being able to pull the correct faces and mouth shapes needed for the production.

Rigging A rigger will put bones in the character, create control handles and make sure that the mesh works with the skeleton. This will involve *weighting* the mesh, so that it moves correctly with the bones. It could also involve the clothing and any other object that the character would have to manipulate.

Texturing A texture artist will apply the texture and colours to the 3D models. These textures must move with the model and not be too distracting from the movement.

3D set builder The 3D set builder and prop maker will build the set and the environments, such as trees, walls, props, rocks and grass.

3D animator The 3D animator will animate the character. Generally, they will do all the animation, from the key positions to the manipulating of the curves that polish the animation.

Technical director A technical director will make sure that the character fits into the background correctly and also sort out the million and one things that need to be done to get the shot correct.

Lighting A lighting director will set up the lights in order to illuminate the shot correctly. They will also be in charge of creating lighting effects like lightning, the glow from fires and any other unique examples of lighting.

Rendering A huge team will organize the rendering of the shots.

There are lots of other jobs that need to be done in 3D. Nobody can do them all (unless you are making your own film).

As you can see, there is a huge amount of jobs to be done on an animated film and you would be expected to specialize in one of them. Animation is an expanding industry and has never been so popular. There are lots of opportunities to make animation to entertain, inform and sell things.

So, give it a go!

Animation can be one of the most fun things in the world!

GLOSSARY OF KEY TERMS

Alpha channel The part of a digital image that is transparent.

Animatic An animatic is a movie that consists of a series of still images. Each still image is given a certain amount of time to be seen. The goal of an animatic is to define the timing for a piece of moving image. When used with a soundtrack and dialogue, they are a quick and easy way to get a sense of a finished piece of moving image. Animatics are created by playing a series of images in order and changing the timing on each frame. Timings changes are used to create a sense of pace.

Animator An animator is the person who is responsible for producing the animation.

Aspect ratio The ratio of height to width of the frame expressed as a ratio (for example, 4:3, or 16:9). For a standard (square) television picture – for every four units wide, the picture is three units high (768 × 576 pixels). For a newer HD television (rectangle) picture – for every sixteen units wide, the picture is nine units high (1,920 × 1,080 pixels); 2k and 4k are 2,000 pixels and 4,000 pixels wide, respectively.

Assistant animator An assistant animator is the person who takes the animator's drawings and cleans them up to make sure that they look like the characters. They will clean up the keys for the final line. They will do the major in-betweens (the breakdowns) and clean those up as well. (The assistant needs to be a better draftsperson than the animator.)

Beat board A beat board is a sequence of illustrations that sums up the look and feel of the film and also tells the story. A beat board is not necessarily exactly how the film will be edited or paced, but is a good way to give an idea of how it will look. It is particularly good to show to clients, who may not understand something a bit more technical, such as a storyboard. These images could be edited together as a movie, to make a beat-board animatic.

Breakdown A breakdown is a major in-between image between two key positions. Generally, this term is used in traditional drawn animation.

Clean up Animation drawings by the key and in-between animators can sometimes be rough, with a lot of movement in the line. A clean-up animator tidies that all up and brings the animation down to just a single, clean line.

Compositing Compositing is completed in a piece of software such as Adobe After Effects. It is the combining of two or more separate elements into one, for example compositing the character, background and foreground elements together. Alpha channels and layers are used.

Cycle A cycle is a series of drawings or key poses that are designed to hook-up and be repeated as many times as required. For example, a walk cycle of a character walking on the spot.

Dope sheet Same as an x-sheet (exposure sheet). Information on how to shoot a piece of animation is contained on a dope sheet. When the animation is completed and the dope sheet filled out, it would be passed on to a camera person to shoot the animation. The word 'dope' is an early twentieth-century slang term for information.

Flicking This is where you have two drawings on your light box and you need to draw an in-between drawing between them. This in-between drawing is placed on top of the two finished drawings. You interleave the three drawings between your fingers and, as you are drawing, you flick the pages to see the movement. This is done by looking at the first drawing, then looking at the in-between drawing, then looking at the final drawing in quick succession.

Flipping Flipping is where you flip the drawings you have done one after another in order to give the impression of movement. It is a good way to check if your animated drawings are working correctly.

Frame Animation is made up of a series of individual frames, which, when played back together, create the illusion of movement.

Frame rate The speed at which frames progress in an animation. Measured usually as frames per second (fps). Since most traditional animation is typically done on twos (that is, each drawing is shown for TWO frames), a second of drawn animation will consist of twelve drawings per second. 3D animation will have twenty-four frames per second.

Graticule Also known as a field guide. Oblong frame lines indicate the desired framing of a scene. It is basically a box inside which you keep your animation. You can have a field guide that indicates a 4:3 aspect ratio for older television displays and a 16:9 ratios for wider HD displays. You will also find field guides in most animation apps.

In-between An in-between is an image between the key images. This refers mainly to traditional drawn animation, but the in-betweens on a computer animation app could also be referred to as in-betweens. These can also be called tweens.

In-betweener A person who does the in-between drawings. An in-betweener should be very familiar with the construction, design and line quality of the character being animated and be able to replicate that character accurately.

Key position/frame/pose A key position is a drawing or image on a computer app that is the main position during the movement of a piece of animation. When the key images are done, images must be drawn or manipulated to produce the complete animation. These could be breakdowns and in-between drawings, or, with a computer animation app, they could be manipulated with a form of curve or graph editor.

Layout and layout drawings When the storyboard and animatic have been approved, a layout artist will draw up the backgrounds and position the characters for each shot on separate layers of paper or digital. A copy of the background layout will be sent to the background artist to be painted up. A copy of the background layout and the character positions will be given to an animator to be animated.

Lieca reel This is a very technical version of an animatic, shot on film. The Lieca is part of pre-production – layout drawings are captured and cut together to length and with dialogue. Every single camera move is reproduced accurately, as well as basic key positions of characters. This is done in an editing suite by an editor and accompanied by the director. This process is meant to lock down the pacing of the show or animation piece. A movie file is created and distributed to the production teams to watch, get a feel for what the director is looking for and to use as a reference. This is more part of the traditional drawn animation process, shot on film.

Limited animation This is pose-to-pose animation with the least amount of in-betweens used. Actions are usually quick and held for longer periods of time during dialogue. A character may remain still for a long period of time, but a small amount of animation (the movement of the hair, blowing in the wind) will keep the character looking alive. Lip movements and blinks help with this too.

Line tester A line tester is a device used for testing drawn animation, in which the raw, uncoloured drawn lines are shot to see if the animation is working correctly. A line tester could be a film camera shooting the drawings; the film is then developed and played back on a projector. A line tester could be a video camera connected to a video recorder that can record single frames. It could also be a computer with a digital camera connected to it and a line-test app used to play back the animation.

Lip-sync The animation of a character's mouth to match the recorded dialogue provided. The sound is broken down first and noted on an x-sheet. The animator then interprets this information to produce the animated actions of the character and mouth shapes.

Mirroring This is when a character or object that is symmetrical moves with both sides in sync and in unison. This mirrored appearance typically appears unnatural and incorrect.

Motion capture This is where the movement of a human can be interpreted by a computer and then applied to a computer animation character. Motion capture tends to need a large amount of work later to make it look convincing.

Moving hold A series of frames where a character is relatively motionless. Usually there is very subtle movement to keep the character 'alive', including blinks and changes in eye direction. This can also happen when there is a very quick movement of the character, but the audience needs to see the expression on the character's face. The character moves through the shot quickly, but the facial expression stays the same.

Onion skinning This term is used in various animation apps on a computer. When drawing frames one by one it can be hard to make smooth animations. Getting the timing and positioning right is difficult. Onion skinning shows you a semi-transparent version of previous and upcoming frames so that you can draw the current frame appropriately.

Pacing Pacing is the rhythm of a sequence, scene or entire film. It is the speed at which actions occur. All animation should have a rhythm to it – some bits should be fast, other parts slow. If everything happens at the same pace, it can make for very boring viewing.

Pan A camera move, in which the camera moves along its horizontal axis; pans to the right or left.

Peg bar A flat piece of plastic or metal with two or three pins on it that register animation paper together.

Pipeline The system that is used by a studio to produce an animated movie (who does what, where things are saved, how you show work to the director and so on). Most studios seem to have slightly different pipelines, so if you are working at a particular studio, make sure you are familiar with their pipeline!

Pitching When a client has a project that they want to make, they will ask animation studios or individual animation directors to pitch on the project. They will supply a brief, then the companies or directors come up with ideas and designs for the brief and pitch their ideas to the client.

Point of view shot Also referred to as P.O.V. – a camera angle that approximates what one of the characters in a scene would be seeing.

Pop-through A puppet animator will move the puppet through a series of key positions, shooting them with a camera and computer for each key position. They will then re-time them in their stop-frame app by adding a certain amount of frames to each image. A note will be made of the timing, then the animator will re-animate the shot straight through, bearing in mind the timing from the pop-through.

Post-production This refers to everything following the animation stage, including editing, sound editing, sound mixing, effects and titles.

Render farm A render farm is a bank of computers dedicated to rendering images to produce the shots for the final movie.

Rendering When a piece of animation is completed on a computer animation program, the shot needs to be rendered. Each frame of the shot needs to be made into a full coloured image that will make up the movie. The rendering could be done with the animation program, or using a piece of third-party software. These images can take a long time to render, so sometimes are done with a render farm.

Rigging In 3D animation, this is where the bones are placed into a character and the skin of the character linked to these bones.

Rolling Rolling is where five animation drawings in succession are placed on to a peg bar on a light box. The animator interleaves the drawings between their hand, then moves the hand in an arc-like motion while looking at each drawing in succession. This will give an illusion of movement and is a way to check how the animation is moving.

Rotoscope The rotoscope is a device invented by Max Fleischer that allows an animator to base a character's animated movements on a film of a live-action actor performing the same movements. The original film is used as a reference for the animator's work. Film of a real person moving is projected on to a screen and an animator can trace these movements on to paper.

Stop-motion animation This is frame by frame filmmaking using small-scale practical sets, props and real lighting.

Storyboard A storyboard is like a comic strip. It is a sequence of images that sum up everything that will happen in a movie from start to finish. It will include different major positions that are occupied by a character, camera angles, special effects, transitions from shot to shot and information about the sound, music and dialogue. These can be edited in an editing app to make an animatic.

Strobing A visually distracting jittering effect can occur when large, highly contrasting images move quickly through frames. You can also get strobing when a similar shaped part of a character's body occupies a position held by another part of the body on a previous frame – for example, the arms on a character in a walk cycle.

Thumbnail sketch A thumbnail is a very small image or sketch used as a reference for a final image. A series of thumbnail sketches can be produced quickly to show other people the ideas you have for the animation you will produce.

Tilt shot Also known as 'Dutch tilt'. It is a shot in which the camera has been rotated upward or downward.

Time code The numeric display that corresponds to the running time in video, usually two digits each for the hour/minute/second/frame, for example 00:22:02:29.

Timing chart A timing chart is a drawn graphic that indicates how in-between drawings should be spaced between key positions. It is drawn at the bottom of a drawn key position and refers to the following drawings.

Tracking shot A shot where the camera moves, similar to a dolly shot, but where a constant distance from the subject is maintained, following the action – for example, a camera following a character walking along.

Tweens *See* In-between.

Two shot A shot in which two characters appear together.

Voice-over The narration track that the audience hears, but which is not heard by the characters in the scene. When using a voice-over, you can be a lot more experimental with the images in the movie.

Weighting In 3D animation, once a character has been built and the bones placed within it, the skin of the character needs to be weighted to the bones. That is, the skin must bend and fold in a way that is natural and looks good, so the skin is weighted in such a way to produce this.

X-sheet *See* Dope sheet.

Zip pan A fast pan in which the visuals are deliberately blurred for effect.

FURTHER READING AND RESOURCES

FOR THIS BOOK

charactermation.org

DRAWN ANIMATION SUPPLIES

chromacolour.co.uk
lightfootltd.com

2D DIGITAL ANIMATION

adobe.com
animationpaper.com
celaction.com
kdanmobile.com/animation-desk
krita.org
pencil2d.org
procreate.art
roughanimator.com
synfig.org
toonboom.com
tvpaint.com

PUPPET ANIMATION

animationsupplies.net
animationtoolkit.co.uk
animatordv.com
dragonframe.com
jwmm.co.uk
milliput.com
newclay.co.uk
stickybones.com
stopmotionpro.com
stopmotionstudio.com
tech4learning.com/frames
tiranti.co.uk

3D ANIMATION

autodesk.com
  (3D Studio Max and Maya)
blender.org
lightwave3d.com

ANIMATION FESTIVALS

animation-festivals.com
animationalerts.com
annecy.org
bfi.org.uk
filmfreeway.com

ANIMATION RESOURCES

animationguild.org/keyframe
animationmagazine.net
animationworld.net
awn.com
cartoonbrew.com
cinefex.com
fxguide.com
nfb.ca/animation/
showmetheanimation.com
skwigly.co.uk
vfxmagazine.com
vfxvoice.com

ANIMATION FACEBOOK PAGES

facebook.com/groups/83549374968
  (London Animation Club)
facebook.com/groups/BYOALondon
  (Bring Your Own Animation)
facebook.com/londonanimation

EDITING SOFTWARE

adobe.com
audacityteam.org
blackmagicdesign.com/products/davinciresolve/

COPYRIGHT FREE RESOURCES

audiohub.com
archive.org
freesfx.com
freesound.org
freesoundslibrary.com
pexels.com
pixabay.com
unsplash.com

INDEX

a: as a vowel 80
acting
    acting exercise 72
    acting out 37, 38, 61
    acting styles 62, 63
    acting with dialogue 79
ah: as vowel 80
anatomy
    bird anatomy 50
    human anatomy 30
    snake anatomy 53
    quadruped anatomy 48
anger
    body acting 66, 67, 69
    facial acting 73
animals
    birds 50
    drawing animals 48
    fish 52
    follow through of tails 46, 47
    in history of animation 10, 13, 16, 17, 18, 19, 20
    puppet animals 111
    snakes 53
    quadrupeds 54, 55, 56
animation paper 82, 83
ankle 34
anticipation 44, 45
appeal 48
arcs
    bouncing balls 25, 27, 29
    human anatomy 30, 42
arm
    2D drawn animation 87
    3D animation 132, 134
    anatomy 30, 31, 32, 33, 34
    animation principles 36, 39, 40, 41, 45
    cut out animation 92
    fluid animation 95
    human anatomy in comparison to quadrupeds 54
    human locomotion 58, 60
    in history of animation 15
    performance 63, 66, 67, 68, 69, 70,
    puppet animation 104, 106, 107, 109, 110, 112
    solid drawing 48
armature
    3D animation 136, 165
    in history of animation 17, 18
    puppet animation 118, 119, 122

b: as consonant 81
background
    2D animation 86, 87, 91
    3D animation 138, 139, 145
    cut out animation 92, 94
    digital drawn animation 98, 100
    film making 150, 152, 155
    in animation history 15
    industry 163, 164, 165, 167, 168
    puppet animation 124, 125
    staging a background 42, 43, 44
balance
    animation principles 35, 36, 37
    human anatomy 32
    human locomotion 58
    in animation history 11
    in performance 64
ball and socket joint
    human anatomy 31, 32, 33, 34
    puppet animation 104, 112
    quadruped 54
bouncing
    3D ball bounce 142, 143
    ball trajectories 25, 26, 27
    drawn animation 89
    human bouncing 28, 39
    lighting 124
    with follow through 46, 47
bowling ball
    bouncing bowling ball 23, 25, 26
    picking up a bowling ball 37, 38, 39
breakdown (as a way to divide up animation) 28, 42, 164

camera
    2D animation 35, 38, 82, 84
    3D animation 129, 139
    case study, David Johnson 126, 127
    case study, Haemin Ko 96, 97, 98
    close up acting 73
    cut out animation 94
    film making 150, 152, 153, 155 156
    fluid animation 95, 96
    in animation history 7, 14, 15, 16, 17
    in industry 163, 165, 167,168, 169, 170
    puppet animation 103, 104, 124
    why animation is better than film with a camera 47
    x-sheets 85, 87, 88
camera angles 150, 152, 156, 170
cantering 57

cats 54, 55
centre of gravity 35, 36
character
    2D digital animation 98, 99, 100,
    3D animation 132, 134, 135, 136, 137, 138, 141, 143, 144, 145, 146
    animation principles 20, 21, 22, 24, 25, 27, 28, 29
    anticipation 44, 45
    basic emotions 66, 67, 69, 71
    character design 48, 49, 50
    cut out animation 92, 94
    facial expressions 73, 74, 75, 76
    film making 147, 148, 149, 150, 151, 152, 153, 155, 156, 157
    fluid animation 94, 95, 96
    glossary 168, 169, 170
    human anatomy 30, 34
    human locomotion 58, 59, 60, 61
    in animation history 15, 18
    in industry 163, 164, 165, 166, 167
    know your character 71, 72, 73
    lip-sync 77, 78, 79, 81, 84, 86, 87
    overlapping action and follow-through 45, 46, 47
    performance 62, 63, 64, 65, 66
    picking up a ball 38, 39, 40
    puppet animation 106, 110, 111, 112, 113, 114, 116, 120, 124, 125, 126, 127
    quadrupeds 54
    secondary action 47, 48
    staging 43, 44
    timing and spacing 41, 42
    two characters on screen at the same time 76, 77
    weight and balance 35, 36, 37
chest
    bird anatomy 50
    human anatomy 30, 31
    human locomotion 59
    performance 66, 67
children 16, 19
closed body postures 66
close-ups 47, 61, 153
clothing 47, 106, 165
cloven feet 54, 55
collarbones 32
colouring
    2D digital animation 101
    3D animation 137

INDEX

film making 157
   in industry 164
   traditional animation 91, 92
combative body language 67
concentration 149
condyloid joints 34
consequence of emotions 66, 148
consonants 79, 80
construction
   animal construction 54, 55
   animation principles 22, 24
   character construction 25
   character design 49, 50
   in industry 168
   solid drawing 48
conversations 72, 76, 77
cow 54, 55
crossing arms 69
crossing legs 71
crossover positions 56, 58, 59
crow's feet 74
cube 36, 129, 135
curve
   3D animation 129, 131, 132, 141, 142, 145
   animation principles 37
   film making 157
   in industry 162, 165
   path of snake 53
   puppet sets 123, 125
   solid drawing 48,
cylinder 11, 12

dabbing 66
deer 54
defensiveness 69
design
   3D animation 18, 145
   birds 50, 51
   character design 48, 49
   facial expressions 73
   film making 156
   in industry 161, 163, 164, 165, 167, 168
   puppet animation 106, 118
   staging 43
dialogue
   2D digital animation 101
   case study, David Johnson 125
   case study, Haemin Ko 97
   glossary 167, 168, 169
   in industry 158, 163, 164
   lip-sync 77, 78
   performance 79, 81
   x-sheets 84
disgust
   animation performance 66, 67, 68, 69
   animation principles 49

facial expressions 73, 74, 76
dishonesty 69
distortion 20, 25, 66
diving 27, 28
dcg 15, 45, 54
dominance 69
double take 47
drag 40, 59, 60, 92
drawing
   2D animation 82, 83, 84, 86, 87, 88, 89
   2D digital animation 97, 98
   animation performance 61, 63, 64
   animation principles 22, 27.28, 36, 38, 40, 41, 42
   birds 51
   case study, Haemin Ko 96, 97
   case study, Steve Roberts 100, 101
   character design 48, 49, 50
   cut out animation 92, 94, 96
   film making 150, 155, 157
   glossary 167, 168, 169, 170
   n animation history 11, 14, 15, 21
   in industry 163, 164
   preface 7, 9
   puppet animation 113
   show reels 162
   solid drawing 48
   traditional drawn animation 89, 90, 91, 92
dropped 22, 26, 39, 67

eagerness 69
editor
   in animation history 15
   animation principles 37, 84
   3D animation 129, 131, 132, 133, 135, 137, 138, 139, 141, 142
   in industry 162, 163, 168
eee: as vowel 80
eh: as vowel 80
eight basic efforts 65
eight basic plots 147
elbows 33, 67
electrical connectors 104, 106, 107, 108, 112
emotions
   animation principles 47, 48
   facial expressions 73
   film making 151
   human locomotion 49, 59
   performance 62, 63, 64, 65, 66, 69, 70, 71
exaggeration 47
excitement 32, 67, 69
exercise
   2D animation 86, 102
   3D animation 141
   about this book 8, 9

animation performance 61, 63, 72, 73, 76, 77, 81
animation principles 20, 21, 22, 25, 28, 29, 35, 37, 42, 44, 45, 46, 47, 48, 49
birds 51
fish 52
human locomotion 59
preface 7
puppet animation 125
quadrupeds 57
snakes 53
expanding foam 118, 122
expectation 69
expressions
   animation performance 62, 66
   animation principles 47
   facial expressions 73, 74
   human anatomy 32
   in animation history 16
   puppet animations 116
eyebrows
   facial expressions 73, 74
   puppet animation 113, 114, 118, 122
eyelids 73, 74, 114
eyes
   3D animation 134, 135
   animation performance 61, 68, 69
   animation principles 42, 44
   facial expressions 73, 74, 75
   in industry 169
   puppet animation 105, 113, 114, 118, 119, 120, 122
   two characters 77
   what is animation 10, 11, 14

f: as consonant 80
faces
   animation performance 63, 66, 67, 68, 69
   facial expressions 73, 74, 75
   film making 149, 151, 158
   fluid animation 96
   in animation history 14, 15
   in industry 165, 169
   lip-sync 81
   puppet animation 114, 115, 116
falling
   anticipation 44
   weight and balance 36
fear
   basic emotions 66, 68, 69
   eight basic plots 148
   facial expressions 73, 74
feet
   3D animation 143
   cut out animation 92
   human anatomy 33

performance 73
puppet animation 103, 107, 108, 110, 111
quadrupeds 54, 55, 56
flicking
  glossary 168
  laban effort 65
  tradition animation 89, 90
flipping
  glossary 168
  traditional animation 89, 90
floating 66
fly 50
flies 51
focus 25
follow-through 44, 45, 46, 47
force
  anger 67
  animation principles 24, 36
  facial expressions 74
foreground 86, 167
forwards body postures 67
four-legged animals 54
frame numbers 38, 85
frames per second
  animation principles 25
  glossary 168
  x-sheets 84, 86
fugitive body language 67

gait 56, 57
galloping 11, 57
gliding 66
glue (for puppets) 105, 106, 107, 108, 110, 112, 115, 116
grabbing 38
graph editor 131, 132, 141, 142, 168
graticule 87, 168
gravity 22, 29, 35, 36

hair
  facial expressions 75
  in industry 165, 169
  overlap and follow through 45
  puppet construction 105, 113, 115, 122
  secondary action 47
hands
  3D animation 133, 134, 143
  animation history 13, 14, 15, 17
  body language 67, 68, 69, 70
  character design 49
  film making 151
  flipping, flicking and rolling 90, 91, 92
  hand to face gestures 75
  human anatomy 33, 34
  in industry 161
  picking up a heavy ball 38, 40

puppet construction 104, 106, 108, 110, 112, 122, 123
quadruped 54
timing and spacing 41
two characters 76, 77
walking 59, 60
happiness 148
happy
  animation performance 66, 67, 68, 69
  animation principles 21
  case study, Steve Roberts 102
  character design 49
  facial expressions 73, 74, 76
  film making 158
  human locomotion 59
  in industry 162
  solid drawing 48
hinge joints
  human anatomy 33, 34, 35
  quadruped anatomy 54
honesty 69
hooves 55
horse 54, 56
human anatomy 30
human locomotion 58, 59, 60

importing sound 137
inanimate objects 17, 41
in-betweening 15, 21, 37, 39

jaw
  animation principles 24
  human anatomy 32
  facial acting 73
  lip-sync 80
  puppet animation 104, 116, 117
joints
  animation history 17, 18
  animation principles 35
  cut out animation 94, 98
  human anatomy 30, 31, 32, 33, 34
  in industry 165
  puppet animation 104, 112
  quadruped anatomy 54
jump
  animation principles 25, 27, 28
  anticipation 44, 45
  human anatomy 32
  overlapping action and follow through 45, 46
  performance 61, 62, 73
  quadruped locomotion 56, 57
  x-sheets 88

keyboard shortcuts (in blender) 129
key frames
  3D animation 131

animation principles 20
digital drawn animation 98, 100
key animation
  animation principles 20
  drawn animation 83
  x-sheets 88
  3D animation 132
  puppet animation 156
kinesphere 63, 64
knees 33, 44, 69

laban movement theory 63, 65
land and landing
  animation principles 23
  film making 154
  overlapping action and follow through 45, 46
latex rubber
  animation history 17
  puppet animation 104, 105, 110, 112, 118
LAVS (live action video shoot) 61, 62
LED lights 104
legs
  animation history 10
  animation performance 63, 66, 67, 68, 69, 70, 71
  animation principles 35, 36, 37
  drawn animation 92
  human anatomy 31, 32, 33
  human locomotion 58, 59, 60
  overlapping action and follow through 45
  picking up heavy ball 39, 40
  puppet animation 106, 107, 109, 110
  quadruped anatomy 54
  quadruped locomotion 56, 57
  solid drawing 48
lift and lifting 26, 37, 38, 39, 40, 50
light boxes
  animation principles 36
  fluid animation 95
  glossary 168, 170
  in animation history 15
  traditional drawn animation 82, 83, 89, 90, 91
lightning and lights
  in industry 165
  puppet animation 104, 123, 124, 125, 138, 139
limbs 109, 116
limited animation 168
the line (that you must not cross) 152, 153
line tester 38, 84, 88, 169
lips 69, 79
lip-sync

INDEX

basic principle 77, 78, 79, 81
glossary 169
puppet animation 117, 137
lying 69, 73, 74

m: as consonant 79
method acting 62
mime 38
mirroring 169
misery 64
motion capture 18
mouths
    animation performance 68
    character design 49
    facial expressions 73, 74, 75
    lip-sync 79, 80, 81
    puppet animation 104, 113, 115, 116, 117, 118
movement
    2D digital animation 100
    3D animation 131, 142, 145
    animation performance 62
    animation principles 20, 21, 22
    anticipation 44, 45
    arcs 29
    cut out animation 94
    case study, Haemin Ko 97, 98
    case study, Steve Roberts 100, 101, 102
    film making 156, 157
    fish locomotion 52
    fluid animation 95
    glossary 167, 168, 169, 170
    human anatomy 30, 31, 32, 33, 34, 35
    human locomotion 59
    in animation history 10, 11, 12, 13, 15, 18
    in industry 163, 165
    laban movement theory 63, 64, 65, 66, 90
    overlapping action and follow through 45, 47
    picking up heavy ball 38, 39, 40, 41
    puppet animation 125
    quadruped locomotion 54, 56, 57
    snake locomotion 52, 53, 54
    squash and stretch 25, 28
    timing and spacing 41, 42
    traditional drawn animation 91
    weight and balance 35, 37, 38
muscles
    animation principles 48
    bird anatomy 50
    human anatomy 32

neck
    facial animation 75
    cut out animation 94
    puppet animation 106, 107, 113, 118, 119
nervousness 69
newplast clay 114, 115, 118

o: as vowel 80
ooo: as vowel 80
open body language 66
overlapping action 45, 46
overshoot 39, 45, 46

p: as consonant 79
pace 59
pain 66, 69, 73, 74
paws 54, 55
peg bar
    glossary 169, 170
    traditional drawn animation 82, 83, 84, 89, 90, 91
pelvic girdle 31, 32, 33
pencils
    animation principles 34
    in industry 164
    traditional drawn animation 82, 83, 92, 98, 106
personal space 63
picking up
    animation principles 37, 38
    3D animation 143, 144, 145
pigs feet 55
pivot joint 33, 34
plane joint 33, 34
plumb line 36, 37, 39
pointing 64
pose to pose
    3D animation 136
    animation performance 78, 81, 86, 88
    animation principles 20, 21, 22
    glossary 167, 168
    timing and spacing 41, 43, 45
posture
    animation performance 64, 66, 67, 68, 69
    human anatomy 31
    lip-sync 79
pressing 65
puppet 103
pupils
    facial animation 73, 74, 77
    puppet animation 113

rabbit paws 54, 55
realism 47
recording 25
reflective body language 67
rendering
    3D animation 129, 139, 140

film making 158
    in animation history 18
    in industry 166
responsive body language 67
rhythm
    2D animation 97
    glossary 169
ribcage 31, 32, 54
rolling ball 21, 22, 27
rolling paper 89, 91
rotation
    3D animation 131
    human anatomy 33, 34
    in animation history 15
running 32, 45

saddle joint 34
sad and sadness
    animation performance 62, 63, 66, 67, 68, 69
    character design 49
    facial animation 73
    human locomotion 59, 60
    solid drawing 48
scale 129, 130, 135, 143
scene
    3D animation 138, 139, 140, 143, 150, 151, 157, 158
    animation performance 61, 62, 65
    animation principles 21, 22, 25, 27
    glossary 168, 169, 170
    in animation history 15
    in industry 164
    know your character 71
    laban movement theory 65
    overlapping action and follow through 45, 47, 49
    puppet animation 124
    staging 42, 43
    x-sheet 85, 87
secondary action 45, 47
self-skinning flexible polyurethane foam 118, 122
seven questions of character 71
shoulders
    animation performance 67
    human anatomy 32
    human locomotion 59
    puppet animation 106
    theatrical acting 63
silhouettes
    fluid animation 95
    staging 42, 43
skeleton
    bird anatomy 50
    human anatomy 30, 31
    in industry 165
    puppet animation 104, 112

snake skeleton 53
solid drawing 48
skin
  3D animation 137
  glossary 169, 170
  puppet animation 110, 111, 113, 118, 122
  solid drawing 48
skull
  animation principles 24
  human anatomy 32
  puppet animation 114
slashing 66
smearing 25, 27
smile 67, 69, 73, 74
soccer balls 25, 26
solid 22, 23, 24, 25, 31, 32
solid drawing 48, 49
sound
  3D animation 137, 138
  animation performance 66, 72
  breaking down sound track 78
  case study, David Johnson 125
  case study Katie Chan 145
  case study, Steve Roberts 101
  glossary 167, 169, 170
  in animation history 16, 19
  in industry 147, 157, 158, 163, 164
  lip-sync 79, 80
  preface 7
  x-sheets 84, 85
space, time, weight and flow continua 64
special effects 158
speech (lip-sync) 77
speed
  3D animation 132
  animal locomotion 57, 59
  blurring and smearing 25
  ease in, ease out 28
  glossary 168
  picking up heavy ball 38
squash and stretch 22
staging 42

stick exercise 35
stress 75
stride
  human locomotion 58, 59, 60
  quadruped locomotion 56, 57
string
  follow through and overlapping action 46
  puppet animation 116
studio
  2D animation 101
  3D animation 128
  case study, David Johnson 126
  in animation history 7
  in industry 161
  puppet animation 103, 104
surprise
  animation performance 66, 68
  character design 49
  facial animation 73, 74

tails 45, 46
teeth
  animation performance 67
  character design 49
  facial animation 73
theatrical acting
  animation performance 61, 63
  animation principles 47
the line
  do not cross the line 152, 153
three-dimensional
  3D animation 124, 128
  in industry 165
throwing
  animation performance 73
  anticipation 44
thrusting 66
timing
  animation performance 61
  animation principles 20, 21, 28, 29
  in animation history 15
  picking up heavy ball 37, 38, 39

timing and spacing 41, 42
trotting 56
two or more characters 76

v: as consonant 79
vertebra 30
video footage 21
views (in blender) 128
visibility (in blender) 145
vowels 80

walking
  animation principles 45
  human anatomy 30, 32
  human locomotion 58, 59
  quadruped locomotion 56
water
  animation principles 23, 24, 27, 28
  animation or timing 42
  fish animation 52
  weight and balance 36
weight
  3D animation 136
  animation performance 67, 69
  animation principles 20, 22, 23, 28
  glossary 170
  human locomotion 58, 59
  in industry 165
  know your character 71
  laban basic efforts 65
  space, time, weight continua 64
  weight and balance 35, 36, 37, 38, 39
wringing 65
wrists
  animation performance 69
  human anatomy 33, 34
  picking up heavy ball 40
  puppet animation 108

x-sheets 84